DOC

THE RISE
AND RISE OF
JULIUS ERVING

Vincent M. Mallozzi

WILEY

John Wiley & Sons, Inc.

This one is for you, Mom—you left us way too soon. I picked up the phone to call you on April 7, 2008, shortly after Mark was born, and then I put it down. For a brief moment, I had forgotten that you moved to heaven.

Contents

Foreword by Dave Anderson   vii

Preface   xiii

Acknowledgments   xvii

1 A Leap of Faith   1

2 Decisions, Decisions   19

3 Doc Signs with the Squires   51

4 Julius and Dave Down by the Schoolyard   59

5 Asking for Another Raise   77

6 Coming Home   85

7 In a League of His Own   97

8 Another Contract Dispute   119

9 A Philadelphia Phenomenon 137

10 Waiting to Hit Pay Dirt 157

11 Swan Song 189

12 The Ghost of Samantha Stevenson 227

13 Cory Disappears 235

14 Up Close and Very Personal 245

15 Just Like Old Times 267

Epilogue 273

Index 279

Photographs follow page 126.

Foreword

By Dave Anderson

The phrase "the best basketball player I've ever seen" is usually attached to a famous name, seldom to an unfamiliar one. However, in the winter of 1971, at a weekly luncheon of New York–area college coaches and basketball writers at Mama Leone's restaurant on West 48th Street, Jimmy McDermott, the Iona College coach, stood up to report on his team and said, "We went up to the University of Massachusetts and lost, but I saw the best basketball player I've ever seen."

The *best* basketball player McDermott had ever seen? As a prominent small-college coach in the New York area, McDermott was respected because he had seen the best of that era come through Madison Square Garden as college and National Basketball Association (NBA) players. His opinion meant something, but who could this *best* player be? Furthermore, if this player was really that good, what was he doing in the woods of western Massachusetts? Even more important, what was his name? Before anyone could ask, McDermott told us. "Julius Erving," he said.

That was the first time I ever heard of the six-foot six-inch basketball player who would soon be better known as Dr. J and widely recognized as one of the best players in history.

Shortly after his junior season at UMass ended in 1971, Dr. J walked into the Long Island offices of the New York Nets, not far from where he grew up playing in Roosevelt Park and at Roosevelt High School in Roosevelt, New York. "I want to play with the Nets," he told Lou Carnesecca, then the general manager and coach. "We'd love to have you," Carnesecca said, "but our policy is not to sign undergraduates."

It was not, however, a policy of the Virginia Squires, for whom Dr. J, in the first year of his four-year contract for five hundred thousand dollars, would average 27 points a game as the American Basketball Association (ABA) second-team all-star and rookie of the year. After that season, he was eligible for the NBA draft because his UMass class had graduated.

The Milwaukee Bucks quickly grabbed him up because their general manager, Wayne Embry, had remembered a visit to a teenage camp in the Adirondack Mountains when he was with the Boston Celtics. "I was playing one-on-one against this skinny high school kid from Long Island," Embry said at the time. "He was six-three, six-four then. I was six-eight, 250 [pounds], going into my ninth season in the NBA, and this kid was beating me."

The day after the Bucks chose Dr. J, the Atlanta Hawks announced that they had signed him prior to the draft as a free agent. Contractually, however, he remained committed to the Squires, which prompted a legal dispute that would require a federal judge's ruling.

On a Sunday afternoon late that summer, with Dr. J's future in limbo, I stopped by the Holcombe Rucker Memorial Playground across from the tall red-brick Polo Grounds project apartments on Eighth Avenue in Harlem. To stay in shape, Dr. J, like many other pros in that era—Wilt Chamberlain, Kareem Abdul-Jabbar, Willis Reed, and Connie Hawkins, to name four Hall of Famers—often played there against other pros and playground legends on the blacktop courts in the Pro Rucker for no pay with no box office and no ticket takers. Anybody from anywhere could join the crowd of 3,500 sitting on the wooden bleachers, standing in the aisles, perched in the trees, hanging atop the wire fence, and enjoying the show in which a player's moves provoked more of a reaction than a routine basket did.

"You really a surgeon, Doctor," somebody shouted that day when Dr. J shimmied, soared, and dunked on an embarrassed opponent. "You really operating on that man." At the Rucker, there were no locker rooms and no showers. The players changed in the Parks Department workroom, and that's where Erving told me how he got his nickname.

"In high school," he explained, "a friend of mine kept telling me he was going to be a professor, so I told him I was going to be a doctor. We just started calling each other that, 'Professor' and 'Doctor.' And later on, in the Rucker League in Harlem, when people started calling me 'Black Moses' and 'Houdini,' I told them if they wanted to call me anything, call me 'Doctor.'"

Not long after that, a federal judge ruled that Dr. J still belonged to the Squires, so he had to return there for another season, in which he averaged 31.9 points per game. On August 1, 1973, he finally joined the Nets, along with center Willie Sojourner, in a trade for forward George Carter, the draft rights to Kermit Washington, and cash.

After the news conference that day at the Nassau Coliseum, I asked him to take me over to Roosevelt Park, where he had developed his game. When we got there, he pointed to a far basket on one of the two green cement courts with white lines.

"That's the best basket, that one there," he said. "That's where I played the most. I'd ride over here on my bike and play one-on-one here, two-on-two, three-on-three. Sometimes on Sunday, kids from other towns would come over, and we played five-on-five all day. The years I was in college, I ran the league in the park. I had the key then; I turned the lights off when I left, sometime around midnight. I worked on shooting and dribbling. If somebody else was around, I'd play 100 points won. We didn't play for money. We just played for ego, for pride."

Dr. J had been playing for money with the Squires, of course, and now he was playing with the Nets for even more money. At $350,000 a season, his eight-year contract was worth $2.8 million—big, big money in those years, before free agency and salary caps. The deal had taken so long to hammer out that Roy Boe, the owner of the Nets, said it was "like the closing of a house," but Dr. J's agent, Irwin Weiner, called it "the closing for a bank."

It really was the closing for a franchise, and the beginning of a franchise, too. The Nets won the ABA championship in the 1973–1974 season, and again in the 1975–1976 season, but the shame was that ABA games were not on national television, in those years before ESPN and other cable channels.

As a treaty with the NBA was being negotiated the summer of 1976, not enough people appreciated that Dr. J had averaged 29.3 points per game that season and 34.7 points in the play-offs. Many thought that if he was in the ABA, he couldn't possibly be as good as, much less better than, the best NBA players. However, when I asked him during those play-offs whether he thought he could do the same things with a basketball in the NBA that he did in the ABA, he did not hesitate.

"Yup," he said, quietly but firmly. Dr. J wasn't being smug or sarcastic. He wasn't like that, on or off the court. I once described him as a showman but never a showboat. He simply knew what he could do, and he knew he could do it on any basketball court against any team in any league. When the NBA absorbed the Nets, the Indiana Pacers, the San Antonio Spurs, and the Denver Nuggets for the 1976–1977 season, Dr. J had the opportunity to prove it.

Sadly, it would not be with the Nets. To keep the Nets franchise solvent, Boe decided to sell Dr. J to the highest bidder. Boe offered him to the New York Knicks, but the Madison Square Garden impresario at the time, Michael Burke, in a rare moment of sympathy for a new NBA member who would be a natural rival, did not want to dilute the Nets as a team.

The Philadelphia 76ers were not as thoughtful. They jumped at the chance to get Dr. J in a six-million-dollar deal: three million dollars for Boe and a three-million-dollar contract for Erving. In his first NBA season, Dr. J took the 76ers to the NBA Finals before losing to the Portland Trail Blazers, with Bill Walton and Maurice Lucas, in six games. By then, everybody in or out of basketball knew that Dr. J was not merely an ABA mirage. He was the real thing.

In his eleven seasons with the 76ers, he would lead them to the play-offs every year, and in 1983 they won the NBA title. He was the NBA Most Valuable Player in 1981 and a five-time first-team All-Star. His career regular-season scoring average was 22.0, with a high of 26.9 in 1980; his play-off average was 21.9, with a high of 27.3 in his first year. He was elected to the Naismith Memorial Basketball Hall of Fame in 1993.

Yup, he did the same things in the spotlight of the NBA that he had done in the low lights of the ABA, and yup, he did them his way: as a showman but never a showboat.

Preface

On Christmas morning 1973, I raced into the living room along with my older brother, Frank, and our five sisters to see what awaited us beneath the tree. I was nine years old and had been asking for a basketball to call my own. Sure enough, I spotted something round that was wrapped in Christmas paper, and my name was scrawled on the tag.

"Guess what this is," Frank said to me, bouncing the wrapped ball on the floor. I ripped off the paper, not expecting any surprises, but I got a big one. Beneath that wrapping paper was indeed a basketball, but it was not the kind that Walt Frazier dribbled on television or that the other kids played with in the schoolyard across the street. This ball wasn't orange. It was red, white, and blue.

Huh?

"It's an ABA ball," Frank said to me. "That's the league with Dr. J in it."

Who was Dr. J, and what in the world was the ABA? I soon knew the answers to both, and it began to make perfect sense that so many of the older kids in the schoolyard were Nets fans and that they finished their finger rolls and dunks by saying things like "The Doc-tah is in the house."

I eventually caught glimpses of Julius Erving playing basketball, flying through the air with the greatest of ease, sporting his giant Afro and star-spangled uniform like something from the circus. I became addicted to watching him play basketball, my favorite sport, and he became my favorite player. I have been following his career from the moment I unwrapped that colorful ball.

I tried to put a little Dr. J in every move I made on the playground adjacent to Public School 206 in East Harlem, where I grew up, and at St. Agnes High School in Manhattan, where I was a member of the 1982 team that defeated Regis High School to win the Catholic High School Athletic Association's Small Schools championship. When I went to St. John's University and rooted for its team, the Redmen (with Chris Mullin, Walter Berry, and Mark Jackson), as well as for my beloved and usually crummy hometown Knicks, I always kept a close eye on what the good Doctor was doing in Philly with a basketball in his hands.

Julius Erving is the most gifted athlete I have ever seen—in any era, in any sport—which is why I leaped at the chance to write this book. I saw Erving do things on a basketball court more than thirty years ago that I have not seen since. There are a lot of retired players out there who still see the bottoms of Julius Erving's Converse sneakers in their worst nightmares.

"I've always taken a very artistic approach to the game," Erving wrote in the foreword for *The Official NBA Basketball Encyclopedia*. "The interesting thing to me is that such an approach now seems to be the norm rather than the exception. In the 1960s and 1970s, anything different was viewed as unorthodox; now I see much more creativity among the players, and it's a beautiful sight."

The beauty of it all is that he was the one who first had the artistic vision. There was only one Julius Erving. He is often imitated but never duplicated, and—with apologies to Michael Jordan—there will never be another like him.

"Erving was the Michael Jordan of his time," Harvey Araton wrote in a *New York Times* column in 1993, "but what a different time that was. He was a bridge between the early fliers like Elgin Baylor and Connie Hawkins [and] today's star trekker, Michael Jordan. When the country was frowning on pro basketball—the widespread thinking that it consisted of too many blacks on cocaine—Erving stepped forward to help change that perception. He wore a large Afro and platform shoes, but he exhibited such class and spoke with such eloquence that he forced people to see beyond what he said was simply cosmetic."

Born and raised on Long Island—like the Nets, for whom he later starred—Erving was the greatest crowd pleaser in the history of sports, stretching the boundaries of the game and, by extension, the boundaries of our imagination. Long before there were video games, he was bigger than life on television screens, stretching his body to rubbery limits far beyond those of mortal men; soaring up, over, and around opponents; always dipping and darting through a maze of players at warp speed and ringing up points by the dozens in New York and later in Philadelphia, where he is held in a reverence reserved for the likes of Benjamin Franklin and the cheesesteak.

"The dunk is so popular because a lot of people who love the game, play the game, and watch it as a pastime can't do [that]," said Vince Carter of the Nets, whose own aerial escapades, largely based on the Erving blueprint, came in handy when he slammed with two hands from the foul line to win the NBA's 2000 Slam Dunk Contest.

"You have a chance of doing a behind-the-back pass, a crossover dribble, maybe even hitting a half-court shot. But how many people are going to do a 360 dunk? I think just the amazement of guys being able to get off the ground that high and do things like that is what draws so much attention to the dunk. I can't imagine where my game would be without it."

For that, he and future generations of high flyers have Julius Erving to thank.

This biography is for all of you who have never had the pleasure of seeing the great Julius Erving play basketball and for those of you who were lucky enough to share that pleasure. I hope to constantly remind you on every page that before there was an MJ, there was a Dr. J, and he injected a whopping dose of entertainment into the once mundane game of professional basketball, turning it into the kind of freewheeling, high-flying spectator sport that it had not been before he swooped onto the American basketball scene.

Acknowledgments

There are so many people to thank for making this book happen. First, major thanks to my old agent, Mark Reiter, for recommending that my pen be put to this project, and to my new agent, Flip Brophy, for putting it all together.

A special thanks goes to all the former players and coaches who gave up their valuable time to share their wonderful memories of the great Dr. J., world-class people and ballplayers like Charles Barkley, Michael Cooper, Darryl Dawkins, World B. Free, Dominique Wilkins, George Gervin, Charlie Scott, and Bill Walton. There were scores of others, including Kevin Loughery, Mike Fratello, Lou Carnesecca, Dean Meminger, Swen Nater, Rick Darnell, Rod Strickland, Kenny Anderson, Kevin Joyce, Willie Hall, Lee Jones, and Rick Pitino.

This book also benefited a great deal from the recollections of the players and coaches from Erving's youth who took me down memory lane, including Al Williams, Archie Rogers, Dave Brownbill, Cal Ramsey, Joe Blocker, Don Ryan, Cecil Watkins, Jack Wilkinson, Mike Cingiser, Ernie Morris, Michele Sharp, and Mel Feldman.

There are also those who crossed Erving's path at the high school and college levels, such as Pete Broaca, Ray Ellerbrook, John Betancourt, Jack Wilkinson, and Rita Leaman, the widow of Jack Leaman, who was Erving's varsity coach at the University of Massachusetts in Amherst.

A special salute is due to those media members and others in the sports community who gave a helping hand: Marv Albert, Bob Costas, Pete Vecsey, Mark Heisler, Phil Jasner, Robert Huber, Malcolm Moran, Alex Tarshis, Eric Handler, Noam Cohen, Elena Gustines, Mark Beal, Dan Schoenberg, Dan Wasserman, Bob Behler, John Temple, and Jason Yellin.

I would also like to tip my basketball cap to Patty LaDuca, Diego Ribadeneira, Phil Coffin, and Wally Patrick, brilliant editors at the *New York Times* whose deft handling of my stories in sports, metro, and regional news have made me a better writer than I was before I crossed their paths.

No one gave a more crucial assist, however, than Dave Anderson, my Pulitzer Prize–winning colleague who is the classiest journalist I have met in my twenty-three years in this often insane business. Dave said to me that he "would be honored" to write the foreword for this book, and his stamp of approval is a gold seal by anyone's standards. In addition, I read and reread many of Dave's great "Sports of the Times" columns on Erving from as far back as the early 1970s, and those insights helped me a great deal in conveying Erving's mood and mindset during the many phases of his brilliant career.

Finally, I owe an enormous debt to the late Roy Boe, the former owner of the Nets, who was as straight a shooter as you can find in basketball.

1

A Leap of Faith

On a summer day in 1958, an eight-year-old boy named Julius took a nasty spill on a patch of broken glass on the asphalt courts in Campbell Park, the playground adjacent to the Park Lake Apartment complex on Beech Avenue in Hempstead, Long Island, where Julius lived with his mother, Callie, his older sister, Alfreda (Alex), and his younger brother, Marvin.

Callie Mae Erving, a deeply religious woman, prayed for the quick healing of young Julius's torn-up knee, which was bleeding profusely as he hobbled up the steps to his third-floor apartment.

How much more could Callie take? Five years earlier, her husband, Julius Winfield Erving, had abandoned the family, leaving Callie to raise three children on a welfare check and the money she made cleaning houses. Nevertheless, Callie, who was heavily involved at the South Hempstead Baptist Church, kept the faith.

She took Julius to see a doctor, who stitched the bloody wound but announced that the young boy would be limping around town for a while. The doctor's prognosis did not prevent Julius from returning to his favorite court, however, where he practiced shooting from sunrise until sundown. Callie, watching her son hone his skills through a window of their apartment, cried at the sight of her young "June"—short for Junior—dragging one leg behind the other as he made his way around the court.

Showing signs of a hoops IQ that would one day put him in a basketball class by himself, Julius found a way to limit the pain while strengthening his bum knee. With each trip up and down the stairs of his building, he would take two, three, sometimes four steps at a time; each leap minimized the painful steps while greasing the springs in a pair of bony legs that would catapult Julius Winfield Erving II from poverty and relative obscurity to fame, fortune, and a place in history as one of the greatest athletes of the twentieth century, a superstar whose gravity-defying theatrics would have puzzled Isaac Newton.

"He is that rarity," Dave Anderson, the Pulitzer Prize–winning columnist of the *New York Times* once wrote of Erving, "a showman who is not a showboat."

Dominique Wilkins, one of the most extraordinary dunkers in the history of basketball, idolized Erving as a child and as a contemporary.

"I think that Julius will go down in history as the most exciting player who has ever stepped on a basketball court," Wilkins said. "He's the one guy that all of us wanted to be like when we were growing up. He set the benchmark really, really high for all the great players who followed, most notably Michael Jordan."

Erving, the first player to glamorize the slam dunk, is now the NBA's professor emeritus of suspended animation. If he were given frequent flyer miles for every one of his majestic flights to the hoop, he could travel around the world, free of charge, for eternity.

"As a longtime broadcaster and basketball fan," said Marv Albert, "I can tell you that Julius is one of the most extraordinary players I have ever seen. Back when Julius was with the Nets, I was a television news sportscaster, and when we did the six and eleven o'clock broadcasts, we always wanted to put some Dr. J footage on the air, so we would go to his play-off games for live shots or to his practices, because we knew he would always do something spectacular that was worthy of being part of the highlights. I cannot recall a time when we sent a camera crew out and they came back disappointed."

Growing up in Honolulu, President Barack Obama played basketball at Punahou High School in the late 1970s, and he idolized Julius Erving, whose poster he once had tacked on his bedroom wall.

"My favorite player when I was a kid was Dr. J," Obama said in a 2008 ESPN interview. "He had those old Nets shorts with the socks up to here [pointing to his shin]. Those Converse Dr. J's, that was the outfit then."

Obama was once asked whether he would rather be president of the United States or Julius Erving in his prime.

"The Doctor," Obama immediately replied. "I think any kid growing up, if you got a chance to throw down the ball from the free throw line, that's better than just about anything."

I totally get it. After all, it is a whole lot easier to become the next president than it is to become the next Julius Erving. With all due respect to Doctors Zhivago, Livingstone, Spock, Seuss, Dolittle, Frankenstein, McCoy, Welby, and Ruth, the most famous Doctor of them all, in my mind, is Dr. J.

"Julius is among a group of players from the 1960s and the 1970s who epitomized style and cool," said Bob Costas, once a play-by-play broadcaster for the ABA's Spirits of St. Louis.

"While he was colorful and dynamic, there was never any sense that he was trying to be an exhibitionist. Out there on the court, he was a stylist, not an exhibitionist, and that's a distinction lost on the modern athlete. This guy was so much cooler than 95 percent of the athletes playing today, it's a joke. He played the game with such style, such flair, but he never did it in a way that showed up an opponent, or to show off in front of a crowd. There was nothing about his spectacular game that lent itself to any of the nonsense that goes on in sports today."

In a February 1993 "On Pro Basketball" column in the *New York Times*, Harvey Araton, writing about Erving as he prepared for Hall of Fame enshrinement, wrote the following: "Those who know Erving well always said family came first [for him], be it the nuclear kind, the team he happened to be playing for, or the league his team was playing in. It was all just part of the game plan to seek out a troubled player or take a rookie home for Christmas, but it worked better way back when. In these dizzying days of global expansion and gargantuan endorsement contracts, of one-man corporations like Shaquille O'Neal rolling off the collegiate assembly line, it is almost impossible to imagine a superstar with the scope, the off-court grace, of Julius Erving."

Despite all the accolades and all the bows, the man who became known as Dr. J, an American icon whose soaring sojourns to the basket revolutionized the way the game was played around the world, suffered his share of bumps and heavy emotional bruises along the way. The tiny scar on the Hempstead hoop prodigy's bloody knee has long since disappeared, but much larger scars have never healed.

Julius and Archie at "the Garden"

It's hard to believe that it all started at the now-defunct Prospect School in Hempstead, a fugitive from the wrecking ball, where a couple of kindergarten students and best friends named Julius Erving and Archie Rogers were introduced to the game of basketball.

On the tired walls of the school's tiny gymnasium—which served as a coal bin in the early 1900s—hangs a dusty clock that ran out of ticks years ago and a faded sign that reads MAXIMUM OCCUPANCY NOT TO EXCEED 150 PERSONS. Beneath a thirteen-foot ceiling are two baskets, each of them eight feet in height, and two deflated basketballs that remain frozen in time, one on each side of the court.

"My first dunk was at Prospect," Erving said. "By the time I was in ninth grade I was dunking on the regular baskets. I never had any trouble jumping. When I was six to seven years old, I was jumping out of swings in the playground. The roll, the parachute, all of it. We had a game called Geronimo. You'd jump, yell 'Geronimo,' float, and land. Then you'd look back at the next guy and say, 'Match that!'"

Erving's first court, terribly small even by elementary school standards, is not quite the length of a normal-sized half-court, and the distance between the top of each backboard and the gymnasium's roof is less than two feet. This is why Erving and Rogers and all the other young basketball players at Prospect had no choice but to develop the art of line-drive shooting.

"As soon as a kid trying out for one of my teams took a line-drive shot at the basket, I said 'Lemme guess, you went to Prospect, didn't you?'" said Don Ryan, who ran a Biddy Basketball team for eleven- and twelve-year-old boys that would eventually include Erving and Rogers. "It wasn't exactly a great place to learn how to shoot."

Nevertheless, to a couple of young boys dreaming a hoop dream, it was basketball heaven—and beyond.

"That little basketball court at Prospect was our Madison Square Garden," said Rogers, now fifty-eight, who works as a laborer for the Village of Hempstead. "Julius and I played a lot of basketball in that gym, and we learned a lot about life in that school."

Basketball Salvation

On a February morning in 1962, there was a series of knocks on the front door of the Salvation Army Center in Hempstead. The door was answered by Ryan, then a nineteen-year-old student at Adelphi University who had played basketball for the Hempstead Travelers of the Police Boys Club and was now running a Biddy Basketball team.

"I open the door and there are these two young kids on their bikes, one of whom introduces himself to me as Archie Rogers, and the other as Julius Erving," recalled Ryan, now sixty-five, who still lives in Hempstead and still coaches a boys' Biddy team there for the Salvation Army.

"They asked if they could join the program," Ryan said. "I put them on the court, and it wasn't long before I realized they were two of the best players on my team."

The two young boys soon joined a roster that included some of the finest talent New York had ever known. Ryan's team already featured a trio of terrific guards, including a slick and savvy ball handler named Al Williams and a pair of sharpshooters named Terry Conroy and Tommy Brethel.

Williams, now fifty-eight and an attendance teacher at Hempstead High School, still regales students there with tales of his old teammate and the glory days when he, Erving, and Rogers, and the rest of the Salvation Army team were at the top of the basketball heap.

"I think we had a smorgasbord of talented players on that team," said Williams, who went on to average 14 points and

10 assists per game at Niagara University. He is now a member of the school's Hall of Fame.

"Everybody played off everyone else's talents, and Julius just fit in perfectly. Julius was longer and taller than the rest of us, and the one thing I can say is that he always had the ability to jump. I recognized that the first few minutes he stepped onto the court with us. But he wasn't really a true standout at that point; he wasn't that explosive—that happened much later for him, at the college level. That's where he really blossomed, and I attribute that to practicing hard, being confident, and being well coached.

"Even at a young age, he was quiet and resourceful. He was the type of player who was always willing to give more than he got out on the court. He was excellent, but he was always humble, and I think teammates and opponents respected that about him. I also think that what made him so great was his dedication to the game. He always practiced and practiced and practiced. In fact, we used to call him 'the Man of a Thousand Dunks,' because he had just about every one of them known to man. And I remember that we used to call him 'Junior,' not 'Julius,' and he never really minded; he was all right with it."

Julius was sent to Ryan by a man named Andy Haggerty, an employee of the New York City Parks and Recreation Department who coached Ryan and the Hempstead Travelers. Haggerty, who also lived in the Park Lake Apartments, had often stopped to watch young Julius play at Campbell Park. Sensing that the five-foot six-inch, 115-pound Erving, then twelve, had the kind of game that might blossom on hardwood, Haggerty approached Erving and told him about Ryan's Salvation Army team. "Go see Don," were the last three words Haggerty said to Erving that day.

Ryan, now a trustee of the Village of Hempstead—"I'm Hempstead born and Hempstead bred, and when I die I'll be Hempstead dead" was one of his campaign slogans in 2007— quickly began to see why Haggerty had taken such an interest in Erving.

"Julius was a very unselfish player who could jump out of the gym," Ryan said. "He had good strong hands, and he was coachable beyond belief. And the one thing I can say about Julius is that he got better and better every day on the court."

In the summer of 1964, Ryan answered an ad in the *Long Island Press* placed by a man named Cecil Watkins, who was running the Ray Felix Tournament on 99th Street and 25th Avenue in East Elmhurst, Queens. The tournament, named after the former Baltimore Bullet and New York Knick who hailed from Queens and died in 1991, was an open competition that featured talented players from the city's five boroughs in various age divisions.

Ryan called Watkins and asked if he could bring a team of fourteen-year-olds to the tournament, which featured more than a hundred teams.

"Are you sure you want to bring a team from Long Island to New York City?" Watkins asked incredulously. "We have a lot of outstanding players in this tournament."

Ryan told Watkins that he had a kid named Julius "who could really jump."

"We have a lot of kids here in New York who could really jump," Watkins shot back.

"Well, not like this kid," said Ryan, adding that he had an outstanding guard named Al Williams who "has a string on the ball."

Watkins told Ryan, "Look, we have a lot of kids in New York who can handle the ball."

Ryan persisted, however, and Watkins relented. Julius Erving and Company were headed for Big City asphalt.

"We didn't know anything about Julius," said Watkins, now seventy-five and the director of New York's National Pro-Am basketball tournament.

"We always had this running joke that Long Island kids could not compete with City kids in basketball, but Don kept saying that he had these kids, especially this one kid named Julius, who would make believers out of us. Well, needless to say, Julius introduced himself to New York City that day. They [the Long Island team] beat a team of New York City kids in the Midgets Division pretty bad. Julius was jumping out of the park, and the crowd was oohing and aahing, but Julius was never out of control.

"In fact, for a young kid, he showed a lot of finesse that day. For weeks after that game, people kept coming over to me and asking, 'Who was that kid?' Everyone knew that he was going to be a hell of a player. After the game, Don came over to me, smiling from ear to ear and saying, 'Hey, Cecil, what do you think about my boys from Long Island now?' "

Watkins worked as a coach and a referee for decades, so he has seen thousands of young players on basketball courts over the years. Of all the young New York hoopsters that Watkins has ever seen, Erving is in his top five. The other four (in no particular order) are Tiny Archibald, Kareem Abdul-Jabbar, Connie Hawkins, and Roger Brown.

"I'll put that starting five against anybody's all-time starting five, from anywhere in the country, from any era," Watkins said. "Julius and those guys are players who come along once in a lifetime."

While they were young basketball studs at Hempstead Junior High School, Erving, Rogers, and Williams became the nucleus of one of the Salvation Army's greatest teams, which finished with a record of 33–1 when they were twelve-year-olds.

"In grade school, sometimes the only recourse you had was to shoot line drives," Erving once said. "The Salvation Army was a newer facility, and I got a chance to bank it better and with a lot of backspin and reverse English."

Having honed their shooting skills on a real court, the Hempstead trio led their seventh-grade squad against West Islip High School's junior varsity basketball team in a scrimmage game that reached every basketball fan on Long Island. The game wasn't ever close; Erving and Company dominated their ninth- and tenth-grade competition.

"I was a pretty accurate shooter; Julius was an unbelievable leaper, rebounder, and outright scorer; and Al had a wicked handle," said Rogers, who recalled scoring 15 points that day; Williams scored 17, and Julius finished with a game-high 21. "Those kids from West Islip were pretty amazed," Rogers said. "I think that's where it all started, especially for Julius. That's when people really started paying attention to him."

Coach Ollie Mills at Hempstead High School figured he would inherit the terrific trio, all of whom were eligible to try out for Mills's freshman team as soon as they became eighth graders. However, in 1964, in the summer before Julius entered eighth grade, Callie Erving met a man and moved her family into his house on Pleasant Avenue in Roosevelt. Just like that, Ollie Mills and Hempstead basketball were on the outside looking in, and Roosevelt High School, where the varsity coach was a man named Ray Wilson, opened its doors to a basketball prodigy who was on his way to becoming the most exciting player on the planet.

Julius at Roosevelt and the Legend of Joe Blocker

One day, during Erving's first year at Roosevelt High School, Earl Mosley, the junior varsity coach, called NBA referee Lee Jones over to the gym to meet an energetic, fourteen-year-old slamming sensation with long arms and a short Afro hair-style who was not yet being called the Doctor. That nickname would come a little later, when Erving called a bright buddy at Roosevelt "Professor," and his buddy quickly responded: "And you are the Doctor."

"You have to see this kid play," Mosley told Jones. "I think he's got some real potential."

Jones, who is now retired, got his start officiating basketball games at Rucker Park in New York, a hallowed hoop haven in West Harlem, where the Entertainer's Basketball Classic now takes place. Rucker Park brings together professional and college players in their off-season who compete for bragging rights along with scores of woulda-made-it, coulda-made-it, shoulda-made-it players who earned most of their fame play-ing on hot summer nights behind chain-link fences throughout New York.

Jones had grown up in Roosevelt, and for a fifty-cent toll that took him over the Triborough Bridge, he got to see, up close and very personal, basketball behemoths like Connie Hawkins and Cal Ramsey work their magic on the fabled strip of asphalt across the street from Willie Mays's former address— the old Polo Grounds, where project buildings now cover the same earth that the Say Hey Kid once covered for the New York Giants. However, Jones had not seen Julius Erving until he shook hands with him that day in the Roosevelt gym.

"He was a nice kid, not that tall yet," Jones said. "At the time, he was considered a very good player, not a great one— there's a difference. In fact, he did not even make the All–Long Island team as a high school senior."

While Jones was traveling to New York to see some of the best basketball the city had to offer, Erving was in the neighbor-hood, polishing his skills before family and friends and leaving them oohing and aahing by taking off for the basket with the same graceful force displayed by the jets soaring off the runway at nearby Kennedy Airport.

"In those years, we'd invite guys from Hempstead or Lawrence or Freeport over to play full court," Erving once said. "The young ladies would come out, [as well as] parents [and] other kids. They'd react to things you did on the court. If you got up 10 or 12 points, you'd want to do more than just win the game. Like if I was coming down on a fast break and there were two defenders back, I'd take the challenge. I'd try to beat both defenders. I'd fake one guy, then try to spin or jump and pump past the other guy. I'd challenge 'em both. I'd do some trickery with the ball and try to score at the same time.

"That's the part of the game I really loved as a kid, that challenge of daring to be great. If you rise to the challenge and are successful, it gives your confidence a definite reinforcement. If you succeed, it's a feeling of accomplishment. If you fail, you don't feel bad about it, [because] you haven't really lost anything. But if you don't try at all, it's as if you tried and failed. So you've eliminated trying for that good feeling."

Erving kept rising, higher and higher, to every occasion and every challenge, putting an eye-opening exclamation point— one of his patented slams—behind many of his towering assaults on the rusted rims scattered around Long Island.

"Dunking is a power game, a way of expressing dominance," Erving once told *Black Sports The Magazine*. "It makes your opponent uptight and can shatter his confidence. My style is an expression of me as an artist. If I develop an aspect of my game to the point where I can do certain things, why not do them? I would relate it directly to other professions like music and writing. Different people have different styles of expression. Shakespeare had a way with words so that they could be poetic . . . they just do it, that's them. The way I play the game, that's me."

On his rapidly developing game as a youth, Erving once told *Esquire*, "I've never felt particularly unique. Even within the context of basketball, I honestly never imagined myself as anything special. I remember back home, when I first started playing, at nine, ten, I had a two-hand shot. Then by twelve-and-a-half, thirteen, I had a one-hand shot. Always went to the basket, that was my way, that pattern was set by then.

"Back then, before I was physically able, I felt these different things within me, certain moves, ways to dunk. I realized all I had to do was be patient and they would come. So I wasn't particularly surprised when they did, they were part of me for so long. I didn't find anything particularly special about them. It wasn't that I didn't think I was a good player, I just assumed everyone could do these things if they tried."

Long before Erving began his high school career at Roosevelt, he was playing ball at Campbell Park, his home court, on the green cement courts at Roosevelt Park, and on any other playground. Basketball provided not just an arena for showcasing his ever developing talents but also a temporary escape from a life of poverty and of never again seeing his father, who was killed in an automobile accident when Erving was just eleven years old.

"I never really had a father," Erving told *Esquire*, "but then the possibility that I ever would was removed."

Julius Erving still had a mother, though, and she was loving, hardworking, and dedicated. Callie Mae was one of fourteen children and was born under the sign of Taurus. Erving once said of his mother, "She's a great lady. She has been a profound influence in my life. Born in meager surroundings in rural South Carolina, she and my dad migrated to New York, where I was born, my brother was born, [and] my sister was born. I view her as a very, very strong-willed person, who understood her values very early in life, learned her lessons about dealing with people, and made her family her priority. The influence on her family, because it was such a priority for her, was clearly felt by all of us.

"She had to work very hard. As a matter of fact, she used to teach school when she was in South Carolina, but she wasn't qualified to teach in New York, and she did whatever she had to do. She did domestic work, she went through the training to become a hairdresser, and she rented a booth in a salon and supported her family as best she could. She always gave us great doses of love and made us feel special about the little material things that she could give us, to help us to understand the merit system.

"If you came home with a good report card, As and Bs, then maybe there was a pair of tennis shoes that went along with that. I remember one instance in elementary school. She knew that I liked white grapes, and she bought me a pound of white grapes, and these were all mine and it was just so special. It was in response to having a good report card, and something simple like that meant a lot to me. I guess it was the gesture on her part that was behind it that still carries through today, in terms of thinking that way. I think I started learning lessons about being a good person long before I ever knew what basketball was. And that starts in the home, it starts with the parental influence."

In addition to Callie Mae, there were always the parks and always basketball.

"When there was a fight at home, or I was uptight, I would go down to the park and play, sometimes just by myself," Erving said. "And when I was through, I would be feeling good again. I could come back and deal with the situation. Being a typical Pisces, I might have experienced mood shifts, but I don't remember any depression, or needing to do anything, or to have someone bring me out of being depressed."

Sometimes Erving would go to Campbell Park just to watch a street-ball phenomenon named Joe Blocker hold court there.

Blocker, one of the most legendary athletes that Hempstead High School ever produced, is sixty-six now and back where he started. A football, basketball, baseball, and track and field star in the mid to late 1950s, Blocker—who was voted Hempstead's "Athlete of the Millennium"—spent a lot of his free time carving his legend into the deep cracks of school yards around Long Island.

Although Blocker played college football as a running back at West Texas State University and went on to play professionally with the Montreal Alouettes of the Canadian Football League in 1967 and 1968, he is best known for having defended playground honor at Hempstead, where Erving first honed his skills, and in Roosevelt Park—now called the Reverend Arthur Mackey Park—where a wooden sign was hung on November 2, 1973, that says, "This court is dedicated to Doctor Julius Erving."

Most weekend mornings before Erving got out of bed, and most nights long after Erving had rested his head on his pillow, Blocker was somewhere within bike-riding distance at a local park, blocking shots or flushing fools with vicious two-handed dunks.

One of Blocker's favorite playgrounds was Campbell Park, where legend has it that he once sent a rising NBA star named Robert Parish running from the park with a bruised ego. A pair of Brooklynites and future pros named Connie Hawkins and Roger Brown, arguably the best high school players ever to come out of New York City, had their share of difficult days in Blocker's outdoor office as well.

"Everybody who was anybody came to Campbell Park," Blocker said. "Robert Parish learned the hard way that Long Island guys could play some basketball."

Long Island guys soon learned the hard way that Joe Blocker could play some basketball as good as, or perhaps even better than, any of them.

"I took on all comers, and there were always fifteen to twenty guys waiting to play next," Blocker recalled. "I never wanted to lose, because losing meant sitting for a half an hour until you played again."

Julius and Marvin Erving, three years apart in age and light-years apart in God-given basketball talent, were two of the youngest neighborhood children who would bike to anywhere Blocker was playing.

"I'm older than Julius and Marvin, but I remember them coming to the school yards, especially Campbell, to watch us play," said Blocker, who grew up on Linden Avenue, across from Campbell Park. "They were both very nice, very respectful kids, and both good basketball players. I never once saw them in any kind of trouble."

By the time Julius was a fourteen-year-old freshman at Roosevelt High, he was beginning to steal some of Blocker's thunder.

"From the minute I saw him play, I knew he was going to be good," Blocker said. "But then he started to get real good, and he just seemed to move perfectly and effortlessly out there on the court. He was maybe five feet six inches tall, something like that, but he could jump pretty well for a smaller player, and he had huge hands. I remember him, at that age, holding a basketball like it was a baseball."

Blocker, now a custodian at Hempstead High School who has been slowed down by gout, limped through the hallways and reminisced some more about the new kid on the block.

"I always got along very well with Julius, but some of the other guys were jealous of his talent," Blocker said. "Julius could jump over guys or drive around them whenever he wanted, and he could shoot, so the older guys tried to bang him around out there, but the physical stuff couldn't rattle him. In fact, it just made him tougher and stronger. He was like this really poised, really cool kid who was just so much smoother than everyone else but never bragged about it and never talked any trash. He just kept playing his game and getting better and better with each passing day. He had the whole nine yards going for him, and he knew it.

"A few years later, the young neighborhood kids were looking up to Julius and going to the parks to watch him play, just as they had done before with me."

Suddenly, a bell rang at Hempstead, and Joe Blocker, weaving slowly through a maze of students with his mop and pail, made his way to an elevator and pressed the down button.

"I'm very proud of the fact that I got a chance to know Julius Erving, and I'm even prouder that Julius did so well for himself, that he became a role model for thousands of kids throughout the years," Blocker said. "Back in the day, nobody gave you nothing. You had to earn what you got, and Julius did just that. Julius is rich now and famous, but until this day he remains well liked and well respected in this area because he is still a down-to-earth guy who always stayed true to his friends.

"My daddy once told me to respect folks, to never think you're better than anybody else or talk about yourself. He always said it's better to let other people do the talking about you. Julius was the same way. He never bragged, despite the fact that he was once the greatest player in the world. People around here still think of me as a legend, but Julius Erving is the true definition of everything a legend should be."

"A Super Nice Guy"

One of the greatest high school basketball games that Jack Wilkinson ever played came at the expense of Julius Erving.

Wilkinson, fifty-eight, played guard for Lynbrook High School during the four years that Erving played for Roosevelt High. Wilkinson's Owls and Erving's Roughriders, division rivals, were members of South Shore Division IV.

"They were a black school, and we were a school filled with mostly white-bread kids," said Wilkinson, now a freelance sportswriter living in Atlanta. "We played them tough at the varsity level, but we never beat them. Julius was a good player at that time, though pretty nondescript, and [there was] nothing to suggest that he would ever become the Doc. He was average size, maybe six-one or six-two, something like that. He wasn't a dirty player, and he never talked s—t. He could dunk, but we always thought that the rims at Roosevelt were a little low. "

On a December day in 1964, the Lynbrook and Roosevelt freshman squads squared off at Lynbrook, and the six-foot Wilkinson, guarded throughout by Erving, rang up 23 points.

"Of course, I wasn't the player that Julius was," Wilkinson said, "but I just happened to be completely on that game."

When it was over, Wilkinson and his teammates were celebrating in their locker room when two players from the opposing team, Erving and Odell Cureton, strolled in to shake hands.

"Here were these two guys we just beat, who were gracious enough to walk into our locker room and shake hands," Wilkinson recalled. "Julius just said to me, 'Nice game, man.' I look back now and I realize how special that moment was. I followed Julius's career all the way through the pros, and every time I read or heard someone say that he was a super nice guy, I knew where they were coming from, because I experienced that firsthand."

2

Decisions, Decisions

By Erving's junior year in high school, he had become a magnet, if not a target, for some of the best playground basketball competition on all of Long Island. While deciding where he would play college basketball, he honed his skills against all comers from all boroughs, including a tall, skinny kid from Power Memorial Academy in Manhattan named Lew Alcindor—later to be known as Kareem Abdul-Jabbar—and a rugged player from Archbishop Molloy High School in Queens named Kevin Joyce, "the White Tornado."

"I remember this skinny, bony kid," said Abdul-Jabbar, who became a Los Angeles Lakers legend. "We measured hands once. His were bigger. He played one-handed and stuffed over everybody."

Joyce, a product of North Merrick, Long Island, who later played for the Indiana Pacers of the ABA and is now an institutional sales trader in New York, remembered hearing about Erving on the schoolyard circuit.

"I was recruited by a lot of big-time colleges, and during that process, all I kept hearing from coaches everywhere was 'You gotta see this guy play, he's unbelievable,'" recalled Joyce, who went on to star at the University of South Carolina. "So I began to take an interest in where Julius was playing, and often I'd catch him in the parks or over at Nassau Community College, and we would just play with or against each other in pickup games. The first thing that struck me about Julius was his long arms and huge hands. He was a terrific, all-around player, and whenever he got ahead of the field on a fast break, you just knew exactly what he was going to do. No one could dunk a basketball quite like the Doctor could."

By his senior year at Roosevelt High, Erving had visited colleges throughout the country, including the University of Iowa and Cleveland State University, but a number of factors weighed heavily against him straying too far from home. Marvin, his younger brother, was suffering from a rare skin disease called lupus erythematosus, and Alfreda (Alex), his sister, had made plans to marry and leave town. Erving was also very close to his mother, and he had a fierce sense of loyalty to Don Ryan and the other coaches who had brought him along and now depended on him.

Erving had options, but as the native New Yorker and former Knick Dean Meminger tells it, those options were limited.

"Julius was not exactly a hot prospect at that time," Meminger said. "People knew who Dean Meminger was, coming out of high school, because I had over a hundred college scholarship offers. People knew who Calvin Murphy was, coming out of high school, because he had a ton of scholarship offers. But who was Julius Erving, coming out of high school? He wasn't a very well-known player. To be truthful, he was a nobody, really. He didn't grow up in the city, he grew up on Long Island, and the general feeling about any kids playing in the suburbs was that they hadn't been really tested yet because they hadn't played against city competition."

Erving, whose scholastic average was in the mid-eighties, gave serious consideration to playing college basketball in New York, so he visited St. John's University, Manhattan College, and Hofstra University.

"There weren't too many people who knew about Julius at that time," said Lou Carnesecca, the longtime St. John's coach. "But we had seen him play and knew that he was one hell of a player and that the potential was there for him to get better. Now, no one in his right mind could ever imagine how great this kid would become, but we saw a tremendous upside, and we were definitely interested because we knew he would have been wonderful for our program. We had the feeling all along that the choice was not going to be Julius's alone, but that he would be influenced by Ray Wilson, his high school coach."

Upon his visit to Hofstra, Erving was given a tour of the cozy campus in Hempstead, New York, by Barry White, the star of the team, and another player named Dave Brownbill, who also lived in Roosevelt.

"I had heard about him and seen glimpses of him playing in the local parks, but I had never met him in person," Brownbill said of Erving. "I didn't know how huge his hands were until I shook one of them. He was a nice guy, though, very quiet and unpretentious. He seemed very mature for a high school kid."

Rather than sell Erving on the Hofstra program, Brownbill dissuaded the rising star. Earlier in the season, Brownbill, a high-scoring guard, averaged 28 points per game, but the Hofstra coach, Paul Lynner, moved Brownbill to forward, where he became ineffective and disappeared from the NBA radar screen. Erving thanked Brownbill and went home, eventually narrowing his choices to two schools: St. John's and the University of Massachusetts in Amherst, where Jack Leaman, a former college teammate of Wilson's at Boston University, was now the head coach.

A few weeks after he shook the hand of the young man who would one day shake up the basketball world, Brownbill was driving home from Hofstra on a cold, snowy day when he noticed a car stalled along the side of the road.

"I see this familiar face standing in the snow next to his car," Brownbill recalled. "It was Julius. He told me his battery had died, so I gave him a lift home and we started talking. I asked him if he had thought about where he might be going to college, and he said that he was still thinking about two or three schools and that UMass was one of them. We stayed in touch and became friends, and over the next few summers, I invited Julius to play basketball with me in some of the parks in Queens. I took him to Sonny Dove's house, and we played some ball. Sonny was very impressed with Julius's game, and soon word spread all over Queens that Julius was a basketball force to be reckoned with."

Before long, NBA players like Dove, Nate Bowman, and Dave Stallworth were challenging Erving to one-to-one games in parks all over Queens, and Erving was leaving them red-faced.

"Julius went head-to-head with Stallworth in a park on Hillside Avenue and more than held his own; he even dunked on him," Brownbill said. "Stallworth, who was a star with the Knicks at the time, didn't like what Julius was doing to him and some of the other pros out there. I mean, I saw Julius dunk on Bowman, who was almost seven feet tall, and it was quite stunning because Julius was just kind of starting out, he was just maturing. But these guys were finding out that he was the best-kept secret on Long Island.

A Perfect 8

To Mike Cingiser, Julius Erving was no secret.

Cingiser, the former Lynbrook High School coach who went on to lead Brown University to an Ivy League basketball title, recalled a day that he spent with Howard Garfinkel, the longtime basketball recruiting expert, at Camp Orin-Sekwa, Garfinkel's five-star camp in the Adirondacks, before Erving's senior year. The camp brought together some of the top high school seniors in the country, and Garfinkel would rate them 1 through 5—with 1 being the least talented—on a scouting report that was used by college hoop recruiters.

"I was helping him rate some of the players based on what I had seen of them," said Cingiser, who coached at Lynbrook from 1963 to 1975. "He asked me what I had for Al Williams, and I said either a 4-plus or a 5, because the kid was like lightning, and he could really play. Howie agreed and gave Williams a 5."

Then Garfinkel asked Cingiser about Erving.

"I responded by asking Howie what he had given Julius. He told me that he gave Julius a 3-plus."

Garfinkel then asked Cingiser again what rating he would give Erving.

"I told him that in my book, Erving was an 8," Cingiser recalled.

"But I only go up to a 5," Garfinkel responded.

"Okay," Cingiser shot back, "I'll give him a 7."

On Cingiser's word, Garfinkel rated Erving a 4.

Garfinkel, who first saw Erving play as a junior, told me that in his mind, "Julius was a mid-major college-type player at that point in his high school career. Now, I thought he had some real potential, and I thought he was athletic, but I still thought his game needed a lot more polish. That said, what I'm most proud of, where my scouting of Erving was concerned, is the fact that I was the only service anywhere in the country that even had him on a list. No one else even knew the kid was alive. Mike really, really loved him, and he and I got into a pretty heated argument over just how good Julius was at the time."

Even Al Williams, Julius's basketball buddy, thought that Garfinkel's rating made sense. "Truthfully, whatever rating Julius got in those days was probably justified," Williams said flatly, "because he would not become the real Dr. J until years later."

Nevertheless, even thirty-two years later Cingiser would still not hear of it, and he continued to restate the case for Erving as a rock-solid 5.

"I explained to Howie that Julius had huge, fabulous hands, which gave him an unbelievable ability to control the ball," said Cingiser, sixty-eight, who coached at Brown University from 1981 to 1992 and is now retired and living in Okatie, South Carolina.

"I told Howie that Julius was not just a very good player, but that he did everything right on the basketball court, which is very unusual for a kid with his kind of athletic talent. Usually, the really talented kids tend to disregard the fundamentals and get by on God-given talent. But not Julius—he was too emotionally grounded, and his game reflected that. That was another big plus in Julius's favor: he did not come with any emotional baggage like so many other players, and that makes life so much easier on a coach and a team. I always saw something new in Julius's game. His game always kept growing, like a sand castle or a snowball, getting bigger and better with each passing day."

Garfinkel, who is a meticulous keeper of notes and records, found Erving's old scouting report in a cabinet in his midtown Manhattan apartment on a rainy October day in 2008. The file is labeled "Preseason Survey" and dated January 27, 1968. The words, scrawled on what is now yellowing typing paper, were written when Erving was a high school senior—or, as Garfinkel put it, "a rising senior."

At the top of the file are listed Erving's biographic essentials: "Julius Erving, G/F, 6-3, 175 Roosevelt, L.I. Coach, Ray Wilson."

Then comes Garfinkel's scouting report: "Hot prospect and can do it all. Goes well to hoop with either hand. Handles ball intelligently. Above average 17-foot jump shooter. Rebounds with desire. Major League Second Guard. Excellent attitude."

Under "Grades," Garfinkel had written, "Top quarter of the senior class. College Prep Avg. 81. Junior Boards (SATs) between 950 [and] 990."

"He was only six-three at the time," Garfinkel recalls, "and who the hell knew he was going to be six-seven? Not even Cingiser knew that." Garfinkel sent the scouting report to approximately one hundred colleges and universities around the country, including Georgetown University, Duke University, and St. John's University. "If Julius had already been that tall when I wrote the damn thing, the report would have been more glowing than it already was."

Two months after sending out his Erving critique, Garfinkel went to see him play so that he could provide a follow-up, or progress report to the schools that had purchased his initial report. The follow-up report is dated March 5, 1968, and Erving is still rated a 4-star player, out of a possible 5 stars. Here is how Erving is ranked in certain categories on a 1–10 scale, with 10 being the best: "Speed, 8; Spring, 8/9; Shooting, 7; Rebounding, 7;

ction 3.....City.....cont.)

OHN BELMONT   F   6-4   180   STEPINAC--WHITE PLAINS, N.Y.   TOM CARNEY
off last year's CHSAA Playoffs is decent mid-range shooter who lacks good speed & variety of moves—
constant hustle & growth potential could prove compensaters at GOOD SMALL COLLEGE--grades unav.--W

RON CARGILL   G   5-11 165   ERASMUS HALL--BROOKLYN, N.Y.   BERNIE KIRSNER
constantly improving guard with those good drive moves & quickness--must continue to elevate jumper
from standpoint of range--nice ballh. & coach says "coachable"--pref.MVC-Big 8--low. ½/CP/70--LOW.MAJOR--N

ED GARRETT   F/C 6-5½ 170   FRANCIS LEWIS--FLUSHING, QUEENS, N.Y.   JACK LOCHE
slender forward being called upon for rebounding duties & not strong or tough enough to handle job
now or in ML frontline--good 15' jump shot & agility lend EX. SC HOPE--pref.Dentistry--low. ½/CP/68--N

BILL GRIMES   F/G 6-3½ 170   TOTTENVILLE--STATEN ISLAND, N.Y.   JERRY POWDER
lanky swingman's offensive excellence (27 ppg) totally negated by condition (tires in locker-room &
plays with limp), court attitude (refuses to run,guard,rebound,hustle & refs a hell of game) & poor
competition--good shooter,dribbler either hand, passer, hands--low. ½/CP/72..SB (V/345-M/462)--NO TIMER--W

DON HURLEY   F   6-2½ 170   ST. PETER'S--STATEN ISLAND, N.Y.   JACK MC GINLEY
with above's talent & his own attitude would be winner--strong moves to goal/good runner & jumper--
shooting's confined to within 12' radius of basket--pref.East--8 of 169/CP..JB (V/450-M/558)--ADQ. SC--W

JAY LIEBERMAN   G   5-9   150   CHRISTOPHER COLUMBUS--BRONX, N.Y.   WILBUR KLEIN
dribbles both ways & heady general--hustles on "D"--jumper inconsistent--top ½/CP/84..JB (1000)--SC QB-W

INGRAM MONTGOMERY F   6-5   175   FRANKLIN K. LANE--BROOKLYN, N.Y.   IRWIN BELL
spindly frontliner with an outstanding touch in or out--good moves & lots of finesse--needs weight
& more defense to go all the way--good rebound potential--runs well--low. ½/Gen./72--MM/BT "SLEEPER"--N

JERRY MOSS   G/F 6-1   180   W.C. BRYANT--LONG ISLAND CITY,QUEENS, N.Y.   LOU HACKER
can't miss...has it all!--built like tank/fine speed & leap/enough bb brains to play guard--kicker
is very good 15-17' jump shot--tough/aggr. "D" potential--low. ½/Gen./68-70--BIG TIMER/SUPER JC--N

BILL PATTISON   F/G 6-2   180   MSGR. FARRELL--STATEN ISLAND, N.Y.   WARREN FENLEY
good qualities for backcourt save top speed...strong/goes tough to boards/nice key area jumper/fluid
inside moves (outside ?) & steady dribbler/ex.att.--137 of 251/CP/78..JB (V/498-M/549)--ML SWING--W

JERRY POTTS   F   6-4   185   ERASMUS HALL--BROOKLYN, N.Y.   BERNIE KIRSNER
2nd year of organized ball & fairly well advanced tho riddled with inconsistencies--soft touch from
mid-range/jumps well/very physical--lacks savvy & positioning/avg.moves--low. ½/Gen./70--LM 3RD-BIG-MAN--N

LEE SCHULMAN   G   5-10½ 150   ERASMUS HALL--BROOKLYN, N.Y.   BERNIE KIRSNER
has come long way in short time...never got into game last season--16-year-old dunks with 2 hands &
& bangs pretty good in rough lg.—right now is immature dribbler & shooter--top ½/CP/80..JB (1000)--EX. SC--W

EARL SHANNON   F   6-3   185   ERASMUS HALL--BROOKLYN, N.Y.   BERNIE KIRSNER
tough moves around the hoop & fair short-range jumper but must elevate touch from out to better our
ADEQUATE SMALL COLLEGE rating--well put together & works hard on "D"--jumps & gets ball--low. ½/Gen.--N

BARRY SHURELDS   G   5-11 165   JAMES MADISON--BROOKLYN, N.Y.   JAMMY MOSKOWITZ
possibly out for season due to recent illness so consider this his progress report till further not-
ice--terrific shooter/good ballh./long arms/coachable/heady vs.press--558 of 1085/CP/76--LM/MM PLAYER--N

Nassau ± Suffolk

JOHN CHAPMAN   F   6-4   205   SEWANHAKA--FLORAL PARK, L.I., N.Y.   STEVE BOKSER
playing the backcourt but natural forward & shoots too much when in control--good ballhandler vs.
pressure/fine jump shooting range/fine spring/rips defensive boards--savvy ?--LM/MM POTN...EX.JC--N

JULIUS ERVING   G/F 6-3   175   ROOSEVELT--ROOSEVELT, L.I., N.Y.   RAY WILSON
hot prospect & can do it all...goes well to hoop with either hand/handles ball intelligently/above
avg.17' jump shooter/rebounds with desire/ex.attitude--top ½/CP/81..JB (950 to 990)--ML 2ND-GUARD-N

EDWARD FIELDS   C   6-4   180   BAY SHORE--BAY SHORE, L.I., N.Y.   MEL BECKEL
hard-working youth whose poor grades stem from Bedf.Stuyv.background (low.½/Gen./D)...needs JC--good
moves in the lane & jumps well--must elevate outside shot for college corner--pref.PE/East--OK SC-N

PAUL SCHAUM   G   5-11 170   ELMONT--ELMONT, L.I., N.Y.   RICHARD MORAN
ex.shooter & quick enough to release against pressure--fair passer--top 30%/CP/85..JB (1000+)--LM--W

DICK VOGELEY   F   6-6   190   SEWANHAKA--FLORAL PARK, L.I., N.Y.   STEVE BOKSER
can face the hoop & hit consistently to 20' with soft jumper--lacks strength & aggr.off the boards
& must learn to drive to keep "D's" honest--decent rebounding potn.—top ½/CP/B..LOWER-MAJORS BEST BET--W

Howard Garfinkel cannot contain his excitement over a then relatively
unknown high school player named Julius Erving.

Ball-Handling, 8; Offensive Moves, 7; Court Savvy, 8; Defensive Potential, 6/7; Aggressiveness, 8; Attitude, 10."

Academic information is listed under "Final Grades": "Class Rank, 70 of 220; Average, B-minus; Senior Boards, Verbal, 420 [and] Math, 549."

"That's almost a thousand on the SATs, so this guy was no dummy," Garfinkel explains. "He was very intelligent, both on and off the court, even at such a young age. Today those grades would easily get him onto an Ivy League basketball team."

The summation on Garfinkel's forty-year-old scouting report of Erving reads as follows: "Young senior with huge hands, long arms, size 14 shoe, growing frame, 2 inches in one year and lots of talent. But in two looks [at Erving], we haven't seen big-time jump shooting range for backcourt, size and strength for corner, or overall defense."

"What I was saying there," Garfinkel states, "is that Julius was an excellent player but that he was not big-time the way I had rated other players over the years, like Kareem Abdul-Jabbar, Patrick Ewing, and Alonzo Mourning. I thought he was terrific, but not the end-all."

The summation did get better: "Tough scorer around basket with either hand. Fine offensive rebounder. Poised and instinctive passer on break, fluid and bouncy. Class kid. Prefers business and away college. Bottom line—mid-major college at least."

"Today," Garfinkel notes, "a report like this would grade out as a 4-plus, and that's what I thought of Erving at that time."

Garfinkel finally boosted Erving's rating to a 5 by late in the player's senior year and admitted that he blew the first two calls on the young hoop surgeon.

"Overall, I guess my two reports sucked, but again, I didn't know Julius would grow to be six-seven, and that extra height made all the difference in the world. I couldn't predict that, I'm

TRAFALGAR 9-3755

HOWARD M. GARFINKEL
EDITOR AND PUBLISHER

HSBI REPORT

944 PARK AVENUE

NEW YORK, N.Y. 10028

Vol. 4 No. 12   <u>ALL-SENIOR EASTERN PROGRESS REPORT # 4</u>   March 5, 1968

10---The Ultimate	5---Fair (Average)
9---Excellent	4---Between Fair & Poor
8---Very Good	3---Poor
7---Good	2---Extremely Poor
6---Between Fair & Good	1---Automatic

<u>NAME</u>	<u>P</u>	<u>HT</u>	<u>WT</u>	<u>SCHOOL--CITY--STATE</u>	<u>COACH</u>

*****CHARLIE BLANK   F   6-8   200   ST. JOSEPH'S--CAMDEN, N.J.   TONY MARTIN

Speed........ 7/8	Off. Moves..... 7	SUMMATION: got to love a strong, well-built 6-8'er who
Spring........ 8	Court Savvy.... 6/7	really pours in jump shot from corners & top of circle/
Shooting...... 8/9	"D" Potential.. 7/8	goes well to the hoop/knows where he is on floor/runs
Rebounding.... 7	Aggressiveness. 8	like athlete (ex. footb. end & baseb. pitcher) & has right
Ballhandling.. 7	Attitude....... 9	attitude--unchallenged rebounder in present company--

GRADES: 146 of 218/CP/C..SB (V/388-M/528) fair dribbler/good passer--pref. PE--MARGINAL BIG-TIMER--W

****STEVE DAVIDSON (6/3)   F/C   6-6½   190   BAYSIDE--BAYSIDE, QUEENS, N.Y.   ELIOTT VINES

Speed........ 8/9	Off. Moves..... 6	SUMMATION: medium-built/slope-shouldered forward-center
Spring........ 9	Court Savvy.... 3	whose poor shot selection, over-reliance on huge-quick
Shooting...... 7	"D" Potential.. 6	1st-step to goal from pivot or corner & savvy-less "D"
Rebounding.... 8/9	Aggressiveness. 8	make him BT GAMBLE despite 32 ppg--hits bottom of net
Ballhandling.. 7	Attitude....... 7	when he sticks to 15' herky-jerk, line-drive jumper/tire-

GRADES: 1453 of 1458/Gen/67..no boards less rebounder/great hands, leap, mobility--Grambling or JC-N

****JULIUS ERVING (7/3)   F/G   6-3½   170   ROOSEVELT--ROOSEVELT, L.I., N.Y.   RAY WILSON

Speed........ 8	Off. Moves..... 7	SUMMATION: young senior with huge hands/long arms/size
Spring........ 8/9	Court Savvy.... 8	14 feet/growing frame (2" in 1 year) & lots of talent--
Shooting...... 7	"D" Potential.. 6/7	but in 2 looks we haven't seen BT jump shooting range
Rebounding.... 7	Aggressiveness. 8	for backcourt/size & strength for corner or overall de-
Ballhandling.. 8	Attitude....... 10	fense--tough scorer around basket with either hand/fine

GRADES: 70 of 220/CP/B-..SB (V/420-M/549) offensive rebounder/poised, instinctive passer on break/
fluid & bouncy/class kid--pref. Bus./away--MM AT LEAST--N

***JEROME FLOWERS (1/5)   F/C   6-5   210   RANKIN--RANKIN, PA.   PAUL V. BIRCH

Speed........ 4/5	Off. Moves..... 4	SUMMATION: very strong/big-boned frontliner with leap to
Spring........ 8	Court Savvy.... 6	be great rebounder but appears to lack extra-effort to
Shooting...... 6	"D" Potential.. 6	go get the ball out of his immediate area--fair mobility/
Rebounding.... 7	Aggressiveness. 5	decent shooter facing but needs time & bothered by pressure
Ballhandling.. 7	Attitude....... 7	methodical moves tho makes right ones/handles ball well

GRADES: 4 of 450/CP/B+..SB (V/404-M/482) for size--Class Pres. pref. Ministry--FINE LM 1ST-FORWARD-N

***BOB GREGORY (1/3)   F   6-5   195   ST. HELENA'S--BRONX, N.Y.   JOHN SILVERBERG

Speed........ 5	Off. Moves..... 5	SUMMATION: strong/horsey frontliner with little speed
Spring........ 7	Court Savvy.... 8	or deception marking his play--overpowers lesser foes
Shooting...... 6	"D" Potential.. 7	on both boards & is especially rugged going to offens-
Rebounding.... 7	Aggressiveness. 8	ive hoop--shooting appears overrated & has good range
Ballhandling.. 6	Attitude....... 8	but little consistency from corner or stripe) & moves

GRADES: 30 of 250/CP/86..SB (V/596-M/555) are mechanical--pref. Soc./Met Area Cath--LM 1ST-FORWARD--W

**MIKE HAGEN (2/3)   F   6-3½   180   CHRIST THE KING--MIDDLE V'GE, QUEENS, N.Y.   JOE RUSSO

Speed......... 5	Off. Moves..... 4/5	SUMMATION: cumbersome but strong & well-developed left-
Spring........ 5/6	Court Savvy.... 6	hander with very limited shot range/moves to the basket/
Shooting...... 6	"D" Potential.. 5	ballhandling talent & quickness--slow hands & reactions
Rebounding.... 6	Aggressiveness. 7/8	deter ability to pitch-out to his speedy guards--aggress-
Ballhandling.. 3	Attitude....... 9	ive rebounder/can make a layup & fairly decent postage-sta

GRADES: 44 of 384/CP/88..SB (V/569-M/636) jump shot within 12' of hoop--pref. Ivy--GOOD SMALL COLLEGE

In this area of his report, Garfinkel delved deeper into young Erving's game, breaking it down into various categories, which he graded. The summation notes that Garfinkel was less than enthralled with young Erving's outside shooting. MM (mid-major), at least, is what Garfinkel wrote. That proved to be prophetic, because Erving chose UMass, a mid-major basketball school in a relatively remote location with respect to the major basketball schools.

not [the Amazing] Kreskin. If I had known, it certainly would have been a different story. But like I said, no one else even had him on their radar screens, so I'm pretty proud about the fact that I put him out there for all of those schools to see.

"Looking back, though, Cingiser was right," Garfinkel finally admitted. "Of the thousands upon thousands of kids I looked at over the years, I would have to say that rating Julius Erving a 4 was my biggest blunder. He was a late bloomer who turned out to be one of the top ten basketball players of all time, so from that standpoint, yeah, I guess I blew that call. Fortunately for Julius, things worked out even better than I predicted they would."

Friendly Rivals

Besides playing basketball, Julius Erving and Archie Rogers also ran track and field at the Prospect School. Away from school, they competed in billiards and Ping-Pong tournaments.

"We were competitive in just about everything," Rogers said. "We won a 440-Relay at Prospect one year, against a whole bunch of other public schools. Julius was fast, man, and I'll never forget that look on his face, the look of a great, fierce competitor, when he handed off the baton to me that day. It is one of my fondest memories of me and Julius together."

The two friends also got their first jobs while attending Prospect: delivering newspapers in Hempstead and Roosevelt on a bike route that took them into the white and wealthy neighboring town of Garden City.

"We were like twelve or thirteen, and we delivered papers from four until seven a.m. then our parents picked us up at the end of our routes and we went home for breakfast, and then we were off to school," Rogers recalled. "We each made fifteen dollars a week back then, which was decent money for a couple of young kids, but we always thought that we were underpaid, and Julius was always riding around saying he wanted a raise."

Rogers, who was born on February 7, 1950, and is fifteen days older than Erving, has always considered himself Erving's "other brother." (When Julius was born on George Washington's Birthday, somebody suggested to his mother that he be named George Washington Erving, but she replied "*You* have a baby and name him after George Washington. My baby's name will be Julius Winfield Erving Jr.")

"We were superclose," Rogers said. "I loved Julius, and I still do, because he has always been such a laid-back, humble brother. I was close to his mom, and he was close to mine. His brother, Marvin, was nowhere near the basketball player that Julius was, but he was a smart kid, the kind of kid who could grow up and become president. In fact, Marvin was class president, and he was also a drum player. Then there was Julius's sister, Alfreda, who everyone called Alex. She was very beautiful and very charming. Like all the Ervings, she had a lot of class. Although our families were poor, we always kind of looked out for each other. We shared our pennies together, we ate welfare cheese together."

To help bring a few extra dollars into their respective households, Erving, Rogers, and Al Williams eventually took a job performing maintenance duties at the Esso gas stations around town.

"Ollie Mills got us the job, and it paid some decent money," Williams said. "We used to have to scrub the tops of the signs and the roofs above the gas pumps, and Julius was the only one in our group who didn't need to use a ladder. He had such a long reach, it was really something to see him scrubbing with that squeegee in his hand. He was very competitive, even in that environment. He would try to get his job done faster than the rest of us, so after a while it became this really fun, competitive game. Julius was quiet, but anything he became part of, he wanted to be the best at it. I guess it was just a part of his nature."

Erving was indeed competitive, but away from sports, he was, by his friends' accounts, rather low-key, almost bashful, not the sort of young man who went around looking to get into a fight. Archie Rogers knew this, which is why he always looked out for his buddy, especially on the day that Rogers turned thirteen.

"Me and Julius and some of the other guys just got through playing ball in one of the parks, and I went and got us a pint of wine to celebrate. We had this saying in Hempstead when it came to wine or any other alcoholic beverage: either drink it or wear it.

"So we're passing the bottle around the schoolyard and everybody is taking swigs from it, and then it gets to Julius, and he very politely says 'No thanks, I'll pass.' A couple of the other guys took it the wrong way, and they started beefing with Julius. I stepped between them and Julius and told them boys, 'Look, if this man don't want to drink, he don't have to drink.'

"I mean, Julius never had a fight in his life, and I wasn't about to let him start there. It's kind of ironic, but despite the fact that Julius never fought, one of his idols growing up was Muhammad Ali. Julius loved everything about Ali, he loved Ali's athleticism, his endurance, his ability to speak his mind and take a stand. Julius always told me that it's hard to be a black man in America, especially when you're being oppressed, but Ali remained true to himself and true to his beliefs, and Julius always admired that."

In fact, Erving often read books about Ali and other, mostly black, role models.

"I started really getting into biographies, and reading particularly about black people," he told the Academy of

Achievement, "Marvin Gaye's tragic biography, *Divided Soul*, [and] *The Autobiography of Malcolm X*. [I had] Abraham Lincoln, Jesse Owens, Bill Russell, Bill Cosby, and people like that as role models, in terms of high achievers. I wanted to read as much literature as I could about their lives. In a lot of areas of my life, particularly in my teenage years, I began to think about the world, and to think about the universe as being a part of my conscious everyday life. I guess in my adult life I began to read biographies more than fiction. I started to want to relate to other people's lives, things that had really happened."

Later, Erving would talk about embracing his role as a shining example for black athletes to follow, about being the man who would help to break stereotypes of the black athlete who was uneducated, on drugs, or in trouble with the law.

"I was very conscious of the stereotypes associated with black athletes," he said. "It was embarrassing to see a guy struggling through an interview. I always thought if I made it, I wanted to help eradicate that and maybe protect some of them."

Although Erving loved Ali the most, the closest that young Julius ever came to fighting, according to Rogers, was in the seventh grade, with a neighborhood bully named Sonny Boy, who was jealous that Julius was the big man on Hempstead's tiny campus.

"I'm not gonna lie and tell you that Julius and I were not scared of Sonny Boy, because we were, because the guy was always threatening us," Rogers said. "So one day, Sonny Boy comes around, and he's ready to beat up Julius, and I just couldn't take it anymore. I attacked the guy, put him in a headlock, and started choking him. We started rolling around [on] the ground and then I put him in a scissorslike hold, and I mean, I was squeezing the life out of this dude, and he starts screaming in pain. I think I would have killed Sonny Boy that day, but

Julius, of all people, started begging me to let him go. As much as Julius hated Sonny Boy, he didn't want to see him get hurt."

Later that year in seventh grade, Rogers also came between Erving and someone else: Wanda Watts, one of the prettiest girls in school. Both boys had a crush on Wanda, and they began competing for her attention with the same intensity they displayed when competing on the basketball court, on the track, in the pool hall, and across a Ping-Pong table.

"I won that one, because I ended up with Wanda," said Rogers, who would father five children by Watts. "Some guys might have gotten angry about losing out on a girl to his best friend. I might have, but not Julius. We never became enemies over it."

In fact, Erving, Rogers, and Williams remained the best of friends. It did not matter that Rogers and Williams continued playing basketball at Hempstead High School while Erving moved on to nearby Roosevelt High School.

"When we played against Julius and Roosevelt, the games were always very competitive, but I think we came out more on top than on the bottom," said Williams, laughing. "Even though Julius was a Rough Rider and Archie and I were Tigers, we always maintained a special friendship. We always went to his house and played ball around there, and we enjoyed playing against all those kids from Roosevelt. We went from playground to playground almost every day of our lives. The Ray Felix Tournament was a real eye-opening experience for our team, because it was the first time most of us had played ball outside Long Island. I remember that all of us played really well in that tournament and that Julius was especially exceptional. As great as we played there that summer, I still think that city kids don't give Long Island guys their due when it comes to basketball respect.

"I also remember one summer when we played for the Salvation Army team. We went to Philadelphia and stayed at a place called the Divine Lorraine Hotel. Even though Philadelphia seemed like another world, we didn't forget how to play basketball, and I remember us doing some real work on those Philly kids. I think we played four games in four days, and we really dominated. We had a lot of camaraderie on that team and lot of great competitive fire. Who knew that Julius Erving would one day wind up back in Philadelphia?

"The kids at Hempstead today, they know the name 'Dr. J'—not 'Julius Erving,' but 'Dr. J.' They know that he is a great figure out of history, and that he once sat where they were sitting. It's pretty cool, actually. Whenever I see Julius, we talk about those great times, and believe me, they were great. Looking back, the best thing I can say about Julius was that no matter how hard he played, no matter how much he wanted to win, he was a real gentleman on the court, and he was a true friend, someone you could always count on. I see him from time to time, and he still possesses those great qualities."

Growing Pains at UMass

Just as Lou Carnesecca had figured, Erving decided to attend UMass, and he was indeed steered there by Ray Wilson, into the waiting arms of Jack Leaman. Wilson went along for the ride, eventually accepting a job on the UMass staff as an assistant coach.

Pete Broaca, coach of the freshman team at UMass and an assistant with the varsity, remembered Wilson calling Leaman to say that "he had a kid who he thought could turn out to be a real good player."

"Now, remember," Broaca said. "In those days, there were no sophisticated scouting services or AAU [Amateur Athletic

Union] programs or ESPN or the kind of traveling you see in basketball today, so you pretty much had to go on someone's recommendation, and Jack went with Ray's recommendation of Julius."

In the three years that Erving would play at UMass, 1968–1971, the National Collegiate Athletic Association (NCAA) did not permit dunking. Kareem Abdul-Jabbar had slammed so often at UCLA that the dunk was ruled illegal in college games from 1968 until 1977. That rule cemented Erving's status during his college days as America's best-kept sports secret.

"Julius pulled off some of the greatest dunks anyone has ever seen," said John Betancourt, a guard from Westwood, New Jersey, and a teammate of Erving's on UMass's 1968–1969 freshman squad, which finished 16–0. "The only problem was that he was doing all that dunking in practice. We had some very gifted players on that freshman team. But from day one, we knew we had something really special in Julius."

When Erving's Converse sneakers first touched down on the hardwood floor of the Curry Hicks Cage, UMass's home court, which seats roughly twenty-five hundred, he stood just six feet two inches tall. Even at that height, Erving was performing the kind of acrobatic feats that Broaca had never seen.

"I remember Julius, in practice, palming one basketball in each hand and walking beneath the rim," Broaca said, "and then, from a standstill position, he would just explode toward the rim, like a rocket, and dunk one ball after the other through the basket. All the guys would just kind of freeze for a second and stare. It was quite startling, really."

Ray Ellerbrook, a junior that season who would often sit in on Erving's practices with other members of the varsity, was one of the players who was wowed not just by the size of Erving's vertical leap but also by his mighty mitts.

"He could really leap, but it was his hands that really caught my attention—they were gigantic," Ellerbrook recalled "I remember shaking hands with Julius and his fingers being so long that they literally wrapped around the entire back of my hand."

There were other feats that Erving routinely pulled off in practices.

"Julius would dribble up the floor as fast as he could, with a defender or two draped all over him," Ellerbrook said, "and then suddenly he would come to a complete stop, palming the ball as he hit the brakes without ever using a second hand to gather the ball. He would then hold the ball in one hand over his head, as if it were a baseball, and, like a shortstop, fire a pass to a teammate who was cutting toward the basket. The whole thing happened in the blink of an eye, and it really threw defenses for a loop. We came to expect that sort of thing from Julius, so we were always ready to respond to that kind of play."

Early on at UMass, Erving displayed the typical New York City game.

"He could run and jump, and he could handle the ball and slash to the hoop and finish with style, all that city stuff," Betancourt said. "But when Julius got to UMass, he couldn't shoot a lick."

As a result, Broaca, whose job it was to groom freshmen for Leaman, said he "encouraged Julius to practice his shooting." Erving, whom Broaca said was one of the most disciplined and respectful players he had ever coached, began practicing his mid- to long-range shooting from each corner of the court and all around the perimeter. He did this hour after hour, day after day, and night after night, just as he had done as a small boy on the asphalt courts in Campbell Park.

"Julius took it very seriously, and he worked on his shot for two hours before practice and sometimes as long as two hours after practice," Betancourt said. "Looking back, I think it was the enormous size of Julius's hands that made it difficult for him to shoot the ball smoothly, but he just kept working at it."

The biggest game on the junior varsity schedule that year was against top-ranked Rockford Academy, an Illinois prep school led by a New Yorker named Henry Wilmore, a six-foot three-inch forward who would become a basketball legend in Michigan, where he would twice earn All-American Honors (in 1971 and 1972), finish with a three-year scoring average of 23.6 points per game, and become a fifth-round draft pick of the Detroit Pistons.

"Julius destroyed him, and we blew them out," Betancourt said. "That was one of the first games where players and fans alike began to realize what Julius could do when matched up against a professional-caliber player."

Tears for Marvin

In the spring after his first season of basketball at UMass, Erving received a phone call at school and was told that his brother, Marvin, the young man who many believed would grow up to be president, had succumbed to his rare skin disease.

"I'll never forget that moment when Julius walked into my room, with tears streaming down his face," said John Betancourt, who roomed with Erving during road trips. "I had never seen Julius like that, and when I asked him what was wrong, he said that Marvin had died and that he needed to get home right away to help his mother. He asked me if I could give him a ride home, and I just said, 'Let's go.'

"The ride home was very quiet, with Julius just sitting there, staring out at the trees and crying. Anyone who knew Julius knew that he and Marvin idolized each other. Marvin was a straight-A student and Julius always admired him for that, and Julius was a phenomenal athlete, which Marvin always admired. He looked up to Julius. The one thing I remember Julius telling me on the way home was that he was going to quit school so he could be closer to his mother and his sister, who were grieving Marvin's death. I kept trying to talk him out of it, telling him that basketball was his true calling and that Marvin would never have wanted him to walk away from the game. But Julius just sat there, crying and staring out into space. It was the darkest moment of his life.

"When we got there, it was a pretty emotional scene. I called our coaches and our teammates back at school to let them know what was happening and that Julius was considering quitting school. All of us waited for Julius to mourn, we even called his mother to express our sympathies at that time, and then we began the process of recruiting him again. We called him and called him and begged him to return to school, not just for basketball, but for his own peace of mind. We eventually got him to come back, and even though he never spoke much about the whole thing, I think he was grateful that we stood by his side and that we showed him how much we cared about him and his family."

Several years later, Erving recalled the day that Marvin was buried. "I cried all day on the day of the funeral," he said. "I went to the cemetery the first two days after he was buried and I cried each day. Then I went the next day and I didn't cry. I told myself I wasn't going to cry anymore. I realized I didn't have any control over what had happened. I haven't cried over anything since that day in 1969, and I don't know what it would take to make me cry again. I don't have any fears. I'm not afraid of dying. That traumatic experience changed my life."

That summer, Julius returned home and took a job overseeing activities in Roosevelt Park. Long after the last person had filed out of the park, Julius was shooting baskets, continuing to hone his skills in preparation for his first season of varsity ball at UMass.

Bigger and Better

In September 1969, a six-foot six-inch, bony-kneed player with a familiar Afro crossed paths with Pete Broaca on the way to his first varsity practice.

"I looked up, and then I had to look again," Broaca remembered. "I almost couldn't believe my eyes. It was Julius. He had grown another four inches."

Ray Ellerbrook recalled Jack Leaman once telling him: "Julius growing another four inches that summer was the greatest coaching move I ever made."

In Erving's sophomore year, his first year with the varsity, he averaged 25.7 points and 20.9 rebounds per game (a school record that still stands), leading Leaman's squad to an overall record of 18–7 and a share of first place in the Yankee Conference with an 8–2 mark.

"The fact that Julius was not able [allowed] to dunk was actually helping his game," Mike Cingiser said. "Instead of jamming the ball after rising, he was developing an arsenal of short-range bank shots and fadeaways and turnaround jumps, and that made him so much more dangerous. By the time he got to the next level, even with bigger people guarding him, he was virtually unstoppable."

Erving's best games during the 1969–1970 season were against Providence (28 rebounds), University of New Hampshire (33 points), Fordham University (37 points, his career high), Boston University (34 points, 27 rebounds), Northeastern University (30 points, 27 rebounds), Rider University (30 points), University of Rhode Island (30 points), University of Maine (28 rebounds), and the regular-season finale at University of New Hampshire (another 37 points).

"People only saw his scoring and rebounding," Leaman, who died in 2004, once said. "But he was a great passer, too.

He could hit a man at three-quarter court during the fast break, and he was a standout on defense."

UMass, one of the top teams in the Yankee Conference, finished with a record of 18–7 and was matched up against Al McGuire's Marquette University team in the first round of the National Invitation Tournament (NIT). McGuire's team, led by Dean Meminger, a talented New York City guard, had built a 20–3 record and was ranked tenth in the country and top among the sixteen participants in the NIT.

Marquette had actually earned a postseason berth at the NCAA Tournament, but McGuire became angry when he learned that the NCAA was shipping his team out west for a first-round matchup against UCLA, so he decided to stay home and play in the NIT.

McGuire had done very little scouting of the UMass Redmen (the team was not called the Minutemen until the 1972–1973 season) and had not really heard of Erving until his name was announced over the public address system at Madison Square Garden. However, McGuire knew Erving's name after the game, a competitive battle that was tied 27–27 at the half and eventually won by Marquette, 62–55, before 14,236 spectators at the Garden, including 5,000 noisy fans who made the trip from Amherst and remained on the edge of their seats until the game was decided in the closing minutes. Erving finished with a game-high 18 points and 14 rebounds.

"They were a well-coached, well-prepared team," McGuire said of UMass after the game. "They gave us all we could handle."

Meminger would capture the Most Valuable Player award in the NIT that season, when Marquette defeated Pistol Pete Maravich and Louisiana State University in the semifinals and St. John's University in the finals. Meminger said he was impressed with the young Erving but not yet blown away by his still-developing talents.

"Truthfully, I didn't think Julius was that impressive—yet," Meminger said. "We really kind of neutralized him that day. Remember, we didn't even belong in the NIT, and UMass was not even on our antenna, so we didn't know that much about their players. Julius was not an All-American yet, so most people still didn't know who he was."

Nevertheless, Erving was singled out by McGuire. "The kid's murder under the boards," the coach said, "and he has the good outside touch. Give him a little more help, and that team would be just about impossible to stop."

Thirty-seven years later, Broaca was still feeling the sting from a game he always believed UMass could have won. "We knew they [Marquette] were good, but we thought we had a chance to beat them," he said. "Sure, we were unknown then and were really just happy to be playing at Madison Square Garden, but deep inside, we truly felt that we had an opportunity to win that game."

Despite Erving's fine showings against some of the nation's better teams, Broaca said that the first true turning point in Erving's career came in the summer after Erving's sophomore season, when the NCAA was putting together a team of the best American college players to tour Europe and Russia as part of an Olympic development squad (in those days, all U.S. Olympians were college players).

Leaman initially made a strong case for Erving to join the American All-Stars during a series of exhibition games, but his star player was overlooked. It was only after another player who had been selected became injured that the door opened for Erving, who glided through it and won the Most Valuable Player award (named so by his teammates), putting him on every NBA and ABA radar screen in the country.

Opposite Directions

When Erving left Hempstead for nearby Roosevelt, he left behind a world that would soon swallow up his best friend, Archie Rogers.

By the time Erving was making a name for himself at UMass, where he majored in personnel management, Rogers began drifting with the same kind of street thugs he once protected Erving from in the Hempstead school yards.

Rogers ended up playing more football (as a running back) at Hempstead than basketball, and he went on to the State University of New York at Cortland, a decision he still regrets.

"It was a completely white school, and I never really fit in because I was black, and I truly felt a lot of racism going on up there at that time," Rogers said. "I tried to play a little basketball there, but I couldn't take the people, or the schoolwork, and I came home after a semester."

Rogers got hooked on heroin. "I sniffed it and I shot it," he admits. Desperate to support his habit, he became a thief, burglarizing homes in the same Hempstead neighborhood where people once cheered for him in the local parks. He was arrested and sent to jail three times for assault and robbery. He served his longest stint, from 1972 to 1975, at "The Hill," the Elmira Correctional Facility, a maximum security prison in upstate New York.

"I'm glad I went to jail," Rogers said. "By buying all those drugs, I was on my way to buying my own death. Going to jail actually prevented me from dying early."

Al Williams said that he and Erving often tried to reach out to Rogers, but they couldn't help an old teammate who refused to help himself. "As far as Archie goes, we were always there to try to help him when things went wrong. I know that

I stood by him all these years, and so did Julius. Once a team-mate, always a teammate, I guess."

Don Ryan, the old Salvation Army coach, still has a difficult time trying to make sense of the fact that one of his former players, Julius Erving, reached for the sky and touched it, while another, Archie Rogers, hit rock bottom.

"When they were starting out, they were two great kids, each of them with a great personality," Ryan said. "People always ask me about the two of them because they were my two stars, and they went in completely opposite directions. I learned through their experiences that as a coach, you shouldn't take too much credit for one of your players going on to great success, because you have to then take just as much blame for the other player who failed. Julius was a bit different from Archie in that he always had more of a serious side to him. In fact, Julius's sister, Alfreda, used to tell me that Julius thought like an adult even when he was a kid. I pray for Archie constantly, and I think that it's great that he is back on his feet and working again.

"Look, they were both my guys then, and they are both my guys now," Ryan added. "We have to realize that there is still enough time left in both their lives to judge them at the end of their days and not anywhere in between."

The Secret Starts Getting Out

By his junior season at UMass, Erving had grown another full inch, topping out at a slinky, strong six feet seven inches.

"Julius grew all those extra inches after he turned eight-een," John Betancourt said. "That late growth spurt was the key to his greatness, because he had learned to do all the things that a faster, younger player can do before he reached his maxi-mum height. He was like a guard trapped in a forward's body. He could handle the ball, and he was a great passer and had finally developed a pretty good outside shot, which made him a Magic Johnson–like player. With the exception of Kevin Garnett and a few others, there aren't too many big men who have those all-around skills, because most of those players were taller when they were younger, so they were trained early on to camp out under the basket and post up. But Julius, by the time he was fully grown, had developed an all-around incredible game."

Betancourt, who, like Erving, was voted to the All-Yankee Conference First Team in 1971, recalled how Erving single-handedly dominated the boards in practices and games.

"The ball would bounce off the rim, and all these sets of hands would go up to try and grab it," Betancourt recalled. "Then there was always just this one hand, skying above the rest, that would snatch the ball out of midair and just rip it away from the rest of the pack. It was one of those giant hands that belonged to Julius. Until this day, I've never seen a basketball player, at any level, rebound a ball like that."

Despite the fact that Julius was a high-flying, freewheeling acrobat in a tank top and shorts, his dazzling game was in stark contrast to Jack Leaman's patient, half-court offense. Despite the fact that Erving was always a step or two faster and could jump an inch, or two or three, higher than anyone who was leaping around him, he never said a word to Leaman about building an offense around his vast talents.

"He never complained, not once," Pete Broaca said. "Believe me, there were times when Jack saw what Julius was doing out there on the floor and was tempted to change his offensive phi-losophy, but Jack stuck to his guns. Julius just kept playing, just kept practicing his shooting and learning the fundamentals, and just kept getting better and better."

Although it was clear that Erving had the kind of talent that warranted his being part of a big-time roster, his teammates insist that being a giant fish in a small New England pond helped catapult Erving to much greater success down the road.

"Julius could have definitely held his own on a team like [the University of] North Carolina or UCLA," said Betancourt. "But on those kinds of teams, he would have found three or four Julius Ervings, three or four guys who had the same kind of explosive talent, and he may have gotten lost in that kind of program. At UMass, he was the star, the main event—case closed. Everything revolved around him, and in a quieter environment he was able to keep his focus, to keep his goals intact."

"Goals determine what you're going to be," Erving once said.

In his second year of varsity ball, Erving was named cocaptain along with teammate Ken Mathias. With Erving en route to a school-record 26.9 points per game, as well as 19.5 boards per game, UMass breezed through the Yankee Conference with a 10–0 mark and an overall record of 23–4.

Erving's best games that season came against St. Anselm College (32 points in the season opener), American International College (31 points), St. Michael's College (33 points, 30 rebounds), Colgate University (31 points), Fordham University (30 points), College of the Holy Cross (32 points), University of Rhode Island (30 points), Syracuse University (36 points, 32 rebounds) and George Washington University (35 points).

"Julius was just having one great game after another—it was absolutely amazing," said Rita Leaman, the widow of Jack Leaman, who attended many of Erving's games. "The crowds coming out to see him just kept getting bigger and bigger, the likes of which the university had never seen. Julius did not disappoint them; he put on a performance every night. He couldn't [wasn't allowed to] dunk during the games, but he would do it during pregame warm-ups, so the gym was always packed long before the games began."

Erving, ever the showman, always loved the crowds. The bigger they were, the harder he would try to impress them. "When the crowd appreciates you, it encourages you to be a little more daring, I think," he once said. "With the crowds on your side, it's easier to play up to your potential."

As in the season before, fans crowded into the Curry Hicks Cage and gymnasiums on the road to see Erving's aerial escapades. They watched him make incredible, if not improbable, shots, some with his body suspended beneath the backboard and his right arm extended parallel to the rim. They watched him sail toward the basket from the free throw lane or one of the corners, the ball held high in one hand as he approached his target, his other hand held out in front of him, like Superman.

"When handling the ball, I always would look for daylight, wherever there was daylight," Erving once said. "Sometimes there's only a little bit of daylight between two players, and you'd find a way to get the ball between those two bodies and you make something happen. Having good peripheral vision, I would always see daylight. Maybe I could see daylight that a lot of other players couldn't see. They see a body there, and they don't want to challenge that body, and they just don't see the daylight. So that's a great optic option to have.

"The flamboyance wasn't intentional. The approach was result oriented, more than reaction oriented. Trying to get the results, [you] stop the team on defense any way you can: block a shot, steal a ball, force a turnover. Offensively, [you] try to score, set up a teammate to score, keep it very simple."

Erving always kept it simple by stressing the fundamentals: "The main dribbling is to handle the ball without looking at it," he once explained. "While you're practicing your dribble, look at anything besides the ball. Then you try to establish a rhythm. There should be one pace you master. Then go faster or slower depending on the situation. Becoming a good dribbler comes with practice and experience. It's important to use your fingertips while dribbling. Spread your fingers out as far as you can. Try not to dribble with your palms or your wrists."

As for defense, Erving couldn't keep it any simpler. "I keep both eyes on my man," he noted. "The basket hasn't moved on me yet."

Of all the years of practice and hard work, Erving said, "The result was the priority; the effect was an added bonus, I guess. That was part of the gift, the blessing. Once it became very sensible businesswise, if you do things with a certain type of result and cause a certain type of reaction or effect, then you increase your market value. It's very much a competition for the entertainment dollar, and that's never been more clearly evident than in today's NBA game."

Erving's greatest forty minutes of college basketball came that season against Syracuse University. The Orangemen, a perennial national power, were led by a player named Bill Smith, a highly touted seven-foot power forward and center who led the team with a career scoring average of 20.7 points per game (more than seventy games)—a mark that stood for more than thirty years before Carmelo Anthony came along to score 22.2 points per game in his one season (2003) with Syracuse. Smith went on to play two seasons with the Portland Trail Blazers of the NBA.

"Julius, despite being four or five inches shorter, just dominated Smith," Ray Ellerbrook recalled. "He raised his game to another level that even we had not seen to that point. He blocked almost everything that Smith threw up there. In the days leading up to that game, Julius never talked about how he was going to handle Smith, but as the game unfolded, it became clear that Julius was playing with a purpose. He was just a little bit higher, a little bit quicker, a little bit faster than Smith on both ends of the floor."

Erving finished with an incredible 36-point, 32-rebound performance—a record that still stands—leading UMass to an 86–71 victory over Smith and Syracuse.

Bob Costas, a Syracuse fan who was majoring in broadcast journalism, was at that game. "I was just a fan, sitting in the stands, marveling at this incredible talent," he said. "Here was this guy, with this underdog team, almost going for 40 [points] on us. I remember him being so distinctive in the way he swooped to the hoop with those big hands. He carried the ball down the lane like he was carrying a softball. He just came swooping in the way no other player did before him, and I attribute that to both his physical gifts and a boldness of imagination.

"Julius at times seemed like he was being improvisational in midair, and there is perhaps no more evidence of that than the great reverse layup he would later pull off against the [Los Angeles] Lakers. He was at times truly making this stuff up as he went along, just creating new and exciting moves on the dead run."

Erving proved, as he had the season before against Dean Meminger and Marquette University and the season before that against Henry Wilmore and Rockford Academy, that he could play with, and maybe even better than, any player with the tools to take his game to the next level.

"Julius was one of the main reasons I wanted to go to UMass," said Rick Pitino, the Louisville coach who played college basketball with the UMass Minutemen. "He generated an incredible amount of excitement about the program, and me and Al Skinner and a lot of other guys who followed wanted to be a part of that excitement."

Against a superior University of North Carolina Tar Heels squad in the first round of the NCAA Tournament, Erving finished with just 13 points and 9 rebounds as the Tar Heels won easily, 90–49.

Nevertheless, the secret that was Julius Erving was beginning to spread through basketball circles across the United States. In just two varsity seasons, he was twice named an All-America and All-Yankee Conference performer, and he remains one of only six players in NCAA history to average more than 20 points and 20 rebounds per game, finishing with career-scoring and rebounding averages of 26.3 and 20.2, respectively.

"Julius put up some great numbers, but he was not a greedy player," Rita Leaman said. "He always shared the ball with his teammates, which is something my husband always promoted to all the players, so there was never any animosity among the guys."

In only 52 varsity games, Erving racked up 1,049 rebounds, and he remains second in that category to Lou Roe, who had to play 134 games to collect 1,070 rebounds. Erving's 1,370 varsity points places him thirteenth among UMass career scorers.

"Julius had a great career," Pete Broaca said. "Looking back, I would say it was the Syracuse game where everyone saw the kind of professional player that he might actually become. Julius did all that damage against a seven-footer who was on his way to the NBA, and he did it while playing forward. After that game, we just knew we had something really special going on.

"One of the highlights of my career was coaching Julius Erving—not just the player, but the person," Broaca added. "Not too many of us in this business get the kind of opportunity to be around a player that special."

3

Doc Signs with the Squires

After playing two varsity seasons at UMass and showing signs that he could become an impact player as a pro, Erving had caught the eye of Earl Foreman, the owner of the Virginia Squires of the American Basketball Association (ABA), an upstart professional basketball league that was competing for players, fans, and television audiences with the older, more established National Basketball Association (NBA).

The ABA began in 1967 with eleven teams spread over two divisions. The league used three gimmicks to help draw audiences to arenas in then obscure professional outposts like New Jersey and Anaheim, California: a red, white, and blue basketball, a 3-point shot, and (unlike the NBA) a no-foul-out rule. The ABA's freewheeling, one-to-one, thrill-a-minute fast breaks and dunkathons were right up Erving's alley.

"People looked down on the ABA the way they had looked down on the AFL [American Football League]," the journalist Dave Anderson said. "These were new entities, with new players and new owners, that were unfamiliar to the American public, and most fans did not take either one very seriously."

The ABA's Eastern Division included the Pittsburgh Pipers, the Minnesota Muskies, the Indiana Pacers, the New Jersey Americans (who had become the New York Nets by the time Erving became a pro), and the Kentucky Colonels. The Western Division included the New Orleans Buccaneers, the Dallas Chaparrals, the Denver Rockets, the Houston Mavericks, the Anaheim Amigos, and the Oakland Oaks.

"There were a lot of young, exciting gunslingers in the ABA," Dean Meminger said. "The NBA was more of a half-court league, more of a white guy's league, to be honest with you. But as far as the gimmicks were concerned, the ABA needed that. The traditional stuff was already being done in the NBA, so the ABA needed to be a somewhat different kind of show.

"As far as style of play was concerned, the ABA suited Julius to a tee," Meminger added. "The NBA, that was more Bill Bradley, but the ABA, now that was Julius."

By the time Erving was ready to soar professionally, the two leagues were competing for the services of many players. In fact, Earl Foreman had sent word to Erving through an attorney that there were several teams in the ABA that were interested in having his signature on a contract.

Erving was more than familiar with the kind of money that the ABA was throwing around at that time. When he returned to UMass for his sophomore season, he learned that Spencer Haywood, who had completed just two years at the University of Detroit, had signed a multiyear contract with the Denver Rockets of the ABA for $250,000 per year. When Erving returned to UMass for his junior season, a University of

Michigan player named Ralph Simpson did not return for his junior season. Instead, he too jumped to the Rockets, signing a three-year deal worth $750,000.

With visions of hundreds of thousands of dollars dancing in his head, Erving huddled with the two people in the world he trusted most, his mother and Ray Wilson, and told them that he was thinking of forgoing his senior year and leaping to the ABA. With their blessings, Erving decided to make that leap.

"I'm educated to a point," Erving said when asked about leaving school early. "I think I might have thrived on life's experiences a bit more than I did on book knowledge to stay on my path. I thrive more on instinct and experience than knowledge. Take basketball. It's a smart man's sport. Now, that may be streetwise or academic, but it's necessary."

Although Erving's departure from UMass initially stunned Jack Leaman, the coach eventually realized that his star player had done the right thing.

"Jack was very close with Julius, but Ray Wilson was like a father figure to him, and Julius really leaned on Ray," Rita Leaman said. "I could never fault Callie Erving for any advice she ever gave her son, because Julius grew up to be such an educated and classy person, and he obviously inherited those traits from his mother, who I met several times and really admired."

Bob Behler, Jack Leaman's former radio sidekick, said: "When Julius left for the ABA, Jack was disappointed—not in Julius, because he wanted what was best for him. But Jack often told me that he would have loved to see what a season with Julius Erving and Al Skinner would have been like. He knew that it would have been really special, and I guess he was just disappointed that it didn't work out that way. Jack was very proud to have had Julius as a member of his team. But he was proud of so many other kids who had played for him who went on to become doctors, lawyers, and successes at other things, and he kept in touch with all of them."

After making the early leap, Erving immediately approached Lou Carnesecca, the coach of the New York Nets, his hometown team, to ask if he might have an interest in signing him.

Carnesecca, who as head coach at St. John's University had lost out to UMass in the recruiting of Erving three years earlier, did not want to lose him again. However, it was the policy of the Nets not to sign underclassmen, so Carnesecca told Erving, "Thanks, but no thanks," after consulting with Roy Boe, the owner of the Nets.

"I'll never forget that call from Lou Carnesecca," said Boe, now seventy-two and living in Fairfield, Connecticut. "Lou says, 'Hey, Roy, you'll never believe who I have sitting here in my office. It's Julius and his agent. They want to sign with us.' It was so difficult to have to pass on such an enormous talent."

For Carnesecca, the memory of losing Julius Erving twice in one lifetime still stings. "The whole thing died right there in my office," he said. "Julius was a little saddened, because he would have loved to play professionally in his own backyard, but he just thanked me and went on his way, and I just knew that someone else out there would grab him."

As Carnesecca sat in his office at St. John's University (to which he had later returned) on a cold, snowy December day in 2007, he looked out a window and confessed to making one of the poorest decisions of an otherwise glorious basketball career.

"For years, I've thought about that day that Julius came into my office [to ask about the Nets], and I realized that I was wrong to have turned him down," he said. "I'm not speaking selfishly here. What I'm saying is that I was wrong to have denied Julius an opportunity to earn a living. Who was I to tell him no? He had every right to come out of school and get paid for his God-given talents. If I had it to do over again, I'd say 'Julius, welcome to the Nets.'"

In early April, Erving, who had hooked up with an agent named Bob Woolf, eventually came back to Earl Foreman, signing a four-year deal with the Virginia Squires for five hundred thousand dollars.

"I realized that in all honesty, my main preference was playing basketball," Erving said. "Going to college was a secondary thing. It would have been stupid for me to deny myself that financial opportunity. I had a list of priorities then. First was school; second, social life; third, basketball. But the offer made me start thinking about how many hours I had spent playing ball. I was amazed. I thought, Why not cash in on it? It was a chance to change my financial situation for life."

By the end of the 1971–1972 season, only a handful of ABA players were keeping the league alive: Rick Barry with the Nets, Artis Gilmore and Dan Issel, the "one-two punch" pair of the Kentucky Colonels, and Zelmo Beaty of the Utah Stars. However, Erving would soon become the main reason that the ABA remained afloat and that the NBA could not ignore the fledgling league when talks of a merger heated up in the mid-1970s.

The Making of the Nets

In its first season, the ABA's New York franchise was awarded to Mark Binstein, who sold it to a prominent trucker named Arthur Brown. From the very beginning, the franchise, much like the league it was part of, seemed doomed, because Binstein's team had no viable New York location in which to play its home games. Brown settled on playing in Teaneck, New Jersey, and calling his franchise the New Jersey Americans. He may as well have set up shop on Mars.

By the following season, 1968–1969, Brown was determined
to have the name *New York* splashed in the daily sports standings and across the jerseys of his players, so he decided to move
the team to Commack, Long Island. Now a true New York
franchise, at least in terms of geography, Brown changed the
team name to *Nets* at the whimsical suggestion of a newspaper-
man who wanted to keep the team's name in rhyming line with
the Mets and the Jets. The team finished last again, and it did so
before an average attendance of 1,108 at the Commack Arena
(total attendance that year was 42,811).

With Brown's team in dire straits and the ABA still on wob-
bly legs, the league was dealt a crushing blow when it failed to
lure Kareem Abdul-Jabbar from UCLA. Brown was looking
to jump ship, so he turned to Roy Boe, a forty-two-year-old
Yale graduate who had made a killing in the women's apparel
business and was an owner of the Westchester Bulls, a minor
league football team. Boe, with the help of financial backers,
bought the team for $1.1 million.

"The ABA was a Mickey Mouse league at the time," Boe
told me. "There was a lot of turnover in terms of ownership
and players, but I thought our ownership group, which lasted
longer than any other in the ABA, really brought some sense of
stability to the league."

With the Nassau Coliseum in the planning stages, Boe
moved the Nets to Hempstead, at the Island Gardens, where
buckets were on hand for whenever the roof leaked and
where the locker room was an annex of the boiler room.

"The Island Gardens was like this tiny little wrestling arena,"
Boe said. "I remember one time when the circus came to the
arena and the owner wouldn't clean up the elephant manure.
I ended up getting into a shoving match with the guy. You can't
make this stuff up."

Boe immediately hired Carnesecca, the St. John's coach, as his new coach and general manager. (York Larese coached the team for one season while Carnesecca completed his commitment at St. John's.)

In the first season under Boe, 1969–1970, the Nets—whose roster included Bill Melchionni, Walt Simon, and Sonny Dove—made the play-offs for the first time, and attendance more than tripled. The following season, Boe pulled off his first huge acquisition, signing the young NBA star Rick Barry, one of the many players caught in the legal cross fire between the two leagues. Barry, who had refused to move to Virginia with a team that had begun as the Oakland Oaks, was a handsome blond bomber who could score and rebound, and he is still considered by many to be one of the greatest passing forwards in the history of professional basketball.

During the 1971–1972 season—Barry's second season with the Nets and Erving's rookie campaign with the Squires—Barry averaged 31.5 points per game, spearheading a charge to the ABA Finals. (By now, the Nets were playing at Nassau Coliseum.)

In the off-season, however, Barry's Nets career ended abruptly because he was forced by the courts to return to a previously made commitment to the NBA's Golden State Warriors. Barry's departure hurt the Nets: they sank to the bottom of the standing under the weight of a 30–54 record. Attendance began to shrink dramatically, and Carnesecca went back to coach at St. John's.

"With Julius and Rick Barry on the same team, I probably would have been hailed a genius of a coach and general manager," Carnesseca said with a raspy laugh. "I would still be in the NBA today."

Boe, however, still had the pieces to rebuild, as well as the savvy and the cash to add to those pieces. His roster would soon include Brian Taylor, the eventual ABA Rookie of the Year who played just two years at Princeton University. Boe had pursued Taylor in an obvious sign that he no longer cared about the policy against bringing aboard undergraduates. After losing out on Erving simply because he believed that signing college players before they graduated was not the right thing to do, Boe had learned the hard way that taking the high road was not necessarily the fastest road to a championship.

With that in mind, Boe had also signed Jim Chones of Marquette University after Chones's junior season, adding him to a roster that already included John Roche, a guard from the University of South Carolina, and Billy Paultz, a rugged center from St. John's who was known as "the Whopper." Boe also rebuilt the top two rungs of the organization's ladder, signing Dave DeBusschere, who still had a year to play with the New York Knicks, as his general manager, and Kevin Loughery, another former NBA player, to coach the team.

"We were doling out all kinds of money," Boe recalled. "I thought DeBusschere gave us a nice legitimate presence, and we really began to put the pieces in place by signing a lot of excellent players to what were very fair contracts at that time."

4

Julius and Dave Down by the Schoolyard

Dave Brownbill played in the Rucker Tournament on the Daily News All-Stars, a team of mostly professional players called the Westsiders and coached by Peter Vecsey, then a sportswriter with the *New York Daily News* and now a basketball columnist with the *New York Post*. Brownbill invited Erving to play at the World's Most Famous Outdoor Arena in 1971, the summer after Erving decided to bolt UMass for the pros. The Westsiders squad included pros like Charlie Scott, Billy Paultz, Mike Riordan, and Ollie Taylor.

"I called Pete and told him about Julius, and I asked if I could bring him down, and he said okay," Brownbill remembered.

Vecsey recalled Erving approaching him that day about the possibility of receiving a paycheck for his efforts. "I had to take a short walk with Julius and explain to him that we didn't pay our players," Vecsey said. "I pretty much told him that most guys were out there for the love of the game and that the high level of competition would only make him a better player."

Erving's first game was against a team led by Sid Catlett, who played at the University of Notre Dame and then with Cincinnati in the NBA.

"On our first possession, Julius takes the ball and sails right by Catlett and two other guys and goes high for a slam, and the place goes crazy," Brownbill said. "His Rucker legend began growing right there."

Indeed, some of the Rucker faithful, amazed by Erving's aerial arsenal, began calling him "the Claw" because of his long hands and an enormous reach that enabled Erving to dunk a basketball like no other human being before him.

"Erving's hands are so big," Pete Vecsey once wrote, "that he could palm Sunday."

Others were calling Erving "Black Moses," "Houdini," or "Little Hawk"—the latter because his flights to the basket reminded them of the "Big Hawk," a high-flying predecessor named Connie Hawkins. Erving asked people to just call him "Doctor," a nickname that most basketball fans believe describes the surgical way that Erving carved up opponents on the basketball court.

That is not the case, however. "In high school," Erving once explained, "a friend of mine [Leon Saunders, his high school teammate] kept telling me he was going to be a professor, so I told him I was going to be a doctor. We just started calling each other that, 'Professor' and 'Doctor.' And later on, in the Rucker League in Harlem, when people started calling me

'Black Moses' and 'Houdini,' I told them if they wanted to call me anything, call me 'Doctor.'"

Brownbill simply called him the best. "Game after game, Julius just dominated," he said. "He was scoring at will and dunking on anyone who tried to guard him. It was like he was toying with these players, and we're talking about some of the best players in the world. He never said a bad word or got rattled on the court, but his dunks were so vicious, he would just shake the place to its core."

NBA referee Lee Jones was also there as a spectator for Erving's first-ever game at Rucker Park. "Julius had grown some six inches since high school," he said. "No one in the crowd, though, believed that kids from Long Island could really play basketball. Everyone always looked at it as strictly a city game.

"The first time Julius touched the ball, three defensive players converged on him," Jones recalled. "Suddenly, Julius just makes a sweeping move along the baseline, glides past all three of them, elevates, and, with his left hand, throws down a tremendous dunk.

"The crowd didn't even cheer because they were in complete shock," Jones added. "That was the first and last time they ever doubted that the kid from Long Island could play some ball."

Willie Hall, who had been a star at Archbishop Molloy High School in Queens and later at nearby St. John's University, still raises his eyebrows when he recalls his first glimpse of Erving at Rucker Park that summer.

"This kid was tall and very lean, with a gigantic Afro, so big he looked like a lion on stilts when I first saw him walk into the park on 155th Street," said Hall, now sixty-five. "What me and everybody else in that park did not know was that this was one ferocious lion."

Hall, who had played two seasons in Germany, was now teaming in the Rucker Pro Division with Tom Hoover, a five-year NBA player whose pro career had just ended after two seasons with the New York Knicks.

Hall and Hoover played for Sweet and Sour, a Rucker team named after a bar on 138th Street and Seventh Avenue. They wanted to whip and tame not only the young lion but Erving's young teammates as well.

"They were a great bunch of young players," Hall said. "They were in a lot better shape than we were, and they could run all day."

From the opening tip, Hoover began talking trash to Erving, which was nothing that Erving hadn't heard before in Campbell Park, in Roosevelt Park, or on any of the other playgrounds where he had left his mark.

"To his credit, Julius never said a word," Hall recalled. "Julius was always like that up there; he was always the perfect gentleman."

With a capacity crowd cheering, the six-foot ten-inch Hoover, who had not been guarding the almost six-foot seven-inch Erving to that point, suddenly found himself in the middle of the lion's den after a switch, and Erving tore Hoover to shreds.

Hoover tried defending Erving along the right baseline, still talking trash as he shuffled his feet. However, Hoover, his arms flailing as he backpedaled, had left a sliver of daylight between his body and the baseline, and Erving, smelling an opening to the basket, slipped past him and leaped high in the Harlem sky toward a steel, netless rim. The Lion was moving in for the kill.

Upon descent, Erving noticed that Hoover had positioned himself directly beneath the basket. It didn't matter; this was a nonstop flight, and Erving was taking it across the other side of the rim.

"Remember that great reverse layup Doc pulled off against Kareem Abdul-Jabbar and the Lakers in the NBA Finals?" Hall asked. "Well, this was the same type of reverse, except Doc finished it off with a powerful dunk."

Erving dipped past Hoover and rose again on the weak side of the rim, slamming the ball through the cylinder with such force that it crash-landed on Hoover's head and, as legend has it, dislodged the dentures in Hoover's mouth. His full set of false teeth fell to the asphalt with a click-clacking sound that had the packed house, including players from both teams, howling in delight.

"You had to see those people going crazy that day, " Hall said. "I mean, they were really out to lunch after that. "Even Tom was cracking up after he picked up his teeth."

By playing against grizzled veterans like Hoover and Catlett on the Rucker playground, Erving knew he was shaping his game and gaining the mental toughness he needed to help him survive at the next level. At the same time, he was able to use the tiny park as an experimental lab in which he created the kind of moves that Elgin Baylor and Connie Hawkins displayed before him—the kind of moves that would soon make him one of the world's richest and most famous athletes, the Michael Jordan of the bell-bottom era who would revolutionize the way professional basketball was played above the rim.

"A lot of my dunks I learned at the Rucker," Erving once told me. "At the Rucker, you had to come ready to do battle, to make your presence felt, to step up or get put down. You didn't have the luxury of playing an average game.

"I was a better professional player than I was an amateur, and it's usually just the opposite," he continued. "Most star players in high school are 30-point scorers, in college they become 20-point scorers, and in the pros they get 10 points a game.

"Well, I was the opposite, the exception. I was a better pro than amateur. I was a guy who got 10-plus points in high school, 20-plus points in college, and 30-plus points in the pros, so I was more a player who developed later. Although I was an all-star caliber high school player, I still wasn't the best player in the country—I mean, maybe in the top 100, but not the best. Then in college, I'd say I was in the top 40, maybe, but not the best. In the pros, I was able to reach the pinnacle of success."

The Doctor versus the Destroyer

Later in the same Rucker season, Erving's star, still rising, collided with that of a playground phenomenon named Joe "the Destroyer" Hammond. Hammond was the star of Milbank, a squad of playground legends with nicknames as colorful as their high-flying games. Milbank featured asphalt gods like Richard "Pee Wee" Kirkland, Eric "the Elevator Man" Cobb, and Pablo Robertson.

In every neighborhood, past or present, in just about every city in the United States, there is a basketball hotshot whose magical game in the schoolyard has earned him the kind of mythical status that travels far beyond the chain-link fence through which people pressed their noses to watch him fly. From the ghettos of Los Angeles to the strips of bubblegum-scarred blacktop scattered around New York's five boroughs, the questions have been asked from generation to generation: Who was the greatest playground player of them all, and despite his great talent, what kept him from making the leap from the playgrounds to the pros? Of the preeminent playground phenomena, none rivals Joe Hammond, whose extraordinary yet sad rags-to-almost-riches tale is beyond even Hollywood's scope and imagination.

Hammond was the greatest playground player in the golden years of the Rucker Tournament, the early 1970s, a time when weekend crowds exceeded ten thousand, including a number of white faces in the large audiences who had ventured into the deepest part of black Harlem to catch the greatest basketball show on earth.

"Virtually all the spectators were black," Dave Anderson wrote of one Rucker crowd on August 12, 1972. "But there were a few white faces, scattered like grains of salt in a pepper shaker."

At that time, the tournament consisted of ten teams that played a single round-robin schedule of nine forty-minute games. Admission was free, but the pro players often made joint out-of-pocket donations to worthy causes in Harlem.

The best playground players during Rucker Park's glory years were all New Yorkers, with Hammond at the head of the class. The best pros were Erving and Nate "Tiny" Archibald, a speedy point guard from the South Bronx who was also on his way to a great pro career.

"Playing in Rucker Park was an ego thing, because there were great players involved from both sides [of the basketball fence]," Archibald said. "In their hearts and souls the play-ground guys believed that they didn't have the same oppor-tunities as guys like myself and Julius Erving did to get to the pros, and they thought they were better than we were. So when I went out there, I had a lot to prove."

So did Erving, and so did Hammond. "The two great-est Rucker players of all time were Julius Erving and Joe Hammond," said Cal Ramsey, a rebounding machine at New York University who went on to play for the Knicks. "I think Joe was that good. He was the one playground player who always stuck out in my mind. You hear a lot of talk through-out the years about 'this guy was this' and 'this guy was that,' but I watched a lot of those other playground guys play, and there was an awful lot of exaggeration attached to their games."

Hammond has a basketball story unlike any player in the history of the sport. He never played one minute of high school basketball, yet at the age of twenty-one, in 1971, he was drafted by the Los Angeles Lakers.

Hammond, who had already achieved professional status in 1970 with the Allentown Jets of the Eastern Basketball League, learned the game on New York City streets. His primary stage became the Rucker Tournament, and once the Los Angeles Lakers—their roster filled with superstars like Wilt Chamberlain, Jerry West, and Elgin Baylor—saw Hammond in action, they drafted him and offered a rookie contract worth fifty thousand dollars. By then, however, Hammond already had another source of income: a lucrative drug trade on the Harlem streets.

"By the time the Lakers made their offer, I had over two hundred thousand dollars stashed in my apartment," Hammond once said to me. "I was making thousands of dollars a year selling marijuana and heroin. What was I going to do with fifty thousand dollars?"

That same season, Hammond also turned down a contract offer from the Nets of the ABA.

"At the time, people were talking about this guy like he was a god, he was that unbelievably talented," said Lou Carnesecca, then the coach and general manager of the Nets. "I made him an offer, but Joe just told me, 'Thanks, Coach, but I think I'll go my own way.' I always say that if he had stuck around, he would have helped me become a real contender."

Eventually, Hammond was swallowed up by the streets. He became a drug addict, was sent to jail three times on drug-related charges, and lost all his prospects and possessions.

"It's a shame, because Joe could flat-out play," Ramsey said. "He was a six-four two-guard who could shoot and slash, a combination of [New York Knicks players] Allan Houston and Latrell Sprewell. He was a bona fide player who could have been an NBA All-Star, and there's no doubt in my mind about that."

Nor was there any doubt in the minds of those in the standing-room-only crowds, many perched like pigeons atop fences and roofs, many others watching from high up on the viaduct leading to the 155th Street Bridge for a bird's-eye view of the battle between Hammond and Erving that came to a boiling point on a summer's day in 1971.

"We want Joe!" the crowd chanted on that steamy, historic day. "We want Joe!"

They stomped their feet as they chanted, but their local hero was nowhere to be found. The chanting continued to fill the Harlem air as players from both teams readied themselves for what would go down in street lore as the most storied playground matchup ever: a once-in-a-lifetime duel between Erving, the great Dr. J, and Hammond, his alternate-universe playground nemesis.

Erving, as skinny as six o'clock, walked into Rucker Park that day with an intimidating reputation that preceded him. Following, in a spectacular shadow that stretched from Roosevelt to West Harlem, were Erving's teammates: Charlie Scott, Billy Paultz, Mike Riordan, and Ollie Taylor, and others.

"The operating table is ready," the league's courtside announcer, Plucky Morris, blared over the public address system, "and the Doctor has his scalpel out."

The crowd, anticipating a series of space jams from a visiting player who was out of this world, gave Harlem's version of a Roman coliseum roar.

As they practiced layups and wind-mill jams, the Milbank players looked over their broad shoulders for Hammond, but their six-foot three-inch shooting god was nowhere to be found, so the game began without him.

Just minutes into the contest, Erving and company delighted the Rucker faithful with a lightning-quick transition game, finishing fast breaks with jaw-dropping swoops to the hoop and thundering dunks. "The Doctor is operating," Morris said as Erving head-faked Milbank's "Elevator Man," Eric Cobb, whipping past him and embarrassing him with a two-handed flush that nearly shook some fans out of the trees. "The operation was a success," said Morris. "The patient died."

By halftime, the Westsiders had built a comfortable, double-digit lead. Just before the start of the second half, as players warmed up on their respective layup lines, a park mascot known only as "Happy" scooted around the blacktop with a large squeeze-bottle filled with wine and poured the sweet red stuff into the open mouth of any player or fan who waved him over. Just as he had done on Archie Rogers's thirteenth birthday, Erving refused the wine. As Happy was making his rounds, a savage roar ripped through the crowd, and the fans began clapping their hands, stomping their feet, and craning their necks.

Across Eighth Avenue, Hammond, who said he missed the first half because he was shooting craps in a nearby social club, was getting out of a limousine. Swarmed by hundreds of autograph seekers and well-wishers, the Destroyer made a move for the court; then suddenly, Hammond said, "the crowd parted for me the way the Red Sea parted for Moses." Hammond rushed onto the court, slipped off his dress clothes to reveal a tank top and shorts, and shouted to no one in particular, "I'm here, Coach, I'm here!"

With the crowd drifting into the outer limits of hysteria, the second half began with Scott guarding Hammond. Soon after, Erving was ordered to lock down Hammond, and offensive fireworks filled the day.

"Everything we gave them, they gave right back," Pete Vecsey said. "All of us watched that day as Hammond, a kid who had surfaced from the cracks of Harlem, became a superstar. But Julius was the top name on the playground marquee, and he wasn't about to let Hammond have all the glory."

On Milbank's first offensive possession after the Doctor locked horns with the Destroyer, Hammond called for a clear-out, which means that he wanted his teammates to scatter so he could arrange for a one-on-one appointment with the Doctor. "Once the crowd heard me call for a clear-out," Hammond said, "the place went hysterical."

A strong leaper who rarely dunked during his playing days, Hammond faked a move to his left from the foul line and went right, with the Doctor in hot pursuit. Deep down the lane, both players elevated, and Hammond, with Erving literally stuffed in his jersey, took the Doctor for a little ride up north, wind-milling a jam over Erving's tall Afro and down through the basket.

"The crowd went off the hook, and Doc was screaming to the ref, saying I pushed off on him," said Hammond. "But the ref said, 'No way, Julius. If anything, the foul was on you.'"

On the Westsiders' next possession, Erving took the ball at the top of the key, and his entire team cleared out of the way.

"All of a sudden, it was like the court was tilted," Dave Brownbill recalled. "It was like the rest of us were on the low side of the court watching, while Julius was on the high side, all alone with the ball in his hands."

The Doctor knew just what to do with it. He took two dribbles while racing to the foul line, then took off from there, like one of those jets leaving Kennedy Airport. He sailed over Hammond and two other Milbank players for a rim-rocking dunk, sending tremors through Harlem that are still being felt by the Rucker faithful.

"Everyone on both teams and in the stands just kind of stood there for a second, frozen," Brownbill recalled. "And then the place just went berserk."

Legend has it that when the smoke cleared, Hammond had 50 points, earning Most Valuable Player honors, and the Doctor had 39. The Westsiders won in triple overtime. However, there are several conflicting versions of the Hammond–Dr. J confrontation, one provided by the Doctor himself. Although Erving agrees that the Westsiders won the contest, he remembers Hammond playing the entire game, not guarding him one-on-one the whole time, and not scoring 50 points.

"Let me start by saying that Charlie Scott showed me the ropes up at Rucker," Erving explained to me. "We were like Batman and Robin, and since it was his team, I was Robin. So any matchup we had was always Charlie versus Joe, Charlie versus Pee Wee [Richard Kirkland], or Charlie versus whoever. But because I became the more significant pro athlete, suddenly the stories get turned around like it was me versus somebody, when that really wasn't the case."

Pete Vecsey also dismisses Hammond's 50-point total, saying that he remembers both players scoring approximately 40 points apiece.

Ernie Morris, a former Rucker player and a park historian who was in the park that day, relayed what he had seen: "Both players were great, Joe did have a great game, and he did come late, but saying that he scored 50 points against Dr. J is a complete fabrication.

"You must remember," Morris added, "that Dr. J was at the height of his run at that time. He was killing everybody back in the day. Now, Joe held his own against Doc, but 50 in a half against the best player in the world? Get the hell out of here!"

Batman and Robin

After the greatest Rucker season of them all had ended in 1971, Charlie Scott watched Julius Erving breeze through the front door of Virginia Squires training camp in Richmond, Virginia. Scott, a six-foot five-inch scoring machine out of Stuyvesant High School in New York who made a stop at Laurinburg Institute (a school in Laurinburg, North Carolina) before taking his high-octane game to the University of North Carolina, was drafted by the Boston Celtics in 1970 but decided instead to sign with the Squires of the rival ABA.

The year before Erving joined the Squires, Scott was the team's greatest attraction, averaging 27.1 points per game en route to being named ABA Rookie of the Year. The following season, the man Julius Erving had earlier dubbed "Batman" at Rucker Park would become half of professional basketball's most dynamic duo.

"When we signed Julius, I knew we had ourselves an excellent player, because I had been a teammate of his at Rucker Park," said Scott, now fifty-eight. "But when I saw Julius playing against seasoned pros at the first camp with the Squires, the first thing I thought was that he was being underpaid."

Both Scott and Erving remember some veterans at that camp being less than enthused about having the high-flying Doctor in the house.

"I went into training camp, and it was like an open tryout," Erving recalled. "We had about 35 guys there, and they had set up three teams. By the second day of scrimmage, I'm running hard and dunking on guys and they're getting mad, so the general manager [Johnny Kerr] goes over to the coach [Al Bianchi] and asks him to sit me down. He says to the coach, 'Take him out, because one of these guys is going to hurt him.'"

Erving, a sleek, 216-pound dunking machine, remembered "running hard, because that was a carryover from my Rucker days."

"Having played in the Rucker, I only knew one way to play as a young pro, and that was hard. It was a confidence gained in believing you could do it. I'd already played against [almost] seven-footers like Connie Hawkins, Tom Hoover, and Harthorne Wingo in the same place Wilt [Chamberlain] had played, and I thought then, 'If I come down the lane and go up and then they jump to block it, if I can still hang there for a while and they hit me on the elbow while I'm throwing it down, well, I can do that to the other guys, too, because these guys are already pros.'

"So my confidence was sky-high. I felt invincible," Erving recalled, "but I guess I needed a little more savvy and moxie in terms of knowing how to pace myself in a pro setting."

This was the year that the nickname "Doctor" first merged with the *J* to make him "Dr. J." Roland "Fatty" Taylor, a member of the Squires, was responsible. He began calling Erving "Dr. J," and the nickname stuck.

Coach Al Bianchi was enamored of Erving the minute he laid eyes upon him. "What struck me most about Julie when I first met him," Bianchi said, "was his maturity and his huge hands. They were the hands of most great players that I've seen through the years."

Charlie Scott, who now runs a travel agency in Georgia, took a trip down memory lane and spoke of Erving in reverential tones. "Doc came in with a ferocity that was not seen at that time," he recalled. "He liked to run, like I did, which didn't go over very well with guys like Doug Moe and Ray Scott, who weren't exactly speed demons.

"Doc was doing everything in the first few days of camp: running, jumping, blocking shots, grabbing rebounds, and dunking on everybody. There was no doubt that he was going to be a success in the league."

The Boy Wonder

While "Batman" was en route to setting the ABA record for highest scoring average (34.6) per game that season, large crowds were turning out to see "Robin," the Boy Wonder from Long Island who seemed to defy gravity with each and every breathtaking swoop to the hoop. He was not allowed to dunk in college, but now he and ABA players like David Thompson, a six-foot four-inch pogo stick out of North Carolina who possessed a forty-four-inch vertical leap, could strut their stuff at an altitude higher than anyone else playing the game.

"It was like 'Free at last,'" Thompson said of his rookie season (1975–1976) with the Denver Nuggets (who by that time had changed their name from the Rockets) of the ABA. "The chains were loosened, and I could really show them what I could do. That was real exciting. I hadn't been able to dunk for four years in college, so that first year I tried to dunk every time I could."

The same held true for Erving, who was now slamming his way into national prominence like some basketball monster let out of the Curry Hicks Cage in the woods of western Massachusetts.

"Julius was just going bonkers; he was scoring 27 points a game and grabbing 15 rebounds," Scott said. "We were mostly a running team, and Doc liked to get out and run, so almost immediately he became instrumental to our success."

Despite the fact that the Squires finished in second place with a 45–39 record and seemed headed toward a championship, Scott was gone the following season, sold by Earl Foreman to the Phoenix Suns.

Fans and media still speculate that Scott had become bitter about sharing the red, white, and blue ball with Erving.
The general consensus was that "Batman" had grown jealous
of "Robin" and bitter about no longer being the focal point of
Virginia's offense, so he took his act on the road.

"I've heard people say that, but it's all nonsense," Scott
insisted. "Julius was not the reason I left the Squires. I had
already played for two years against the ABA's best players, and now I wanted to experience the challenge of playing in the NBA against guys like Wilt Chamberlain, Oscar
Robertson, Jerry West, and Kareem Abdul-Jabbar. I yearned
to play with the best, and those guys were the best. I was
also tired of playing in arenas in the middle of nowhere.
I mean, I'm all excited about coming to New York, but then
we [would] go out to Long Island to play the game—who
wants to play on Long Island, man? I didn't want to play ball
in places like Long Island and Louisville as much as I wanted
to play in cities like New York, Chicago, Detroit, and Los
Angeles.

"As far as playing with Julius was concerned, I was still
scoring 34 points a game, so what wasn't I getting? Julius and
I got along great together, and I think we each helped enhance
the other's game. I know the one thing I instilled in him as a
rookie was tenacity, to play hard every second, every minute
of every game, no matter who the opponent was. We played
games in Pittsburgh in front of two thousand fans, but we still
played hard."

"Batman" was asked what "Robin" had instilled in him.

"Julius taught me to play the game with grace and humility," Scott said. "He had a quiet confidence on the court that
I had not seen in any other player, and I always admired
that quality."

Like a UFO

By the end of Doc's first ABA season, people well-versed in professional basketball knew the name Julius Erving. By now, coaches, players, and astute fans alike were describing his meteoric rises to the hoop the way they might have described a UFO's blazing ascent into the heavens. Erving was fast, sleek, powerful, almost otherworldly, a rocket ship marked by the number 32 that blurred the line between fantasy and reality. He was on the ground one second and out of sight the next, leaving a fascinatingly eerie impression after every liftoff and spine-tingling dunk that what you had just seen, you would never see again.

"I tell people that if you think you saw the great Julie all those years in the NBA, you really didn't see him flying to the hoop the way we saw it in the ABA," Bianchi said. "The game was tailor-made for him in those ABA days. It was wide-open, a quicker pace, and there were not as many big men as there are now to challenge his aerial act."

Al Williams, Erving's old buddy and teammate on Hempstead's Salvation Army team, said that "with the Squires, and later the Nets, all that wide-openness of the ABA played right into Julius's strengths. He had great speed, an enormous wingspan, and a great first step. At that point in his career, he could get by anyone on the basketball court. He was virtually unstoppable."

Dave Anderson, one of the only, if not the only, New York sportswriters to cover Erving on a steady basis in those years, first heard of Erving at a Metropolitan Sports Writers dinner at Mama Leone's in Manhattan.

"All the coaches were recapping their games and looking ahead to others, when Jim McDermott, the head coach at Iona [College], stepped up to the podium," Anderson recalled.

"He starts talking about a game that his Gaels played against UMass [Amherst] and then says, 'We went up to the University of Massachusetts and lost, but I saw the best basketball player I've ever seen—Julius Erving.'

"Now, this was a basketball coach who had seen a lot of great players in his day, and Julius was virtually unknown, so McDermott was really going way, way, way out on a limb to be making that kind of statement. But it really aroused my curiosity, especially since Julius was a local kid, so I began to follow his career more closely, and I soon realized how much sense Jim McDermott made that day."

In his rookie season, Erving averaged 27.3 points per game and finished second to Artis Gilmore of the Kentucky Colonels for ABA Rookie of the Year. He was also named to the All-ABA Second Team and to the league's All-Rookie Team, helping the Squires to a 45–39 record and play-off series victories against Kentucky and the Floridians. Erving scored 53 points in one of four games during a sweep of the Floridians, before the Squires lost to Rick Barry and the Nets in the Eastern Division Finals.

Here is how *Black Sports The Magazine* described Erving's game during that time: "On the court he looms as a stutter-stepping, high-leaping poet in short pants; a soulful artist, who seems capable of moving his audience with gyrations, surpassing the best of James Brown. Indeed, in his own way, he is a genius of a performer."

5

Asking for
Another Raise

By the start of Erving's second season with the Squires, the ABA and the NBA were involved in a nasty tug-of-war over big-league talent. Erving was now the latest in a group of college and pro players who were caught in a bidding war between the two leagues.

For the second time in his life, Erving, now twenty-two, believed that he was being underpaid. Back in the early 1960s, he thought he was being short-changed on his paper route through Hempstead and Garden City. A decade later, he was now feeling shortchanged in Virginia, where he and Squires owner Earl Foreman had already agreed to a four-year deal worth half a million dollars.

In an attempt to maximize his earning potential, Erving dumped his Boston-based agent, Bob Woolf, from further contract negotiations, for Irwin Wiener, the thirty-nine-year-old manager of Walt Frazier Enterprises, a company that handled many pro athletes, including Archie Clark and Mike Riordan of the Baltimore Bullets. Wiener also represented two other members of the Squires: Bernie Williams and Roland "Fatty" Taylor.

"Woolf will continue to handle my financial matters," Julius told the late great *New York Times* sportswriter Sam Goldaper. "but Wiener will handle my contract negotiations. I have spoken to many players in both leagues, and I have learned a lot since I signed with the Squires. I was naive when I decided to turn pro. I didn't know much about contract negotiations, and my college coach recommended Bob.

"I'm happy playing with the Squires, but the life of a pro athlete is a short one, and after hearing about the money that is being tossed around, I don't think my contract is a fair one. I have proven myself, and I don't think I'm being paid the market value for the type of player I think I am. I deserve considerably more money. My contract needs restructuring so that I can receive more money now."

Erving, knowing full well that Foreman was listening, or at least reading, told Goldaper that "NBA representatives have talked to me."

Returning to Rucker Park

While the legal eagles were trying to determine the basketball fate of Julius Erving, the good Doctor kept practicing in his favorite lab: Rucker Park. He returned to the Harlem tournament for a second season as a more skilled hoop surgeon than he had been the season before.

Dean Meminger, who was somewhat underwhelmed by Erving's game when the two met in the 1969–1970 NIT tournament, was now getting a second look, and he was form-ing a second opinion about the young Doctor, who had been making headlines in sports pages around the country.

"In the summer of '72, I had a chance to encounter Julius Erving again," recalled Meminger, who was playing for the Sports Foundation team while Erving was still with Pete Vecsey's Westsiders.

"Julius was a whole different guy, a whole different player; the maturity level was completely different. I had never in my life seen anybody who was six-six or six-seven with the ability to hang up in the air so long and to be able to use both hands to dribble, shoot, and dunk. He had such great dexterity. This was the second coming of Connie Hawkins and Elgin Baylor, but at the next level, because Julius was faster and he could jump higher than those guys.

"I kept saying to myself that this could not be the guy I played against when I was at Marquette and he was at UMass. He had evolved into this unbelievable player. Once he got inside the foul line, he would just take off, like a jet. He was practically flying through the air, man, and it was like 'How do you stop this guy?' I was astonished."

Meminger, who had played hoops at Rice High School, a perennial Catholic power in West Harlem, was at the time just the second New York player, behind Kareem Abdul-Jabbar, to have earned All-City First Team honors three years in a row. He had become a college champion at Marquette University and was now living a dream by playing with his hometown Knicks.

Dean Meminger brought all those credentials to Rucker Park, but Julius Erving brought the crowds. "The good Doctor man, he went from being this skinny, relatively unknown guy at UMass to one of the greatest players, if not *the* greatest player, in the world," Meminger said. "He truly is one of a kind. He's what I'd like to call a generational pioneer. He added something to professional basketball that had not existed before he arrived: a small forward who could play like a guard but yet rise higher than any big man on the court. It's a rarity even in today's game."

The Wrong Kind of Bucks

On April 10, 1972, Wayne Embry, the Milwaukee Bucks general manager, made Erving his number one draft pick. Erving, had he stayed at UMass, would have been part of the school's senior class that season, and this made him eligible for the NBA draft under the league's four-year-college rule.

On April 11, the Atlanta Hawks announced that they had signed Erving the night before the NBA draft. Erving, of course, still had three years remaining on his contract with Virginia.

Suddenly, a three-ring circus the likes of which professional sports had never seen was in full motion. When Erving decided he no longer wanted to play for the Squires, he filed suit against the team, charging that a man named Steve Arnold, who initially acted as his agent, was also an agent for the ABA and could not simultaneously represent both parties.

So instead of reporting to the Virginia training camp before the start of his second professional season, Erving reported to the Atlanta camp, where he would sign a five-year contract for more than a million dollars and play in two exhibition games for the Hawks that season. (Erving's initial defection from Virginia followed that of Jim McDaniels from the ABA's Carolina Cougars to the NBA's Seattle SuperSonics and of Charlie Scott from the Squires to the NBA's Phoenix Suns.)

Playing alongside the great "Pistol Pete" Maravich, Erving scored 28 points in his first game for Atlanta, which defeated the Kentucky Colonels, 112–99, in an exhibition game in Frankfort, Kentucky, on September 23, 1972. In forty-two minutes, Erving grabbed 18 rebounds.

A week later, in his second and last game with the Hawks in Raleigh, North Carolina, Erving scored 32 points—shooting fourteen of fifteen shots from the field—in a 120–106 victory over the Carolina Cougars, who were led by Joe Caldwell's 24 points.

"I remember those exhibition games," Erving told *Basketball Digest* in October 2004. "I would just grab a rebound, throw it out to Pete, and get on the wing. Pete would always find you. He got his points, but he loved to pass the ball. He could hit you in full stride in a place where you could do something with the ball. That was a measure of his greatness.

"It really was one of the joys of my life to play with Pete, to be in training camp with him," Erving continued. "We used to stay after practice and play one-on-one. We would play for dinner after practice. I did the same thing with George Gervin once he became my teammate [in Virginia]—I pretty much learned that from Pete. If this guy is going to be your teammate, you really need to stay after practice and get to understand his game and know his likes and his dislikes—where he likes the ball and that kind of stuff. The best way to do that is to just play—go play each other one-on-one, two-on-two, three-on-three. Play away from the coaches, away from the whole team practicing in unison."

While Erving and Pistol Pete were sharing a ball—and having one—all the legal confusion resulted in the Squires filing suit in federal district court in Norfolk, Virginia, to bar Erving from playing with any other team. In the meantime, Embry and the Bucks and the rest of the NBA were angry with the Hawks for swooping in on Erving and ignoring the traditional drafting procedures the league had in place.

League officials had met five times to settle Erving's case, and at their fifth meeting, in September 1972, it was determined that Erving was indeed the property of the Bucks.

Walter Kennedy, then commissioner of the NBA, had pushed all along for Erving to go to the Bucks, who were salivating at the thought of teaming Erving with Abdul-Jabbar, creating a combination of talents that could have transformed the Bucks into a championship team, perhaps even a dynasty.

However, the Hawks contended that Erving was not subject to the NBA draft because he already was playing for the Squires of the ABA, and they filed a two-million-dollar antitrust suit against the NBA. The Hawks also charged the NBA with violating antitrust laws because the league's draft and four-year rule restrained competition for Erving among the NBA teams. Because the Hawks were acting in defiance of Kennedy, the NBA imposed fines against the team totaling fifty thousand dollars.

As the legal squabbling ensued, Erving missed the first four games of his second season with the Squires, until the courts eventually ruled that he return to play for Virginia.

"Most players who have switched leagues are no longer welcome in the cities whence they jumped," *Sports Illustrated*'s Peter Garry wrote at the time. "When Erving came back to Virginia, he was warmly greeted by his coach, his teammates, and the Squires' front office. The fans seemed to mistake him for General [Douglas] MacArthur."

It wasn't long before Erving regained his dominant form. "Not even two months into Erving's second season," Garry wrote, "one school holds that he is already the best forward ever to play the game, [and] another claims he needs a year or two more to polish up his defense and outside shot before he inevitably becomes the best."

Erving, now soaring beneath a different kind of spotlight, had a spectacular sophomore season with the Squires. With his high-voltage act electrifying the large, curious crowds who were coming out to see him, Erving led the ABA in scoring with a career-best 31.9 points per game.

"There was never any question that I wanted Julius back or how well he would play once he got here," Squires coach Al Bianchi said. "He had a great season as a rookie, averaging 27 points and 16 rebounds, but he was even better in the play-offs. He scored 33 [points] a game and 20 rebounds. That means he actually played better for us after he had signed with the Hawks. That's the kind of guy he is."

Erving was selected to the All-ABA First Team squad, an honor he would receive for four consecutive seasons.

"At that point, you might get an argument that Julius was or wasn't the best player in all of professional basketball," Lou Carnesecca said. "But nobody could argue [against] the fact that Julius was the most exciting player in the game. I mean, the guy was like a ballerina in short pants who floated on air. You had to see it to believe it. Connie Hawkins, who came before Julius, could really get up there, but even he couldn't jump like Julius.

"The most beautiful part of Julius's game was that he was never out of control. Every leap, as beautiful and breathtaking as it was, had a purpose, like it was choreographed for some performance at Lincoln Center, and there were only a few players in the world who could even attempt to imitate his moves because no one could jump that high," Carnesecca concluded, his voice reaching a raspy crescendo. "No one!"

6

Coming Home

On August 1, 1973, Erving was back in the headlines. Roy Boe, the owner of the ABA's New York Nets, had taken the moral high ground and made the mistake of a lifetime by passing on Erving a few years earlier. Now he put together a four-million-dollar package to bring Erving back to Long Island, where the Nets were based, and to satisfy the Virginia Squires, with whom Erving had played for two seasons, and the Atlanta Hawks, with whom Erving had played for two games.

"You heard of a three-ring circus. Well, this was more like a fifteen-ring circus," Boe said. "I mean, there were so many players and agents and team executives and league officials involved, and we were spending so much money in legal fees, it was just insane. Remember, we weren't fighting just to get Julius Erving on our team, we were also fighting to keep him in the ABA, because he was our biggest bargaining chip down the road.

If we had lost him at that point, there's no telling what would have become of the ABA."

Boe was still smarting from the loss of Rick Barry, who had been sent back to the NBA's Golden State Warriors after a judge ruled that the contract Barry originally signed with that team took precedence over any later agreement with any other team.

Now Boe sent a reported $750,000 in cash to the Squires as compensation for Erving's departure. The Nets also sent George Carter, their leading scorer from the previous season, to the Squires in exchange for Willie Sojourner, a six-foot eight-inch forward. The Squires also received the draft rights to Kermit Washington of American University, a fourth-round draft choice of the Nets who had led the nation in rebounding the two previous seasons.

The transaction, which remains one of the most complicated in sports history for a single player, consisted of a reported $425,000 payment to the Hawks, which included a $250,000 signing bonus that Erving had received from them. The balance of the payment made by the Nets was meant to cover the legal fees spent by the Hawks during their fight to add Erving to their roster.

Then there was Erving himself, who had filed suit against the Squires to get out of the remaining two years of his four-year contract. He received an eight-year deal from the Nets at an annual salary of $350,000 per year. (The Nets also helped themselves greatly that season by signing Larry Kenon, or "Dr. K," a six-foot nine-inch forward from Memphis State University who was one of the most highly rated players in the NBA. The Nets also signed John "Superfly" Williamson, a talented free agent from New Mexico State University.)

"I'm making an investment," Boe said at the time, "figuring [that] with Julius Erving on our side, were going to win."

As for the Milwaukee Bucks, who had done little more throughout the Erving saga than sit on their hands and hope that NBA justice would prevail, they received nothing but heartache. William H. Alverson, their president, described the historic and bizarre transaction as "the rottenest caper I've ever seen."

Roy Boe's Four-Million-Dollar Gamble

Before Erving had played his first regular-season game for the Nets, it was obvious that Roy Boe's four-million-dollar gamble would pay handsome dividends. During the exhibition season, Erving exploded with 42 points in a game against the Baltimore Bullets, and he followed that with a 27-point outburst against Walt Frazier and the New York Knicks at Madison Square Garden.

"There was so much excitement surrounding our team at that time," Boe said. "We felt we were as good, or even better, than any team in either league."

Anyone in the Garden crowd of 17,226 who had not seen or heard of Erving by now knew not only that he was a force to be reckoned with but also that the Nets, who handed the defending NBA champion Knicks a 97–87 defeat on their home court, had certainly become one of the better teams in all of basketball.

Erving played his first official game in the red, white, and blue star-spangled uniform of the Nets on October 10, 1973, against the Indiana Pacers before a near-capacity crowd of 8,300 at the Fairgrounds Coliseum in Indianapolis. In forty-six minutes, he scored 42 points and pulled down 18 rebounds in the Pacers' 118–99 victory.

"I remember that first game against Indiana," Nets coach Kevin Loughery said. "Just before halftime, we had the last shot in a close game. The clock was ticking down and the ball went to Doc, who was standing alone in the right corner. Doc put the ball down and headed full steam toward the rim. George McGinnis and Darnell Hillman, who was just as big as George, both tried to prevent Doc from getting to the rim. Doc picked up his dribble and just soared right over both of them and slammed it down. In all my years as a player and a coach, I had never seen anything like that. I just thought, 'Damn, that was something. Things are going to be okay around here for a while.'"

Two nights later, on the eve of the opening of the World Series between the New York Mets and the Oakland Athletics, Erving made his home debut against the Squires at Nassau Coliseum before a crowd of 7,207. He scored 38 points in a 116–105 victory.

Squires coach Al Bianchi called the performance "typical Julie."

After a poor start, the Nets made a midseason move, acquiring Mike Gale and Wendell Ladner from the Kentucky Colonels for John Roche, a six-foot three-inch guard from the University of South Carolina. Jim Chones, who was no longer needed by the Nets, had been passed on to the Carolina Cougars. With a starting forward line of Erving, Larry Kenon, and Billy Paultz and a talent-laden team with an average age of twenty-three, Roy Boe had put his team in a position to dominate the ABA for years to come.

"We knew we were good," Boe said, "and we knew we were going to be good for a long time."

In February 1974, word began to spread through the basketball world that Erving, one of America's most eligible and wealthy bachelors, was about to get hitched.

"Everyone wanted to know who Doc was marrying and when he was getting married," said Dave Brownbill, a member of Erving's wedding party. "Julius just wanted us to keep everything private, and we respected his wishes."

Nevertheless, the word somehow got out that Erving would marry Turquoise Brown of Winston-Salem, North Carolina, at 2:30 p.m. on February 9 at the Americana Hotel in Manhattan.

"By the time we got to the Americana, it was past two-thirty and a huge crowd had gathered," Turquoise recalled in the *New York Times*. "We took one look at all the photographers and reporters and decided not to hold the wedding there. The judge who was to marry us suggested a suite at the Waldorf, so we got the word to Julius to meet us there."

"I never did get to the Americana," Erving said. "But I got the word to go over to the Waldorf."

The wedding finally did take place at the Waldorf—at 12:05 a.m. on February 10. "My mother was late arriving," Turquoise said. "When we finally took the vows, it was morning and only three friends of ours were present as witnesses."

After marrying Turquoise, Erving failed to make the starting lineup in the next game, against the Memphis Tams at Nassau Coliseum. His new bride was there watching.

"At that point, Doc had the world on a string," Dave Brownbill said. "He had a dynamite game to go along with a dynamite wife. He really had it all."

By the end of his first season with the Nets, Erving had indeed become one of the biggest success stories in all of professional basketball. He led the ABA in scoring for the second straight campaign, with a 27.4 average. He also finished seventh in the league in rebounding, sixth in assists, and third in both steals and blocks en route to capturing his first Most Valuable Player award. He was the only unanimous choice on the 1973–1974 All-ABA team.

That year, the league's best players rounded out the All-ABA team, including George McGinnis, a forward with the Indiana Pacers; Artis Gilmore, a center with the Kentucky Colonels; Jimmy Jones, a guard with the Utah Stars; and

Mack Calvin, a guard with the Carolina Cougars. The second team featured Dan Issel, a forward with the Kentucky Colonels; Willie Wise, a forward with the Utah Stars; Swen Nater, a center with the San Antonio Spurs; Ron Boone, a guard with the Utah Stars; and Louie Dampier, a guard with the Kentucky Colonels.

Erving explained to the *New York Times* that season why he was now in a class all by himself. "As a pro, most of my moves are impulsive, instinctive," he said. "I can do the things I do because I put in the time experimenting with them, developing them, and polishing them. I watch players, all players. I watch them on television, at college games, on the playground—you can learn from anybody.

"Even now I'll be watching a game somewhere, and I'll see somebody do something that'll remind me of something I've forgotten, some little move, maybe. I'll practice it a little, and I've got it back, and when the right situation comes along against some player, maybe I've got a little edge I didn't have before. I know what I should do in certain situations, and that's what I do. It doesn't require thinking about [the moves]. It's a court awareness of knowing what the situation is and what it calls for. But you can't be inhibited.

"Many players feel that if they make a mistake their coach is going to take them out. They play with the ball on a string all the time. I know players who can do fantastic things with the ball, but they never do them. They fear that if they don't play a mechanical game and stick to the patterns, they're going to be taken out. I'd hate to be in a position where I had to play like that. Mentally your head has to be where you don't place limitations on yourself. You never say I can't make the steal or I can't hit a three-pointer. You never deal with negatives. You never give up trying. Over the long haul that's the way good players are made."

Erving once famously quipped to *Sports Illustrated*, "When it's my turn to solo, I'm not about to play the same old riff." That line, in this author's mind, runs a close second to the line Erving once used to describe his gliding to the hoop: "When you're up there, you just float."

After posting a 55–29 record, Erving and the Nets floated into the postseason, where they beat the Virginia Squires in five games, swept the Kentucky Colonels in four, and won the ABA championship by knocking off the Utah Stars in five games.

"There he is," Coach Loughery said of Erving shortly after the Nets won their first championship. "Pound for pound, he's the greatest basketball player in the game."

In the first game of that championship series, Erving made an amazing 47 points. Here is how Dave Anderson described two of them: "On 45 of those points, his teammates reacted casually. They had seen all the shots before: the slam dunks, the floating layups, the twisting jump shots. But the other two points were something special. Dr. J was loping around the left corner in front of the Nets bench when he started to drive the base line. But he was being angled out of bounds by Bruce Seals, the 6-foot-9-inch forward guarding him. Although far behind the plane of the backboard, Dr. J sprang high, reached out with the ball in his right hand, and flicked it over Seals' outstretched hand, past the side of the backboard and through the orange rim. On the bench, his stunned teammates snapped their heads from side to side. Some even shrieked, Whooooo, Whooo, the way small boys might. His teammates hadn't seen that move before."

Erving said that the Nets' recipe for success was a mixture of youth, experience, and savvy coaching. "Even though I was the leading scorer and rebounder on that team," he explained, "we had some veteran players, particularly Billy Melchionni, who had great experience. He had been a champion in Philadelphia.

"I thought we had a nice mix of young players, but it's the whole package put together that makes you a team that can be a champion, because we were playing against a pretty veteran team in the Utah Stars, with Zelmo Beaty, Willie Wise, Ron Boone, and that crew—they were actually more experienced than we were. Our coaching staff of Kevin Loughery and Rod Thorn were seasoned veterans of play-off wars [as NBA players] and guys who really knew what to talk to the players about in the locker room. I was maybe the horse, so maybe they loosened up the reins and let the horse do what the horse had to do, but the brain trust was way beyond what my understanding of the scope of the situation was."

In the first championship series, Mike Gale averaged 8.3 points per game in the play-offs, ranked third on the team in assists (4.1 per game), and played strong defense. Gale considers that championship the most memorable moment of his career, and he says he will never forget the kind of creative force that Erving was at the secondary gyms, just beyond the reach of the national spotlight during the helter-skelter days of the ABA.

"Doc came out, and he was an awesome player," Gale said. "Because of the way the ABA was at that time, not having a national television contract, most of America did not get to see him in what we would call his prime. Some of the moves that he made you will never see again. If you talk to him about it, he'll tell you that it was not something that he consciously knew he was doing but it was just what the situation called for. It was a sight to see. We sat back as teammates and would say, 'How'd he do that?'"

A Familiar Ring

On the morning the Nets would clinch their first championship, the phone rang in Erving's hotel room. The Doctor picked it up.

"Hello, Doc," the voice on the other end said. "This is Jack Wilkinson."

It was the same Jack Wilkinson who had squared off with Erving ten years earlier at Lynbrook High School, ringing up 23 points on the man who was now considered by many to be the number one basketball talent on earth.

Wilkinson was covering sports for the *Miami News-Record* and decided to write a feature on Erving, trying to capture the Doctor's mood as he closed in on the title of number one basketball talent on earth.

"I call up the hotel room and ask for Julius Erving," he explains. "The phone rings, and all of a sudden he picks it up. I say, 'Hi, Doc, this is Jack Wilkinson. I played high school ball against you when I was at Lynbrook. The first thing he says to me is 'How's Weiss?' He was talking about our cocaptain, Richard Weiss, a talented forward on our team. He then starts rattling off all these other names. I couldn't believe he remembered half the guys he remembered.

"During the conversation, I hear a knock on the door [of Erving's room], and I find out it's room service. So Doc puts me on hold, comes back with his meal, and keeps talking while he's eating. This is a guy who is a few hours away from playing the most important basketball game of his life, and he just stays on the phone, calm as can be. Finally, he says he needs to get a little rest before the game, so he has to go.

"But the time he took with me on the phone, and just the fact that he remembered all those high school players and wanted to know how they were doing, really spoke volumes about who Julius Erving was, not only as a player but as a human being. He was as much a gentleman as he was a professional superstar, the same classy person he was as a high school kid. All those years later, nothing much had changed."

Grounded

After winning the first championship with the Nets, Erving was suffering from aching knees. He visited seven orthopedic specialists in New York, New Jersey, Philadelphia, Oklahoma City, and Los Angeles.

"Maybe it was a psychological kind of thing," Erving said at the time. "But I had to make sure about my knees. You hear so much about knee problems curtailing careers of athletes that it scares you. I had to make sure the pain I experienced last season wasn't doing any permanent damage to my knees. I wasn't looking for any drugs to give me temporary relief."

As a result, Erving was unable to play at Rucker Park or on the playgrounds during the summer of 1974. It was the first time in his life he could not play pickup basketball in the parks, and he was crushed.

"It was a mind-blowing experience," he said. "At times I felt like I was going stir-crazy. I would go down to the basement of my home and move boxes from one side of the room to another, just to find something to do."

While Erving was keeping his knees on ice, his place in the game had become a hot topic to sportswriters like Anderson and basketball fans everywhere, all of whom were beginning to wonder if Dr. J was perhaps the greatest forward the game had ever seen. Those conversations included the likes of Elgin Baylor, Rick Barry, John Havlicek, and Dave DeBusschere.

"He's got the greatest potential of any forward I've seen," Rick Barry, then with the Golden State Warriors, said of Erving. "If he works hard, he could be the best forward in the game."

Certainly, there was no better small forward; Erving had revolutionized the way the game was played, if not controlled, from that position.

"Baylor was the best for a longer time," Loughery told the *New York Times* shortly after winning the championship, "but Doc is a better all-around player than Baylor ever was. He could do everything Baylor could do on offense and more, and he plays better defense."

Willie Wise of the Utah Stars, then one of the best defensive forwards in the league, said simply: "If Doc's not the best, I'm in for a real treat."

At age twenty-four, Julius Winfield Erving II, aching knees and all, was at the top of his game and on top of the world. Forget P. T. Barnum; Dr. J had become the greatest show on earth, but his future seemed more secure than the league in which he was playing.

7

In a League of His Own

By the 1974–1975 season, Erving's second with the defending-champion Nets, they were no longer the *other* team in New York. In fact, they had all but stolen the spotlight from the Knicks, who had begun to fade from the glory of their 1970 and 1973 championship seasons. In much the same way that Joe Namath of the American Football League's New York Jets had stolen a considerable amount of local newspaper ink from the long-established New York Giants by winning Super Bowl III, Julius Erving had done the same for the Nets by winning an ABA championship. The Nets were now as good as any team in professional basketball, and their leader, Julius Erving, had become the game's greatest attraction, Joe Willie in a tank top and shorts, the best bang for basketball bucks anywhere in the country.

"With him," Dave Anderson wrote of Erving in February 1975, "the Nets have upstaged the Knicks, at least in artistry if not appreciation, in New York basketball. No longer do knowledgeable basketball people wonder how good the Nets are, they wonder how many members of the current Knick team would be able to make the Nets squad. Walt Frazier and Earl Monroe would be the starting guards, but Bill Bradley and Phil Jackson would be backup forwards and John Giannelli would be the backup center. And so the pendulum swings, with Doctor J riding it as if he were floating in for a dunk shot. In the fourth American Basketball Association season, he is the game's most exciting player. But beyond that he is an old pro, with an attitude and an understanding that some players never develop. And for all his remarkable repertory on the court, he prefers to understate everything else."

That same month, the Doctor completed his longest operation en route to a 63-point performance at the International Sports Arena in San Diego.

On February 14, 1975, the Nets and the San Diego Conquistadors did battle in a four-overtime thriller with San Diego eventually winning, 176–166. It would become the longest game in the ABA's nine-year history, the first and last four-overtime game in league history, and the highest scoring game to that point in professional basketball, with a two-team total of 342 points. Erving, who scored 45 points in regulation, scored a total of 63 points, which surpassed the total of 58 points that he once scored against the Nets and which represented the league's individual high for the year.

The Nets had a 5-point lead, with only forty-four seconds to go in regulation time, but lost it when Warren Jabali was fouled by Willie Soujourner while scoring a basket for a 3-point play and then Travis Grant hit a twenty-two-foot jumper at the buzzer that made the score 129–129. Erving's basket, with seven seconds to go, tied the first overtime at 144–144. It became 152–152 on a 3-point basket by Bill Melchionni with twenty-three seconds to go in the second overtime, and Brian Taylor tied up the third one the same way, at 161–161, with twenty-two seconds to go. But the Conquistadors, who had lost eight games in a row before this one, broke the contest open midway through the fourth extra period. The game took three hours and ten minutes of real time to complete, or sixty-eight minutes of actual game time.

In the quiet of the Nets dressing room after the game, Erving had his feet buried in ice bags. "I've never seen a game like this before," he said, "and nobody else ever did."

The historic contest, played before a sparse crowd of 2,916, which was actually a decent turnout for the troubled San Diego franchise, was littered with 72 personal fouls, and a whopping 128 rebounds were pulled down. The final score remained a record until December 13, 1983, when the Detroit Pistons, led by Isiah Thomas's 47 points, squeaked past the Denver Nuggets, 186–184, in a triple-overtime NBA game in Denver.

"It's disheartening to lose when you have put so much into it," said Erving, who played sixty-six of the sixty-eight minutes, made twenty-five of fifty-one shots, and pulled down 23 of the Nets' 57 rebounds.

"I hope I'm never in one like this again," the Doctor said of his extended house call, pausing for a second before adding, "unless we win."

By season's end, the Nets had improved on the fifty-five victories they had compiled the previous season, winning fifty-eight games, a team record that still stands. Erving had another dynamite year, finishing with averages of 27.9 points, 10.9 rebounds, and 5.5 assists.

The Nets, however, were eliminated by the Spirits of St. Louis in the first round of the play-offs. The series, considered one of the greatest upsets in basketball history, was a microcosm of Erving's season: he averaged 27. 4 points and 9.8 rebounds over five games. The Nets won the first game but lost the next four. Erving said that the second game of that series was the turning point.

The Nets and the Kentucky Colonels each finished with a 58–26 record in that 1974–1975 season, but the Colonels claimed the Eastern Division title by beating the Nets 108–99 in a special one-game play-off. As a result, the Nets faced the 32–52 Spirits of St. Louis in the first round of the play-offs. The Nets had gone 11–0 against St. Louis during the regular season and took the first game of the series, 111–105, but then the Spirits roared back with an unexpected vengeance, eliminating the defending champions.

The shocking end to the Nets' season led Roy Boe to make some very rash and highly criticized personnel moves. He made three separate deals with San Antonio Spurs owner Angelo Drossos: the Nets acquired Swen Nater, who led the ABA in rebounding in 1974–1975 with 16.4 per game, for Larry Kenon; acquired Billy Paultz for Rich Jones, Chuck Terry, Bob Warren, and Kim Hughes; and sold Mike Gale for cash.

"We had beaten them twelve straight times that season, but they came ready to play," Erving said of the Spirits of St. Louis. "We won the first game on some lucky plays, but we didn't give them the proper respect. I think I had 6 points by the middle of the third quarter, Kevin Loughery had been thrown out of the game, and I got pulled by an assistant coach. We threw in the towel with a quarter and a half [of another quarter] left, and I decided that I would never let that happen again."

A month before, Peter Garry of *Sports Illustrated* offered an intimate portrait of Erving that made it easy to see why he was quickly becoming one of America's most beloved superstars.

Under the headline "Big Julie Is Doing Nicely-Nicely," Garry wrote, "Julius Erving was near the front of the line as the New York Nets snaked out of their dressing room in the Nassau Coliseum and jogged down the tunnel heading for the gleaming floor where they would play host to the ABA's Eastern Division–leading Carolina Cougars one night last week. But by the time the Nets began their layup drill, Erving was no longer with them. He could barely be made out in the dim passageway doing something pro players rarely deign to do, something most would consider uncool immediately before a game. He was talking animatedly and signing autographs for a boy and his father, a small man wearing a black velvet yarmulke. Erving had never met them before, but when he heard that the rabbi had driven 150 miles from upstate New York to fulfill his boy's fondest Chanukah wish—to see Dr. J play—Erving, quite naturally for him, could not resist stopping to chat.

"Amenities completed, he rejoined his teammates, slammed a few perfunctory pregame dunks, did a quick sideline critique of Center Billy Paultz's father's basso profundo rendering of 'The Star-Spangled Banner' ('Not bad at all, but I could teach him a few things about projection'), and then went out and put on another ho-hum performance against Carolina. He scored 23 points. He grabbed 12 rebounds. He stole the ball three times. And he tipped in the deciding basket as the Nets won 99–96, knocking the Cougars out of first and moving themselves within a half game of the new leader, Kentucky, in the hottest three-team race in the pros.

"Yes, Julius Erving has brought his Dr. Nicely-Nicely routine back home to Long Island. He has done nicely on the floor, where he has led the youngest starting lineup in the pros—average age 22.6 years—back from a skitterish start and into title contention. He has done nicely off it as well, charming the clergy, his employers, the recently reelected Nassau County Executive (whom he endorsed after extracting pledges for recreational programs for his hometown of Roosevelt), and even the Madison Avenue types who are after some endorsements of their own. Naturally enough, Dr. J now spiels for Dr Pepper."

The Prisoner and the Pro

While behind bars at the Elmira Correctional Facility in Elmira, New York, in the winter of 1973, Archie Rogers had seen Erving play as a first-year member of the Nets on a small black-and-white television set at the prison, and he began a soul-searching mission that ended in his becoming a Muslim.

"The whole time in prison, while I was searching for God, I was thinking of Julius and about the great times we spent together as kids," Rogers said. "The difference between me and Julius was that he was a leader and I was a follower, and it ain't any simpler than that. But when I was in prison I wanted to find that same God who created Julius perfectly, who gave him that beautiful gift of basketball greatness. I wanted to find this God to learn what gift he had in store for me, and I found Allah. When I got introduced to Islam, it was a serious awakening."

When Rogers left prison in 1975, he owned nothing except for a newfound faith, and he had not yet kicked his drug habit. He borrowed money for a train ticket and hopped on the train to Long Island to visit his schoolboy pal. Erving was now living in upper Brookville, Long Island, in a beautiful seventeen-room home with seven bedrooms and six bathrooms on more than three acres of prime property, complete with a pool, a sauna, a play area, and a wine cellar. The house was in an excellent school district and near the Long Island Expressway, which made traveling to and from the Nassau Coliseum a breeze for

Erving, who was now a millionaire in his third season with the Nets.

"Julius invited me up there, and he offered me some money to get back on my feet, but I was still using drugs and too ashamed to take it, and I turned him down," Rogers said. "Here was this guy, after all the bad I had done, still sticking with me like a brother."

After Erving offered Rogers money, Rogers offered Erving something in return: religion. "I brought the Koran a few times to his house, and we sat down and had some very deep, very inspiring religious conversations," Rogers recalled. "To tell you the truth, I was trying to convert Julius, and I think that behind my back, he went and did a little research into the Muslim faith, but in the end, he didn't embrace it. In fact, he used to call himself a born-again Christian."

Indeed, Erving often talked about embracing his Christian faith. "When I gave my life to Jesus Christ, I began to understand my true purpose for being here," he said. "It's not to go through life and experience as many things as you possibly can and then turn to dust and be no more. The purpose of life is to be found through having Christ in your life, and understanding what His plan is, and following that plan. My Christian faith has helped me put my priorities in order. If I put God number one and my family after that, along with my social existence and my job, I can withstand any attack or criticism."

On Father's Day that year, Erving brought Rogers up to the front of his church and introduced him to the congregation. "Before I speak to this congregation, there is an individual here I would like to introduce to you who has played a very important part of my life," Erving said.

Rogers was speechless. "Here I was, this drug addict, this ex-convict, and Julius Erving is telling the people he loves and respects the most that I played an important part in his life.

Until my dying day, I will always know that God blessed me when he made Julius my friend."

One Last Charge

After a disappointing season, the Nets retooled for another run at an ABA championship. Erving made that run in Converse sneakers. He had become the company's first pro pitchman in 1975, promoting Converse's new line of performance footwear, and he later became a member of the company's board of directors.

That season, the team added Swen Nater, a shot-blocking center from the San Antonio Spurs, who was immediately blown away by Erving's work ethic and the aura that surrounded his legend.

"One of the things that people don't know about Doc was that most of those great moves and spectacular dunks of his, he actually worked on in practice," Nater said. "It seemed improvisational on the court, but Doc already had most of those moves choreographed, and the trick was to know when to pull them out. And don't let all that flash fool you, because Doc was a very fundamentally sound player. People came to see Doc because they wanted to witness one of his spectacular breakaway dunks. I can't think of another player, with the exception of Michael Jordan, who was that spectacular and yet that fundamentally sound. In terms of who are the most spectacular and exciting players in the history of the game, I'd have to rank Doc right behind Michael, but it would be close.

"The one thing that Doc's creativity did for me, and I'm sure for many of the other players, was to get us to start thinking outside the box in terms of creating shots on offense," Nater added. "Watching him perform those aerial feats made us think of ways that we could be more creative and improve our own games. Doc was a serious student of the game. I don't know where the nickname 'Doctor' came from, but in my eyes, he became a doctor through all those years of researching the weaknesses of opposing defenses, experimenting with great moves during thousands of hours in the gym, and then using the great moves he had created to attack those defenses. The game of basketball is all about reading defenses, and Doc was the master of that. Of course, it's a lot easier to read a defense when you can simply fly over it."

In his quest for a second ABA crown and a burning desire to avenge the loss to the Spirits of St. Louis in the play-offs, Erving remained on air attack all season. He averaged 29.3 points a game during the regular season on the way to winning the ABA scoring title and his third consecutive Most Valuable Player award.

"He creates," Lou Carnesecca said of Erving that season, speaking of the Doctor in reverential tones. "It just flows out of him. Erving has great imagination on the court. Every night he upstages himself. You can talk about this guy like a poet, an artist, or a great dancer. He is all three on the basketball court. Julius plays with such flair. Yeah, that's the way I want to put it. Julius is more creative, more imaginative."

Despite the fact that Erving was the biggest star in the ABA, Nater recalled, he always made time for his teammates and the fans. "It would not have been a good situation if Doc was a prima donna," Nater said. "But even though he was so much better than the rest of us, he worked hard at fitting into a team concept. He was a very team-oriented, approachable guy.

"After games, Doc would just stick around and sign autograph after autograph. We would go back to our hotel by bus, and he would jump in a cab and meet us there later."

Nater remembers one play in particular that season that illustrated the many athletic gifts that the basketball gods had bestowed on Erving. "It's the one Dr. J play I'll never forget," he said. "We were playing defense against a team, and the ball was going out of bounds deep along the left sideline near some courtside seats. Doc leaped into the air, and we all thought that he was just trying to save the ball, but he had spotted Billy Melchionni streaking up the court, about eighty feet away, with a defender in close proximity. So Doc leaped, and while he and the ball were still in the air, Doc grabbed it with his left hand and just fired it, underhand, downcourt, like it was a bowling ball. He actually put some kind of left-handed spin on it, because the ball kept sailing up the sideline, almost at a ninety-degree angle, away from the defender and right into the hands of Melchionni, who dropped it in for an easy layup. I have never seen another human being do something like that on a basketball court."

Almost everyone connected to the Nets has a Julius Erving story to tell.

Rod Thorn, a former Nets assistant coach and now the team's president, recalled a fast break one night in San Antonio when Brian Taylor bounced a long pass ahead of Erving, who was steaming down on the right. However, the ball appeared to be on its way into the crowd.

"Doc just extended his right arm and caught the ball," Thorn said, "but he never brought the ball into his body and never dribbled. In one motion, he just grabbed it, went up, and slammed it in. No other human could have done that. Another time, in San Antonio, he drove in and James Silas undercut him. I don't know how Doc did it, but he came down on his feet—like if you drop a cat upside down, it'll still land on its feet."

Stan Albeck, a former head coach for the Nets, recalled a time when Erving was still with the Virginia Squires and Albeck was coaching the San Diego Conquistadors. "He leaped in the air away from the boards, grabbed a defensive rebound, and was about to start the fast break when one of my players jumped in front of him. Doc was still in the air trying to pass, but sensing that the right-handed pass he was about to throw might be deflected, he turned 360 degrees, changed hands and flipped a high left-handed pass off his hip before his feet reached the floor. The ball dropped into Bernie Williams's hands, and he took off full speed for the layup. Man, I thought I'd seen everything. But that 360-degree job, nobody has done anything like that. It was unbelievable."

Bob Costas shared with me another tall tale about Erving: "Julius had a play in Louisville that I didn't call but have heard about from several eyewitnesses," the broadcaster said. "The Nets were in town, and during a game, Julius was playing defense at the top of the key when he deflected a pass and batted the ball forward, to himself. As Julius raced up the floor, Ted 'Hound Dog' McClain, a pretty good defensive guard, raced down the floor and tried to cut Julius off at an angle just inside the foul line. McLain beat Julius to the spot and went down to ready himself in a defensive position. Well, by the time Hound Dog looked up, Julius had soared right over his head, leaping from just inside the free throw lane for a dunk. This of course, is the stuff of legend, but whenever Julius Erving's name is a part of any story that involves defying gravity, you tend to believe the legend.

"I saw in many cities what a lot of other people saw, just how great a basketball player Julius was. I saw so many of those fast breaks and steals and blocked shots and dunks, the whole arsenal. But the one thing that people have always overlooked about Julius's game was just how great a rebounder he was. He used that great leaping ability not only to score points but also to rebound like few players could, especially in his prime.

"You have to also remember that most of Julius's great moves were not the result of some broken play where he just ran out ahead of the field and dunked. A lot of those dunks came at the back end of plays, after Julius had a done a masterful job of evading a defense. Sometimes, the way he split two opponents, slithering through them or just leaping past them, was more beautiful than the dunks or other finishing touches he put on a given play. Julius was a showman in every sense of the word. "

In 1976, Bob Bass, the former coach of the Floridians, recalled a game that Erving played against his team. "He took the whole building through the net on one stuff shot. He took off from behind the free throw lane and flew along in the strato[sphere]. When he dunked it, he created such a vacuum that everyone's ears cracked on the bench."

At the All-Star break that season, the financially troubled league—which by then had been reduced to one division—staged the very first Slam Dunk Contest.

"The ABA promoted showmanship because it was fighting to survive and find its niche, so the players were willing to try more spectacular stuff," said Rod Thorn. "That's when Dr. J really brought the dunk into focus. He dunked everything. He was a high-wire act. He was like a totally different kind of player. When he was in his physical prime, he'd bring you up out of your seat four or five times a night with some of the stuff he did. He got a lot of publicity for it, and the game started changing."

The high-flying field included Erving and four more of the ABA's most exciting players: Larry Kenon (Erving's team-mate with the Nets), Artis Gilmore, George Gervin, and David Thompson. Erving, the odds-on favorite, slammed his way to the crown. The Doctor's final dunk—in which he clutched the ball in one hand, motored the length of the floor, leaped from the free-throw line, and stuffed the ball in an authoritative, stratospheric way—became one of the signature moments of his glorious career. Shown on many local newscasts around

the country, that one celestial jam spawned an entire generation of dunkers and enhanced the legend of the legendary
Dr. J. The NBA took notice of an ABA superstar who was out
of this world.

"I think that the Slam Dunk Contest was one of the things
that really caught the attention of the NBA," Gervin said to me
during All-Star weekend in Las Vegas in 2006. "At the time,
both leagues had been considering a merger, and I think that
me and Doc and the rest of the ABA stars, all of whom had an
abundance of talent and always put on a show, made it impossible for the NBA to continue without us."

Black Sports The Magazine published an interview with Erving
that covered his thoughts on life as a rising basketball star with a
sky's-the-limit potential that he would eventually realize.

"I developed the dunk shot," Erving said, "because it was a
challenging thing to learn to do. After you learn to do it one
way, it's a challenge to learn to do it another way and right on
up. There's an infinite number of dunk shots which I don't possess. And there are psychological considerations, too. I wouldn't
like to start feeling that I've done all that I could do and the
coming years would be a matter of repeating what I've already
done. I guess it's not such a bad thing to feel that I can repeat
what I've already done, but that's not my goal, to do it over, do
it over, and do it over. I want to do it better and do it better.
I want to have fun, too, and you can't have fun unless you're
winning.

"My thoughts have always been aimed toward becoming a
total player," he added. "I'm always trying to reach my outer
limits. I watch the things other players do and try to imitate
them. Then you have to develop your own thing through experience and practice. You experiment all the time and develop
your game individually. You try all these different things, and
in trying, you make discoveries about yourself. You realize what

you're good at and what your weaknesses are. Put enough time into it, then you'll be a true individual, an innovator, and people will take notice and the more gratifying it will be for you."

During a game at Nassau Coliseum during the second half of that season, Coach Loughery half-jokingly spelled out Erving's overall value to the ABA, and professional basketball as a whole, in an exchange with official Wally Rooney. Erving, at the height of his ever rising tenure, led the Nets to a 134–130 overtime victory over the San Antonio Spurs, scoring 51 points, grabbing 12 rebounds, and adding 8 assists. In the process, however, he took a physical pounding from Spurs rookie forward Mark Olberding. At one point, Loughery yelled to Rooney, "Hey look, the guy's killing Doc, and you know if Doc gets hurt we can all pack it in and start looking for jobs. If anything happens to the Doctor, the league goes down the tube."

In the play-offs that season, Erving averaged 35 points per game.

On their way to another championship showdown, the Nets had to get past the San Antonio Spurs and their beloved "Iceman," George Gervin, once a teammate of Erving's with the Virginia Squires. The two forged a healthy friendship, and an even healthier rivalry, almost from the moment that Erving first got a glimpse of Gervin's electric game when the rookie guard joined the team midway through the 1972–1973 season.

"I've seen a lot of long, skinny guys, but George came in about 6-foot-7 and a half, and 155, 160 pounds," Erving said to SportsIllustrated.com. "Ice palmed the ball fairly easily, but he was so thin and so wiry, the ball looked huge in his hand, but he had the ability to just move with it like he was going down the court with a yo-yo."

Gervin had his own special memories of Erving. "Doc wouldn't let me go home after practice," he said. "He made me play him one-on-one all the time. So credit Doc, it really made me a better ballplayer. Doc was like my mentor coming in, so I've got a lot of respect for him."

The Nets outlasted the Spurs in seven games that included a bench-clearing brawl in Game 4. "As the story goes," SportsIllustrated.com reported, "New York's Rich Jones—a former Spurs captain who was among several players on both teams who had been traded for one another in previous seasons—bloodied four different Spurs before order was restored. Fourteen players were fined a total of $2,200 for the fight."

"We always played each other hard," Gervin said. "Erving was my former teammate, so I wanted to beat him, and he wanted to beat me, so it was always a competitive game."

Said Erving, "The guys knew one another so well, which made it a shoo-in for being a long series and a hard-fought series. You can't be great unless you're playing against somebody great to bring it out in you."

A bit bloodied but eager to keep mixing it up, the Nets moved on to play the Denver Nuggets in what would be the last ABA championship series. The Nets would win the series, and Erving would win the postseason Most Valuable Player award on the strength of one of the most, if not *the* most, remarkable five-game performances in basketball history: 45 points, 12 rebounds; 48 points, 14 rebounds; 31 points, 10 rebounds; 34 points, 15 rebounds; 31 points, 19 rebounds. With Erving in the pilot's seat, the Nets won their second ABA championship in three seasons.

On May 17, 1976, Pat Putnam of *Sports Illustrated* wrote an article, entitled "The Doctor Opens Up His Medicine Bag," that recapped the first four games of the series, in which the Nets had raced out to lead by three games to one.

"Too bad, America, but you missed one of the greatest basketball shows on Earth," Putnam wrote. "Or, rather, one just a few feet off the Earth. That was Julius Erving last week, launching himself from various points on courts in Denver and New York, soaring and scoring, passing, rebounding, blocking and stealing—all in the undeserved obscurity of the ABA championship finals. By Saturday night Erving and his underdog New York Nets had Denver down three games to one, which is what can happen when humans go five-on-one with a helicopter.

"The games were not nationally televised, but they should have been. Dr. J's heroics merited more than just local exposure. In the first four games he scored 158 points, pulled down 51 rebounds, had 22 assists, blocked seven shots, and had eight steals. Most of them came with the Identified Flying Object's feet well off the ground, his body twisting and turning. Even the Nuggets felt like applauding.

"Denver had assigned the task of stopping Erving—or, rather, slowing him down—to Bobby Jones, the 6'9" second-year man out of North Carolina who may be the best defensive forward in basketball. But by the end of last week the most Jones could do was smile and shake his head.

"'The thing about him is that you know he is going to get to the basket, you just never know how,' he said. 'In the first game I tried to make him go baseline, and he went right by me. After that I tried to make him pull up in the lane. So he made his jumpers. Or he went right by me. But I really enjoy watching him because every time he does one of those moves I know it's something I may never see again.'"

At one point in the final game of that championship series against the Nuggets, the Nets trailed by 22 points, with about fifteen minutes left. Riding Erving's wave of sheer determination, however, New York managed to come back and win the game. *Sports Illustrated* called Erving's body of work "the greatest individual performance by a basketball player at any level anywhere."

Loughery recalled that "Denver had a good team with David Thompson and Dan Issel, and Thompson was killing us. During a time-out, I told Doc, 'Thompson's killing us, go get him.' Doc stopped him, we got going, and we won. On the Nets we called on him to do everything, and he did it. He led us in scoring, in rebounding, in assists, and in blocked shots."

Erving was well aware that in the minds of the media, the fans, and the players alike, the Nets were a clear underdog to the Nuggets.

"They dominated us during the regular season, but I think that at play-off time us having the championship experience from 1974 really helped," Erving said. "It was something for us to draw on. Brian Taylor played a very significant role during that time, too. The battle with San Antonio before that, going seven games and coming through that healthy, gave us an edge. If you look at the first two games in Denver, I had sensational games, scoring 48 and 45 points, and we got the split. Getting the split was everything for us, because that set the stage; we pretty much played even after that, but we had taken the home court advantage."

Loughery, now sixty-seven and living in Atlanta, where he plays lots of golf, said, "What Doc did in his last year against Denver was just unbelievable. That was part of his greatest season with the Nets. In all my years of coaching, I have never seen a player have that kind of season. Nobody ever had a better year in terms of statistics and performance—nobody.

"Larry Bird, Magic Johnson, and Michael Jordan are great, but as far as handling every situation, on and off the court, Doc was the best. Doc had the best hands in basketball, the biggest and the best. It was like he was playing with a grapefruit. He could play defense, too. One time in Indianapolis at the end of the first half, he drove to the hoop over three guys. Two of them wound up lying on the floor. To me, Doc was Earl Monroe with wings. Doc did in the air what Monroe did on the floor.

"Look, I coached Michael Jordan, Dominique Wilkins, and Bernard King, but I will tell you that the three years I had Dr. J were the best three years I have ever seen from any basketball player in any league, in any era. He never had two bad games in a row, and that's the mark of a true professional. Of all the superstars I have ever coached, Doc was the easiest to get along with.

"In those three years, Doc never once missed a practice, and he never once turned down an interview request or an autograph request. He would give everybody the same amount of time and the same amount of respect. As far as the team went, he would treat the twelfth man the same way he would treat a starter. He was a superstar in every sense of the word, but he never wanted anyone to treat him like a superstar. Through it all, he was really just a regular guy."

How many regular guys have size 13 hands?

"Doc, like Michael Jordan, had the biggest set of mitts I'd ever seen on any other players," said Charles Barkley, one of the NBA's 50 Greatest Players. "I truly think that those giant hands had a lot to do with their overall greatness, because they were able to control the ball like few players could."

After winning his second championship with the Nets, Erving credited those big mitts with much of his early ABA success. "Having big hands helps," he told the *New York Times*. "If I can get my fingers on the ball, I feel I can control it. But it's not only my hands, it's my legs and that I'm a student of the game. Nothing I do on the court is new. I tried it out in the Rucker League and on the playgrounds a long time ago. I was doing it for free in those days. Sure I'm quick, but you have to work at being quick. There are guys who can sprint 100 yards in 10 seconds but can't do that on the basketball courts— it's something that takes developing. Body control comes with hard work. You slow down on your opponent, let him catch up, then you make him freeze by accelerating around him. That's when quickness counts."

Billy Cunningham of the Philadelphia 76ers, an All-Star forward in both leagues, said of Erving after that season, "He's the greatest talent I've seen as forward. He has the flair for the game the way Bob Cousy and Elgin Baylor had."

Al Skinner, a Nets guard who followed Erving at UMass and is now the head coach at Boston University, once said of his predecessor, "A lot of players have his physical talent and tools, but in Doc's case, he combines those with a heart, a mind, and a dedication like no other player I know. Sure, he has big hands and God-given jumping ability, but it's his dedication that gives him his greatness."

By the end of the 1975–1976 season, there were just six remaining ABA teams. "The ABA, when it got down to six teams, was a really tough league," Loughery said. "It was filled with a lot of extraordinary players like Artis Gilmore and George McGinnis, but Doc, he was the best of them all. Pound for pound, he was the greatest and most exciting player in the game. Creativity just flowed out of him. His greatness was in his big hands. There were several pros with hands as large, but none had his size, strength, and sensitivity. If he could get a couple of fingertips on the ball, he could control it."

Merger talks between the two leagues began, and negotiations centered more on initiation fees, television income, and indemnities than on basketball itself. There was also the undeniable talent that the ABA had to offer, with Erving the most talented of the entire lot.

"The NBA can't call itself the best basketball league until it includes the best basketball player," Dave Anderson wrote in a "Sports of the Times" column in May 1976. "Without the merely spectacular Doctor J, the NBA hasn't fulfilled its commitment to the public."

Rick Darnell, who played in the ABA at that time, echoed Anderson's remarks. "Julius was the face of the ABA," said Darnell, who played briefly with the Virginia Squires in the 1975–1976 season, after Erving had left the team to join the Nets, and is now a financial analyst in Newport Beach, California.

"Julius was the first small forward who could really fly," added Darnell, a forward from San Jose State University. "Without him, the ABA would not have lasted as long as it did, and there probably would not have been a merger. He was the one player gifted enough to get two professional leagues together. Without him, how could the NBA claim it had the best players in the world?

"I played against Julius in Virginia and in New York, and fans loved him in both of those cities," Darnell continued. "I can't tell you how many times I saw him fly from the free-throw line and dunk the ball. People came out to see him then the way people come out now to see Kobe Bryant and some other NBA superstars, the only difference being that while the NBA has a lot of great one-on-one players, Julius always played within the framework of a team game. He could have gone to the basket almost anytime he wanted, but he wasn't a ball hog. As spectacular as he was, he was a very unselfish player who just kind of blended in with the rest of his teammates and always got them involved.

"He had such great big hands. I remember him constantly grabbing a pass on the run with one hand, taking two steps to the basket, and then just windmilling the ball into the hoop in one fluid motion. It was a thing of beauty, something you really don't see anymore, and that's saying a lot, because most of today's players are bigger, stronger, and faster than players from previous eras."

Four ABA teams—the Nets, the San Antonio Spurs, the Indiana Pacers, and the Denver Nuggets, eventually joined the NBA. The Kentucky Colonels, the Spirits of St. Louis, and the Virginia Squires all agreed to take cash settlements and close up shop. Immediately their players were dispersed across the new twenty-two-team league.

"Julius had influenced so many players in terms of his overall greatness, his unique style of play, and his approach to the game as a true gentleman that the NBA had to have him," Bob Costas said. "The NBA wanted two teams from the ABA, and the Nets were not one of them, but they had to take the Nets because they had to have Dr. J. It was the move that made the most sense, and it did have an extremely positive result.

"Julius, in my opinion, is one of the fifteen or twenty greatest players in the history of the game, maybe somewhere between one and ten at the time, so the NBA wasn't just going to pass on him and continue business as usual. I don't mean this as a slight, but I'd put Julius at the top of the group of players that come just below the Michael Jordans, the Larry Birds, and the Magic Johnsons. Now, were some of his early years in the ABA, and even in the NBA, just as good as some of the years that Jordan and those other guys had? Absolutely. Again, it's not a slight. If I put Lou Gehrig just a notch below Babe Ruth and Willie Mays, that's not exactly insulting to Gehrig. In fact, it's pretty high praise."

At the time, Dave Anderson asked Erving if the limited recognition he received in the ABA bothered him at all. "Not individually," Erving replied. "I have more feelings about the other ABA players who aren't recognized for their talent: Ron Boone, Marvin Barnes, Bird Averitt, Jim Silas, Ron Buse, Billy Knight, George Gervin. But the players in the other league know these guys. The public doesn't, but the players in the other league do."

Anderson asked Erving if he would like to enter the NBA with the Nets as a complete team.

"Absolutely," Erving said. "And we would be a winning team."

"Are you satisfied that people know who you are?" Anderson asked.

"I think most people know who I am," Erving replied. "But they might not know what I look like." They were about to find out.

"Julius Erving and George Gervin were the two biggest ABA stars at the time of the merger, but there were many others, like Rick Barry and Billy Cunningham, who had played in the ABA," Dean Meminger said. "The ABA guys really brought a new culture into the league and changed the style of play. Prior to the merger, the NBA game, outside the Boston Celtics, was still essentially a half-court, slow-paced, white man's game, but the assimilation of all that young black talent coming over from the ABA changed that, and once the NBA accepted the merger, it had to accept the ABA players. They were a new breed of athlete: young, strong, and fast and with the ability to leap to the moon.

"Now, they might not have been as fundamentally sound as their NBA counterparts, but most of those guys could cover up some of their deficiencies with other areas of their games that were a lot stronger. Take Julius, for example. He wasn't the world's greatest shooter, but because he could jump out of the gym, because he could get to the basket anytime he wanted, on anyone in the game, the lack of an outside shot was never that noticeable. Sometimes more talented players might be a bit less fundamental, but when you're talking about players with the skill level of a Julius Erving, you can more than make up for any part of your game that might not be as strong.

"The bottom line," Meminger added, "is that the merger allowed the greatest players in the world an opportunity to play one another in one united league. I mean, ABA guys like Doc and Gervin and Spencer Haywood and George McGinnis, they were an integral part of American basketball."

8

Another Contract Dispute

In a sad and ironic twist, Erving, the face of the ABA, would never again play for the Nets. He became involved in yet another contract dispute, and he decided to hold out, telling the Nets that he would not report to training camp at Manhattanville College to open the 1976–1977 season.

With four years remaining on a eight-year contract for $1.9 million, Erving was not thrilled about the financial situation of Nate "Tiny" Archibald, a high-scoring playmaker and fellow New Yorker whom the Nets had recently obtained from the Kansas City Kings. Archibald was being paid four hundred thousand dollars a year. The team was marketing Archibald and Erving with the slogan "Dr. J and Tiny A" and charging as much as $357 for season tickets to forty-one games, or lesser packages at either $294 or $231.

The only package Erving cared about was his own. He said that he had been promised several bonuses but had not received them. "I'm giving a lot of myself in every game," he told reporters at the time, "and I expect that when I'm told something, I [can] believe [it]. I want to be in an atmosphere of trust and good faith. Until now, I have heard promises that were not kept. Now, I'll wait until these promises are kept, but I don't want them verbally anymore. They have to be in writing."

Roy Boe was now furious with Erving's agent, Irwin Wiener. "Wiener was going around telling people that all we had was a handshake agreement with Erving and so we needed to renegotiate his deal, which was not true," said Boe, sounding as angry during a 2008 interview as he must have sounded more than thirty years before.

"I had a ninety-page agreement that Erving had signed, and now Wiener was going to the press, basically saying that I was a liar. Well, we had a real falling out. I took Julius out to lunch, just the two of us, to try to maybe smooth things over. Julius was wonderful with me, very polite, as always, but in the end he left me in Wiener's hands, and that was just a disaster, because Wiener talked him into sitting out all of training camp."

Billy Melchionni, who played with Erving during the three Net seasons and was the team's general manager at the time of the trade, recalled the memories of Erving's last days with the team. "I had just been on the job two or three months," he said, "when we realized Erving was not going to go to training camp. I can remember Kevin Loughery calling Julius on the phone and talking to him. We also got some assurances from Roy Boe that he was going to improve Doc's contract."

While Erving stayed away from the Nets, financial bedlam ensued in every NBA city where the Nets would play a preseason game and on the advance ticket sales in those cities.

The Knicks, anticipating a full house to see Erving during an exhibition game at Madison Square Garden, had run this ad in the *New York Times*: "Thursday, Oct. 7, THE BATTLE OF NEW YORK. The New York Knicks with 'Clyde' Frazier and Earl 'The Pearl' Monroe take on the New York Nets with 'Dr. J' Julius Erving. Game time 7:30 p.m."

In Erving's absence, that ad was quickly changed to read: "TONIGHT, YOUR KNICKS VS. NETS. Game time 7:30 p.m."

"Many of the promoters who gave the Nets big cash advances to play, hoping to capitalize on Erving's popularity and drawing power, are now sorry," Sam Goldaper wrote in the *New York Times*.

Erving had become such a draw that even Las Vegas had booked his act. However, in the absence of the ultimate showstopper, the Aladdin Hotel eventually canceled a scheduled game between the Nets and the Seattle SuperSonics.

"We booked the Nets into Vegas because we thought of it as a big happening," Mitch DeWood, the entertainment director of the Aladdin said at the time. "Without Erving, it was nothing."

Lee Fisher, then the hotel publicity man, said, "Not having Erving is like the Los Angeles Lakers coming in without Kareem Abdul-Jabbar or having a championship fight without Muhammad Ali."

When the Nets were accepted into the NBA, the New Orleans Jazz jumped at the chance to bring Erving to the Superdome for a preseason game, giving a twenty-thousand-dollar guarantee to the Nets. Without Erving, all they got was a meaningless, 105–69 victory before a paltry crowd of 13,714.

"We would have drawn thirty thousand if Erving had been in the lineup," said Barry Mendelson, then the executive vice president of the New Orleans Jazz and Heritage Foundation. "We had twelve thousand tickets sold two weeks ago when the announcement was made that Erving would not be coming.

The ticket sales stopped right there. When we booked them [the Nets], I never gave a thought to the possibility that Erving would not be playing. Aside from maybe [Brazilian soccer player] Pelé on the international scene, Erving is the greatest single drawing card in professional sports."

Worst of all, CBS canceled its coverage of the Nets' season opener against the Golden State Warriors at Oakland. The game, which had been billed as a bragging-rights bonanza that featured the 1976 ABA champion Nets versus the 1975 NBA champion Warriors, was to have been the first of forty NBA games televised by the network that season.

"We had scheduled the game to show the national audience Julius Erving in action," Barry Frank, vice president in charge of CBS Sports, said at the time. "Without Julius, the game did not have quite the same interest."

Roy Boe, ever the competitor, reminded me, just for the record, that the Ervingless Nets beat Golden State, anyway.

The financially troubled Nets, who had a difficult time raising the $3.8 million to pay the NBA for entrance to the league and to pay the Knicks for territory infringement, eventually sold Erving for $3 million to the Philadelphia 76ers of the rival NBA, just before the start of the season. (That decision still haunts the franchise, which has not won a championship since.)

"A number of teams were interested in acquiring Erving," Boe said. "The Knicks, especially, were interested in pulling off a deal, but I chose not to go that route." The route he did choose was Interstate 95. He sent Erving straight down the New Jersey Turnpike.

"When he was traded, it was the worst moment I experienced in all the years of involvement in sports," Billy Melchionni said. "I not only lost a great friend, the Nets also lost a great player, a loss the franchise has not recovered from. I played with some of the greatest players: Wilt Chamberlain, Rick Barry, Billy Cunningham, and Hal Greer. Who can say who is or was the best ever? But Doc in his prime had to rank with the greatest. He couldn't rebound with Wilt or shoot like Rick, but he had a certain flair, the ability to do things they and others couldn't do."

Erving's departure infuriated many Nets players. "I don't want to know why, man," said forward Tim Bassett. "I just want to know what possessed them to do that."

John Williamson, knowing that the Nets had just gone from reigning champs to reigning chumps, said, "Everybody's laughing at us now. They got the old draggedy Nets coming in last. This is a helluva way to come in the NBA now. I like those dollar signs, but I hate to lose, man, I hate to lose."

Boe, who still considered himself a Nets fan, said that money was not entirely behind Erving's departure. "Don't forget, Erving was having knee problems," he said. "We were wondering if he would bounce back and be the same player he once was, so that factored into our decision-making process as well."

Boe, who also owned the New York Islanders hockey team at that time, worried that renegotiating Erving's contract would upset the financial balance of his top skaters, many of whom were on their way to becoming part of a dynasty in the National Hockey League.

"Denis Potvin meant as much to my Islanders as Julius Erving did to my Nets," Boe said. "I didn't need Potvin, or any of those other players, forming a line outside my office asking for raises, and that's what would have happened if I had given Erving more money."

Regardless of his reasons, Boe had to deal with being labeled as the second coming of Harry Frazee, the owner of the Boston Red Sox who sold Babe Ruth to the New York Yankees. "I've heard that before, and I don't think it's very fair," Boe told me.

"I took my lickings for selling Erving, but I had legitimate reasons for doing it."

The Nets, who spent nineteen hours in continuous negotiations with the 76ers before agreeing to a price on Erving, felt the immediate departure of their superstar in the locker room, at the ticket window, and in the standings. Many Nets players criticized the ownership for selling off the most popular player in the league and one of the most popular athletes on the planet. In addition, more than a hundred Nets ticket holders lodged complaints at the team's headquarters in Carle Place, Long Island, and at the nearby Nassau Coliseum.

"Doc was basically sold to Philly to help keep the Nets financially afloat," Kevin Loughery said. "We were down and our fans were down when Doc went to Philly. When the heart and soul of your team gets ripped out, it's very difficult to continue to be successful. But despite what was written back then, Roy Boe was the last person on earth who wanted to part with Doc, believe me. We had Tiny Archibald that year, and he and Doc would have made for quite an explosive combination. It would have been tremendously exciting to play in every city on our schedule."

Instead, long lines began forming early in Philadelphia to purchase tickets. Erving was heading to the city where the seven-foot one-inch Wilt Chamberlain had made the dunk a common occurrence. ("That's where his nickname, 'the Big Dipper,' came from," Wayne Embry, who played against Chamberlain, said. "Whenever he would dunk, the public address announcer in Philadelphia would say, 'Dipper Dunk!'"

Meanwhile, back on Long Island, the Ervingless Nets would fall from the ABA throne to the NBA cellar with a 22–60 record.

"As a coach," Loughery said with a sad chuckle, "I got dumb overnight."

Erving, who participated in the negotiations himself before agreeing to the six-year contract with Philadelphia, said, "I thought that my contributions to the merger should have put me higher on the list of priorities. But there was a conflict of egos between my agent and Roy Boe. He said that it wasn't club policy to renegotiate. So I was content to sit and not play."

Pat Williams, the general manager of the 76ers, was asked why he was investing so much money in Erving. After all, the team was already doling out monster salaries to a roster of colorful and talented players such as George McGinnis (another scoring machine, who had come over from the ABA's Indiana Pacers), Doug Collins, Fred Carter, Caldwell Jones, Darryl "Chocolate Thunder" Dawkins, World B. Free (who had changed his name from Lloyd Free), and Henry Bibby, the team's floor general.

The reserves included Harvey Catchings, Joe "Jelly Bean" Bryant (Kobe's dad), and Steve Mix, who was moved from starter to sixth man when Erving arrived. Mix was initially angered about losing his starting job, but he eventually got over it and had SIXTH MAN painted on his tires.

Erving's "availability got the juices flowing," said Pat Williams. "He is a great attraction, and we're trying to sell out a building of almost eighteen thousand seats."

At the time, it was estimated that a sellout crowd in Philadelphia was worth $108,000, which meant that even if all the games were sold out, it would still hardly be enough to meet the 76ers' hefty payroll.

Nevertheless, Williams explained, "There is a lot more to income than ticket sales. If we're successful and get deep into the play-offs, there are revenues from local television, cable television, radio, ads for programs, the sale of novelties and other merchandising. We're looking to Erving as a long-range thing, playing out his career here. All we have to do is win, and we'll do all right.

"I saw an example of his drawing power when we sold more than 250 tickets in the first few hours of the morning," he added. "I tried to call my office for more than two hours and couldn't get through, and we had just installed twelve new phone lines."

People everywhere were buzzing about the Doctor and his new digs. "He's got something to prove in every new city he plays in," Dave DeBusschere said. "Whenever I see Erving play, I come out of my seat. He has extreme quickness, and his presence on the floor carries respect and leadership. His every acrobatic move blends with the chemistry and makeup of his team. The way Julius controls himself and the ball in the air defies gravity. David Thompson can hang in the air like that, but not with the ball. Julius does it while he's doing something with the ball. But on the floor, Julius is incredible, too. He does more than Rick Barry does. He plays defense better, he rebounds better. I've heard said that it would be different if Erving played in the NBA. Hell, no! It would make no difference. No one is going to stop him. He is the best forward in the game. He might be even better in the NBA than he was in the ABA."

Dave Anderson asked Dr. J if he thought he could do in the NBA what he did in the ABA. "Yup," Erving replied.

"Not even John Wayne ever justified a *yup* the way Dr. J has," Anderson wrote.

In a rare photo, Julius Erving (right) waits at the free-throw line for a potential rebound during a Roosevelt-Lynbrook high school basketball game in the mid-1960s.

Another rare photo shows Julius Erving, as a member of the Westsiders, dribbling the ball up a sideline at Rucker Park in the early 1970s.

In September 1972, Julius Erving arrived at the Atlanta Hawks' camp, where he would play two games before the courts summoned him back to play for the Virginia Squires. Erving is huddling here with Hawks coach Cotton Fitzsimmons.

Julius Erving and New York Nets owner Roy Boe at a press conference held at a restaurant in Carle Place, Long Island, in August 1973, to announce the team's signing of Erving, who had previously starred with the Virginia Squires.

Julius Erving of the New York Nets skying past Walt Frazier and the New York Knicks in an exhibition game at Madison Square Garden in October 1973.

Julius Erving bursting past Eugene Kennedy of the visiting San Antonio Spurs in an ABA game in October 1973.

Julius Erving of the New York Nets gliding to the basket in a regular season ABA game against the San Diego Conquistadors at Nassau Coliseum in March 1974.

Julius Erving floats a finger roll over Len Elmore of the Indiana Pacers in a regular season ABA game at the Veterans Memorial Coliseum on Long Island in January 1975.

Julius Erving leaping high to score over Len Elmore of the visiting Indiana Pacers at a Nets regular season ABA game at Uniondale, Long Island, in February 1976.

Julius Erving celebrating in the Nets locker room after the Nets defeated the Denver Nuggets in six games in May 1976 to win the last ABA Championship.

Julius Erving of the Nets soaring over Dan Issel and the Denver Nuggets during an ABA Finals game in May 1976.

Julius Erving driving for a basket during a regular season game in Uniondale, Long Island, in October 1976.

Julius Erving driving past the Denver Nuggets' Bobby Jones in an ABA regular season game in October 1976.

Julius Erving of the Philadelphia 76ers watching from the bench during a regular season NBA game against his old teammates, the New York Nets, at Nassau Memorial Coliseum in January 1977.

Turquoise Erving watching her then husband, Julius, during a March 1977 game in Philadelphia when Erving was a member of the 76ers.

Julius Erving of the Philadelphia 76ers dunking against the Knicks at Madison Square Garden in a regular season game in November 1980.

Moses Malone and Julius Erving sit together on the 76ers' bench during a game in Houston against the Rockets in October 1982.

Larry Bird and Julius Erving talk to an official before a 76ers-Celtics game at the Boston Garden in December 1984.

9

A Philadelphia Phenomenon

W hen I went to Philadelphia, I was twenty-six years old
and really sitting on top of the world," Erving told the
Academy of Achievement in Washington. "[I had] family life, a
professional career, plenty of friends and associates, and a good
reputation, a wish list that could be the envy of many.

"In Philadelphia, our team was put together, and I became
the last component of that team. It was sort of parallel to what
happened with the Yankees: George Steinbrenner getting all
these players together and winning the World Series. There
were a lot of assumptions that, in basketball, that's how things
worked: if you put together a lot of high-priced talent, they were
going to win."

On October 23, 1976, Erving pulled into the players' parking lot at the Spectrum in Philadelphia, a city in a frenzy over

the acquisition of the great Dr. J, which they thought for sure would prove to be the last piece of a championship puzzle.

"Doc was not hired in Philly to play defense and shut the other team down," said Darryl Dawkins, who was the starting center on the Philadelphia squad. "He was hired to provide offense, and he could do that in a way that only a few other guys could. The guys who were assigned to guard him had to do a lot of worrying before each game, and they had a heck of a time keeping up with him during the games."

On a Friday night in the City of Brotherly Love, Erving was the first to arrive in the team locker room for the NBA opener against the San Antonio Spurs. He still had a bundle of things about New York on his mind, including his new child, Jazmin, an eight-pound six-ounce girl born twenty days earlier at Long Island Jewish Hospital. Jazmin was now Erving's third child, joining his two sons, Cheo, 4, and Julius, 2.

"Doctor," Doug Collins shouted, "how you doing, man?"

As a small army of reporters watched Erving dress for the game—"Too big," he said of his new uniform, the one with the number 6 stitched on it, "gotta get a taper job"—his new teammates seemed amazed about all the attention he was receiving on his first day at the new job.

"I haven't played in competition for months," Erving said into a crush of notepads and tape recorders. "In my mind, I feel I can do anything I want on the court. But I don't think my body can do what my mind wants it to do. My body will tell me when it's ready. It'll take time."

Just then, George McGinnis, Erving's friendly rival from their ABA days and now arguably the best forward in the NBA, walked into the room and said to Erving, "You sure look funny in that uniform, man."

The players soon took the floor for pregame warm-ups, and the fans began clapping for Erving and pointing at the man who they thought would surely bring an NBA title to Philadelphia. Except for the lights on an overhead message board that read IS THERE A DOCTOR IN THE HOUSE?, the Spectrum was dark when Erving's name was announced over the public address system to the crowd of 17,196. "From Massachusetts," the man behind the microphone blared, "number 6, Julius Erving."

The Spectrum erupted in applause, and the crowd gave Erving a two-minute standing ovation. The decibel levels rose higher when a fan handed Erving a doctor's bag.

"Looking back at that first game in the Spectrum, after all these years, still sends chills up my spine," said Lloyd Free, an awestruck teammate of Erving's that season. "There were eighteen thousand people standing the whole time before they announced Doc's name. The whole building was hyped up for the big moment. When that black man ran onto the court and put a doctor's bag in the middle of the floor, the place just went nuts. At first, we didn't know what the guy was doing. Back in those days, no one was thinking about bombs or terrorists or anything. We just kind of looked out there, and when we realized it was a doctor's bag, we just cracked up. Security grabbed the guy and hauled him away, but the message was already delivered: Welcome to Philly, Dr. J.

"When they finally introduced Doc, the place went bananas. It was the most electrifying experience I have ever been part of. It felt like the building was moving. Back then, people could smoke in the stands, so when Doc ran out, it was as if he were running in slow motion, through these clouds made by all the cigarette smoke, like a scene from some kind of Disney movie. It was really storybook kind of stuff, and we just stood there in front of the bench looking at one another and saying. 'Oh, my goodness, this is really kind of hard to believe.' Remember [the movie] *The Fish That Saved Pittsburgh*? This was like 'The Fish That Saved Philly.'"

When the applause died down, Erving took a seat on the bench. With five minutes and fifty-one seconds left in the first half, the Philadelphia coach Gene Shue sent Erving into the game for Steve Mix.

Erving's debut was more than a bit rocky. As nervous as he was rusty, he had his first pass stolen. He missed his first shot, a jump from the right side, and all four of his free throws.

"Had he been a fringe player fighting for a job," wrote Tony Kornheiser, the ESPN commentator who was then working for the *New York Times*, "he might have been cut at halftime."

In the second half, however, the Doctor was back in form. He scored his first two NBA points on a layup with two minutes and forty-one seconds left in the third period and finished with 17 points in sixteen minutes. Nevertheless, the 76ers lost, 121–118.

After that first game, Erving said simply, "Outstanding. Probably the greatest ovation I ever received. I almost didn't know what to do. This is going to be a good situation for me. I see potential here. Give us some time. We won't be losing many more games this season."

Dawkins remembered the buzz that Erving caused in his first days with the 76ers. "Doc fit in nicely with our team," he said. "We had people coming an hour before the game just to see what he was going to do on the layup line. He was the best basketball entertainment you could find anywhere on the planet, so in that sense, basketball fans in Philly were extremely lucky, and so were we, his teammates.

"Doc was the kind of player who could get to the basket anytime he wanted, on anyone. He just had such a flair for the game and an unbelievable imagination when it came to his arsenal of moves. The guy was making things up as he went along in midair. I often found myself stopping during the course of games just to watch him work his magic out there."

The Honeymoon Is Over

Despite Erving's artistry and hard work on the hardwood, his Philadelphia honeymoon was over by New Year's Day 1977. Although his teammates were in awe of his great athletic abilities, proven scorers like Doug Collins and Lloyd Free were not about to sacrifice any of their offensive game to appease the good Doctor. Furthermore, to be quite frank, Erving was not having the kind of season that management, his teammates, and the Philly fanatics had expected. Instead of looking like champions, the 76ers were just four games above .500 and struggling, and much of the blame was falling squarely on Erving's broad shoulders.

"Here was the problem," said Free, a rookie that season who now works in the 76ers' community relations office. "A lot of us were young and wanted to make a name for ourselves; we had pretty big egos, and we wanted some of the accolades, too, so we went out there and did our thing. Sometimes, looking back on it, maybe we didn't always get the ball to Doc when we should have gotten it to him. I think there was a lot of ego involved. We wanted to show the organization and our fans that we could play some ball as well. We wanted some of the respect that Doc always got.

"I guess what I'm trying to say is that Doc was our leader; he knew how to lead, but we didn't know how to follow. I went out there and took all my shots, [Doug] Collins was off doing his own thing, Darryl [Dawkins] was just trying to rip down as many backboards as he could, and Joe Bryant was out there putting the ball between his legs and doing all of this fancy stuff. Doc did get frustrated at times, and I can't blame him. He had a lot of meetings with the veteran guys like Billy Cunningham and George McGinnis and Steve Mix, but the guards just kind of stayed away from all that talk. We let the older, bigger guys try to hash it out, but it never really got resolved. That's why it's not always such a good thing when your team is as loaded [with big-name players] as we were, because you can just lose your way."

Mark Heisler, a 76ers beat writer during Erving's first season with the team who is now a sportswriter with the *Los Angeles Times*, said that what he first noticed upon Erving's arrival was that "Doc had a certain cachet, the kind of cachet that Connie Hawkins had before him. In a certain sense, he [Erving] and George McGinnis were equals. They were pretty close."

When the Doctor began to struggle, Heisler, like thousands of others in Philadelphia and beyond, began seeing a version of Erving that was slightly different from the image they had of him. In fairness, Erving was not just trying to get used to a new team, he was trying to get used to a whole new league.

"Julius was still a star player, and there was still this aura surrounding him in Philadelphia," Heisler said, "but he was not as spectacular as we all thought he might be."

Heisler and other basketball experts thought that Erving's difficulty in adjusting to NBA life revolved around the 3-point shot that was a staple of the ABA. In the ABA, a successful shot made behind a semicircle twenty-five feet from the basket counted as 3 points. ABA teams would set up offenses around the 3-point semicircle, luring defenses away from the basket and farther out on the perimeter. With the defenses so spread out, there were more available lanes to the basket, and a player as quick and graceful as Erving could soar to the rim almost untouched. In the NBA, with no 3-pointers allowed and the defenses clogging lanes and stacked tight around the basket, the wind was taken out of Erving's sails.

"The one thing we figured out was that the ABA did not have a lot of centers," Heisler said. "The league did not have the depth of centers that the NBA had. There weren't a whole lot of people in the ABA who could block Erving's shots or his dunks when he went to the basket, but in the NBA it was a whole different story."

Erving thought that he could still be spectacular, that he could do more if only he got the ball more. But how could he be hot when the 76ers kept freezing him out?

"I used to have the ball more," he told the *Philadelphia Bulletin*. "The guy guarding me had to do an honest night's work to hold me down. He doesn't have to do a good night's work now."

Erving blamed his new team's shortcomings on a lack of leadership. "When I came here, I thought in terms of being a leader," he said. "I figured George McGinnis and I should be the leaders, but we haven't been accepted. It's not an easy group of guys to talk with."

Addressing his own poor play, Erving said, "I'm not a water faucet. I can't be turned on and off. I can't go without handling the ball eight or nine times down the court and then do it."

Heisler recalled a conversation he once had with Erving in which the frustrated star complained about his supporting cast. "Julius was not dominating like he had been doing in the ABA, so I guess in that sense, he was disappointing to us and disappointed in himself," Heisler said. "His act was no longer spectacular and high-flying; it was more of a mild disappointment, to be honest. Four months through that first season, there was a lot of transition going on. Julius was unhappy with young guys like Lloyd Free, who was getting his shots up no matter what.

"I remember Julius telling me that he and Lloyd had a talk in the shower about there not being enough air in the basket-ball for the two of them. I was just getting to know Julius, and he told me, 'They have to give me and George [McGinnis] the ball more.' He had a real disenchantment with the young guys, because they weren't giving the older guys the ball.

Doug Collins was a 20-point scorer per game, and he always needed somebody to throw the ball to him. Lloyd would come off the bench and shoot from everywhere—there was a lot of ego conflict going on there. The bottom line is that the 76ers were a pretty wild team in terms of shot selection and playing together out on the floor. They were a bunch of talented guys, but they were a little crazy, a little wild, and there was always a lot of competition for the ball.

"The press never turned on Julius," Heisler concluded. "They just loved him because he would talk until the last guy at radio station XYZ asked his last question."

Bob Behler, Jack Leaman's former broadcast partner, said that it was Leaman who helped weave the qualities of grace and humility into Erving's character. "Jack was just such a caring, sincere person, and everyone who had ever crossed his path knew that," Behler said. "His kindhearted nature really rubbed off on Julius, who would give you the time of day even if he didn't know you. When meeting someone for the first time, he would often act as if he had known them forever. I speak from personal experience. I interviewed him six or seven times on our radio broadcast, and every time he would come on the air he would say things like 'Hey Bob, it's great to see you again.' I would think to myself that I had never seen this guy play at UMass and wasn't really a close friend, but the person listening at home would be thinking we had known each other all our lives.

"Julius was a gentleman that way, and I credit Jack—a wonderful, kind, clean-cut gentleman himself—for instilling a lot of that elegance and grace into Julius's character, as well as Al Skinner's and [that of] many other guys who played for Jack. He helped them with basketball, yes, but I think Jack helped Julius and a lot of those guys become better people off the court as well. He cared about them and they appreciated that, and I think they became disciples, in a sense. Those guys were greatly influenced by Jack's personality, no doubt. Jack always cared more about the person than the player, and sometimes it's the other way around with certain coaches."

Maybe it was Leaman's even-keeled demeanor shining through when Erving once said, "I firmly believe that respect is a lot more important, and a lot greater, than popularity."

Lloyd Free also explained why Erving was so loved, regardless of Philadelphia's won-lost record. "Doc was like a politician on the basketball court," he said. "No matter how frustrated he may have been, he always took the time to stop and say a word or two to a teammate and nod to the crowd when the moment was right. He carried himself with elegance and grace before, during, and after games, and his postgame press conferences were more like question-and-answer sessions with the president or some other head of state.

"I realized that the guy wasn't one of those great players who acted like a snob. He was just a down-to-earth guy. You could talk to him about anything, anytime, and you wouldn't always have to seek him out. If he noticed a teammate was having a problem on or off the court, he would sit him down and chat about it, just trying to impart some of that Dr. J wisdom. Everything he did was perfect, the way he walked and talked and greeted people and smiled; it was all put out there just so perfectly, and it was all real. I found that out when I was Doc's chauffeur."

Doc's chauffeur?

Driving Mr. Erving

After Erving joined the 76ers in a last-minute shocking transaction, there was no time for him to find a new home, so he commuted as often as possible from Philadelphia to Long Island.

The player responsible for getting the world's most exciting player to and from practices and games on time was Lloyd Free, the colorful and free-spirited guard who thought so much of his own game that he would legally change his name from Lloyd to "World B."

"Doc was a childhood hero of mine coming out of Guilford College," Free said. "He didn't realize it, but when he joined the 76ers that year, it was like the ultimate for me. I was in my second year as a pro, but I had grown up idolizing Doc."

As fate would have it, Free would soon get to know his idol a lot better. "I had a place in Philly, but I still lived in Brownsville, Brooklyn, so for two months, I would just drop Doc off at his house on Long Island and be on my way to Brownsville. I was happy to do it because I just wanted Doc to like me; really, he was one of those guys whose respect you wanted on and off the court."

One day, Free was speeding down the New Jersey Turnpike in his brand-new Cadillac with the great Dr. J sleeping by his side. "We were running late for a game, and I started doing like ninety miles an hour, and I was like, oh man, I hope Doc don't wake up, because he's going to be real mad that I'm going this fast. But he looked like he was sleeping pretty good, so I just stepped on the gas and kept going."

A few seconds later, Free looked at his rearview mirror and saw flashing lights. "I thought, 'Oh man, Doc's really gonna be [angry] when he wakes up. He'll never talk to me again.'" Free was pulled over by a police car, and two state troopers approached his side of the Cadillac.

"License and registration," one of the stone-faced troopers demanded. Free handed over his paperwork and glanced over at Erving, who was still sleeping.

"I'm sorry, Officer," Free said. "I play basketball for the Philadelphia 76ers, and I'm running late for tonight's game."

One of the officers peeked toward the passenger seat. "That's my teammate, in there," Free told him. "Julius Erving."

"Julius Erving?" the officer shot back. "C'mon."

"It is, man," Free replied. "He lives on Long Island, and he just joined our team, so I've been taking him back and forth. I'll wake him up."

The officers, peeking in again to see Erving out cold, his large Afro tilted to one side, became giddy.

"Oh, my goodness, it *is* Dr. J," one of them said.

"Don't wake him up," the other said. "Let him sleep, he needs his energy for tonight. I'll tell you what, follow us."

By the time Erving awoke from a dead sleep, he and Free were being given a police escort to the Spectrum.

"Doc looked at me and said, 'What's going on?' Free recalled. I just said, 'Nothing, Doc. Those nice guys are escorting us to Philly so we can get there a little faster.' Doc was still a little groggy, so he just said okay and closed his eyes again. I never told him what really happened that day."

Getting It Together

In only a handful of games that first season in Philadelphia, Erving was able to play, as he had all those years in the ABA, with the shackles off. In the All-Star game, he scored 30 points and grabbed 12 rebounds and was named Most Valuable Player.

Heisler recalled a Friday night game against the visiting Washington Wizards on November 12, 1976, when "all of a sudden, Julius turned back into Dr. J. He did two or three really spectacular things. I remember talking to Lloyd Free about it after the game, and Lloyd was in awe, as were the rest of the guys. When Doc was doing his thing out there, those guys could have caught flies in their mouths."

The 76ers won, 143–104.

"I remember that game, all the oohs and aahs from the crowd," Heisler said. "Julius was putting on the kind of show that he used to put on every night in the ABA."

However, those nights were now few and far between.

In January that season, Erving talked to the *New York Times* about loyalty and high-skilled athletes like himself who leap-frogged from one team to another for bigger bucks.

"Loyalty doesn't enter into it," he said flatly. "That is a term of another era. Today the market value of a player is dictated by what the people are willing to pay. I keep seeing guys come and go. It's a constant cycle. But the player has to be careful that he doesn't get used, abused, and cast aside."

That is exactly what Erving, the great Dr. J, believed was happening to him in Philadelphia. His frustrations led him to declare, "I'm seriously considering bringing Dr. J out of the closet for the remaining forty-one games."

That never really happened, but by the end of the regular season, Erving and the 76ers, easily the most talented group in the NBA, had gotten their wild act together, and they made the play-offs with a 50–32 record. Dr. J and Company dusted Boston and Houston in the postseason before fixing their championship gaze on the Portland Trail Blazers, who were led by Bill Walton, the dominant but often injured redheaded freckled-faced center from UCLA.

Although the stakes were higher than ever, the 76ers remained as carefree as they had been all season, which eventually came back to bite them.

Heisler recalled an afternoon shootaround in Portland, Oregon, that spoke volumes about a team with more than enough talent, but not nearly enough desire, to win it all. "Before one play-off game that year, George McGinnis was out on the floor shooting around with the guys, smoking a cigarette," Heisler said. "He was just shooting around in a pair of sweatpants, smoking. I had never seen anything like that before."

Despite their lackadaisical approach, the 76ers went up 2–0 in the series.

Erving set an energetic tone in the opening of Game 1 with a rim-rocking dunk. He finished with 33 points, and Doug Collins had 30, as Philadelphia won, 107–101. Although Bill Walton finished with 28 points and 20 rebounds, the Blazers committed 34 turnovers.

At one point early in the series, play-by-play man Len Berman said, "I have never seen anybody do the things with a basketball that Julius Erving can do."

In Game 2, the 76ers seemed to have a stranglehold on the series, winning a brawl-filled contest, 107–89. With about five minutes left in the game, a series of scuffles broke out between Portland's Lloyd Neal and McGinnis, Maurice Lucas and Erving, and Bob Gross and Dawkins. Eventually, both benches cleared. Coaches, fans, security guards, and officials were all involved in the zany mix, which resulted in Lucas and Dawkins being ejected and fined twenty-five hundred dollars each. Doug Collins had to have four stitches because of a blow he received from Dawkins that was intended for Gross.

The Trail Blazers, led by Coach Jack Ramsey, kept their fighting spirit high throughout the rest of the series and stormed back to win the next four games, capturing their only NBA championship.

"That was a really tough series to lose, because we knew how good we were and how capable we were of beating the Blazers," Free said. "And we knew how great Doc was when he joined our team, but I think most of us were so young and immature, we really didn't know how to handle a situation of that magnitude. We respected Doc, but we wanted him to respect us, too. Most of us started trying to impress him; it's like everything we used to do: we'd do it to try to impress him and to try to do it even better, because he was now on our team, and he had arrived with such a swagger. In that sense, I guess he really motivated us.

"When you were a teammate of Julius Erving's, you knew you always had a chance to win, and you always had a chance to see something spectacular, something breathtaking from that offensive arsenal of his. George McGinnis was a great player, too; he and Doc were our two superstars. Even though we never got it done together in terms of winning a championship, I used to think back then that this was it, I'll never be on a team this talented again. Just being part of all that talent, with Doc at the head of the class, was an incredible experience for me.

"This may sound crazy, but sometimes I think we didn't win the championship when Doc got to Philly because we were too loaded [with big-name players]. We had Doc and McGinnis and Billy Cunningham and Doug Collins and Darryl Dawkins and Joe Bryant and Steve Mix and myself. Man, nobody had a team like that."

As much as Philadelphia had benefited from having ABA stars like Erving and McGinnis, Portland's attack was bolstered by the arrival of Maurice Lucas, one of the most explosive power forwards in the game. Lucas, a muscular six feet nine inches and 215 pounds who had played for the ABA's Kentucky Colonels the season before, led the Trail Blazers in scoring at 20.2 points per game and averaged slightly more than 11 rebounds per contest. The Trail Blazers also started the former Virginia Squires guard Dave Twardzik, who shared backcourt duties with Lionel Hollins, a second-year player from Arizona State University who averaged nearly 15 points per game.

Lucas led the way in Game 3 with 27 points and 12 rebounds, while Walton added 20 points, 18 rebounds, and 9 assists. The Trail Blazers won easily, 129–107.

In Game 4, Portland raced out to a 17-point lead and never looked back, coasting to a 130–98 victory that tied the series, 2–2.

In Game 5, at Philadelphia, the Trail Blazers opened up a 20-point lead in the fourth quarter and held off a 76ers rally, winning 110–104. Bob Gross scored 25 points, Lucas finished with 20 points and 13 rebounds, and Walton had 24 rebounds and 14 points.

A dejected Erving, who scored 37 points, said afterward, "I had a good feeling about tonight. It all backfired. It's a bad scene."

The Trail Blazers returned home to clinch the series, holding off a Philly flurry in the closing seconds. After McGinnis connected on a jumper, with 18 seconds left in the game, the Blazers' lead was sliced to 2 points. After a Portland turnover, with eight seconds left, Erving hoisted a jump shot in the lane, but it missed. Free retrieved the ball and put up a shot along the baseline that also missed. With one second left, McGinnis got off a final shot that clanked off the rim, sending the Blazers and their fans into a state of delirium and the heavily favored 76ers back to the state of Pennsylvania with their heads hanging low.

"They were tremendously embarrassed after blowing that lead and losing to Portland," Heisler said. "The next season, the team had a slogan that said to the fans, 'We owe you one.' There was [an ad with] a hand in[it], wearing a red, white, and blue wristband, and many people took it to mean that it was Julius's hand. The players were affronted by this campaign. They didn't think in terms of owing anyone anything. Eventually, the team starting getting rid of some of its talented players."

Darryl Dawkins, now fifty-one and living in Allentown, Pennsylvania, still can't fully explain how he and the 76ers lost that series to Portland. "When Doc got to Philly, we did feel like we were going to win a championship," he said. "We already had a great team, but we felt we were missing something. When we signed Doc, we felt like he was the missing link. But I think one of the things that happened to us was that teams like Portland, who had played us a number of times and really studied our game plan, figured out what we were trying to do out there, and they just kind of knew how to shut us down.

"But I have no idea, really, why we didn't win a championship with Doc. It just wasn't in the cards, I guess. The thing all of us realized as we started getting traded away from Philly is that the game of basketball is a business just like any other business, and it made perfect business sense for Philly to try and build a championship team around Doc."

In an interview with the Academy of Achievement years later, Erving spoke, as he so often did, diplomatically and intelligently about falling short his first year in Philly. "The first year that we were together, we were the second-best team in the world. We went to the finals and we lost in six games. We won the first two, and we lost the next four. The team suddenly became stigmatized. It was like, those guys are good, but they're not winners. If you get depressed about being the second-best team in the world, then you've got a problem. I tried to take a leadership position and kind of explain that to my teammates and whoever would hear me. I found myself suddenly becoming defensive about something I really didn't think I should be defensive about.

"Basketball is a five-man game," Erving continued. "The Blazers played as though they invented the concept. We were a team that possessed great individual one-on-one skills, but Portland played like a committee, with no part greater than the whole. In the end, the team concept prevailed.

"There were, at that time, 23 teams in the league. We were better than 21 of them. There was one that was better than us, and maybe we'd have another shot at that team. As it turned out, we never got another shot at them."

According to Free, Erving did not become the target of the fans' wrath after the 76ers fell short of realizing their championship dream. "For a moment, a brief moment, the fans seemed to place the blame on Doc," he said. "But the fans were most angry with George McGinnis. I mean, they booed this poor guy unmercifully. They didn't put anywhere near the kind of hate on Doc that they put on George, it was real bad. They never forgave George for that loss to Portland, but people have to realize that George had never come up against two players like Bill Walton and Maurice Lucas before. These were two very big, very talented, very physical players. Up until that Portland series, George was smoking everyone, but against those two guys, his game was just off."

The Turquoise Letter

By most accounts, Erving's first season in Philadelphia was viewed as a failure because the heavily favored, ultratalented 76ers had failed to win a championship. In the eyes of most Philadelphians, impatient and volatile sports fans who in later years would boo Santa Claus and cheer for Pete Rose, the Doctor, despite all the hype, had not yet delivered.

"With the Nets, we asked Doc to do everything, and he did," Kevin Loughery explained. "He was our leader on and off the court. He had a pretty good cast around him with the Nets, but when he went to Philly, the 76ers had so many talented players, so many big-time scorers, that Doc just kind of blended in. I'm not saying he still wasn't a great player, because he was. But he didn't have the kind of personality to just take over a team. It wasn't his nature. A guy like Michael Jordan, he would have taken over that team in about a week, but that wasn't Doc's style, Doc preferred to lead by example."

Hallelujah, Darryl Dawkins said. "Doc was always a leader. He always worked hard to set an example for all of us to follow. Because Doc came before a whole lot of big-name stars, they had something to follow, a level of excellence to achieve or try to surpass. They had a lot of work cut out for them, something to strive for. I'm not so sure that it could have been the other way around. If Doc had followed them, it would have been a different story."

Nevertheless, the first season in Philadelphia had taken an emotional toll on Erving and his family. His wife, Turquoise, was so unhappy about the change of scenery that she penned a scathing letter about how she felt for the sports pages of the *New York Times*. It was a venomous tirade that did nothing to improve relations between the Ervings and Philadelphia's players and fans.

"The Turquoise Erving letter was set up by a freelance writer named Samantha Stevenson," Heisler recalled. "Samantha would address a lot of different subjects, like lesbianism, and [anger] a lot of people. I tried to go out with her once, but I had no luck, although we did have a good working relationship. Anyway, Samantha got to be friendly with Turquoise and they wrote this letter, which basically announced that the other players on the team were being greedy with the ball and not allowing Julius to reach his greatness."

The letter was published on the "Views of Sport" page, on Sunday, March 13, 1977. Here are some of Turquoise's more inflammatory comments.

> Julius and I miss New York. We would have preferred that the Nets not sell him to the Philadelphia 76ers last October, because New York is home. It has always been home for Julius, but now it's home for me.

I don't know. Maybe if Philadelphia had treated us differently I would have felt better and thought of Philly as home. The treatment in Philadelphia is not like the treatment we received from the Nets. It was like a family in New York, including Coach Kevin Loughery and his wife. We were one. In Philly, after a game, we go our own way.

It's not exactly like being a new kid in school, but close. No one was overly nice when we arrived. The papers said the team was "in awe" of Julius. I don't think so. It's more like we weren't wanted. I feel as if I were stepping into someone else's territory in the wives' lounge.

The press said there would be a problem with Julius and George McGinnis playing together. That was the big thing. George would be jealous of Julius. But it's not that. It's not George. It's those other guys. They shoot that ball like crazy. They forget that Julius and George are paid well to handle the ball, too.

Julius is happy because he's playing basketball, not because he's playing for the 76ers. He knows how it was in Virginia and New York. He was happier there than in Philadelphia. He doesn't have animosity toward the other players or Coach Gene Shue. He just hopes things will get better.

I don't think the 76ers will win the National Basketball Association championship. I feel we have the talent to win, but I don't think they're playing much like a team. No one here respects Shue. How many guys want to win one for Shue? Not one. And sometimes, not even for themselves. . . .

Many players in New York looked at the playoffs in terms of how much money they would get if they won the championship. How many players in Philly even care about the money? None. All of them are so highly paid.

I sat by Billy Melchionni's wife for three years right under the basket in the Nassau Coliseum. When we lost in the first round of the playoffs in 1975, we sat and cried. We were hurt because we lost. If we lost in Philly, do you think I'd care? I wouldn't shed a tear. . . .

In New York, fans had respect for the game and the players. Not just because Julius was their superstar; it was that way for everyone on the team. If a player did one thing wrong, no one booed him. If you make a mistake in Philadelphia, they stand up and boo loudly. But come back and make a basket, and they're jumping for joy.

One thing would be nice—if the fans in Philly could really see Julius play. They haven't seen all of him yet.

Julius is an unselfish team player. He would never say the things I say. Sometimes I don't think he can play on a team like this, where most of the guys are out there for themselves. He plays the game from the first minute until the end. Julius cares.

This letter led Mark Heisler to suggest that one of Erving's biggest problems may have been his own wife.

"Julius may have had his complaints, but he was always discreet about it, whereas Turquoise was high-maintenance," he said. "Her list of expectations was a mile long. She wanted Gene Shue to do in Philly what Kevin Loughery had done for Julius in New York, which was to tell all the other guys on the team to stop shooting the ball and just let Julius shoot it."

10

Waiting to Hit
Pay Dirt

Three times in the next six seasons, Erving and an ever changing cast of 76ers returned to the NBA Finals. By the 1978–1979 season, Philadelphia management had rethought its strategy. The team decided to make Erving its captain, dump all the other huge-salaried players, and build a new team around Erving's vast talents.

The 1979–1980 squad lost to the Los Angeles Lakers, 4–2 in a six-game series.

In the fourth quarter of Game 4, the 76ers trailing 2 games to 1 in the series, Erving executed the most legendary baseline move in the history of the game, which helped the 76ers win, 105–102. In one of those magical sports moments, Erving ran down the baseline and was blocked at the basket. He floated under the basket, kept floating, and stretching his long, right arm to its rubbery limits, wrapped his body around three defenders, including Kareem Abdul-Jabbar, to complete an incredibly improbable reverse layup from behind the backboard that surely had Isaac Newton cheering in his grave.

"The reverse layup on Kareem was a once-in-a-lifetime play that will never be duplicated," said Michael Cooper, a Laker at that time. "No one will ever do it, because no one will ever come along with that kind of hang time and that kind of sheer athleticism and basketball smarts, no one. On that one play, Doc looked like an angel floating across the heavens.

"What made it so special is that he really didn't know what he was going to do until he finally did it. He went around not only Kareem but two other players. It was like he was looking to pass the ball at first and then he just said, 'Oh man, I'm here at the basket, let me take this thing all the way.' He just kept the play alive and turned what for anyone else would have been nothing into one of the most incredible moments in the history of sports.

"You know, it's hard enough to be creative when you're a part of some exhibition or you're standing alone in a gym somewhere," Cooper added. "But Julius was able to maintain his creativity with all those long arms and tall bodies swarming around him on just about every play. Michael Jordan and Dominique Wilkins were the only other players I have ever seen who could dunk in traffic like that, but neither one of them could dunk like Doc.

"Today there are guys out there popping steroids and enlisting the help of trainers to try and be superman out on the court. Well, Doc was Superman without all those things. He was just born with basketball greatness. Yeah, he worked at it, but his gifts came from God, not from some trainer or out of some bottle, and Doc didn't need an entourage around him to prove to everyone how popular he is and that he's a basketball celebrity.

"Doc went to the gym by himself, and he went home himself, and in both places, he was one of the all-time greats. From a fan's perspective, what was great about rooting for Doc was that he was someone you could walk up to and talk to, someone who would shake your hand and give you the time of day. A guy like Kobe Bryant, he's a great player, but unless you're playing against him out there on the floor, you really can't touch him. He's really out of reach."

Magic Johnson, then a rookie playing for the Lakers, said later of the reverse layup, "My mouth just dropped open. He actually did that. I thought, What should we do? Should we take the ball out or should we ask him to do it again? We cut him off, and there was nowhere for him to go but out of bounds. It's still the greatest move I've ever seen in basketball, the all-time greatest."

Johnson, of course, provided his own heroics in Game 6, when he filled in at center for an ailing Abdul-Jabbar and finished with 42 points, 15 rebounds, and 7 assists as the Lakers won the game, 123–107, and thus the series.

That year, Erving joined another cast of characters by playing the lead role in a wacky sports film called *The Fish That Saved Pittsburgh*. It told the story of the Pittsburgh Pythons, the laughingstock of a professional basketball league, led by their star player, Moses Guthrie, who was played by Erving, a Pisces (a water sign represented by two fish). The season is turned around by the team's water boy, Tyrone Millman, through his favorite hobby: astrology. "I thought the movie was low budget," World B. Free said with a laugh. "I told Doc to stick to his day job."

Another Lost Opportunity

The next season, 1980–1981, Erving was named the league's Most Valuable Player, the first time that award had gone to a noncenter in seventeen years. The 76ers made it to the play-offs again, but this year they came up against their old rival, the Boston Celtics, with their second-year superstar, Larry Bird, and lost a heartbreaking series after being up 3–1.

In the 1981–1982 season, the 76ers got past the Celtics in the play-offs but lost in the finals again to the Lakers, in six games, the grand finale a 114–104 clubbing of Julius and Company. For the Lakers, it was their second championship in three years, both times at the expense of the 76ers.

"I feel relieved more than anything else," said Pat Riley, the Lakers' coach, who was hired eleven games into the 1981–1982 season and had never previously been a head coach. Magic Johnson, voted Most Valuable Player of the series, finished Game 6 with box score numbers that included 13 points, 13 rebounds, and 13 assists. The Lakers had pulled ahead by 7 points to open the final period, but the 76ers made the score 103–100, as Andrew Toney made an eighteen-foot shot with three minutes and fifty-five seconds left to play.

The Lakers soon pulled away, however. Kareem Abdul-Jabbar scored on a hook while being fouled by Toney and tacked on a free throw to put Los Angeles up by 6 points with three minutes and seven seconds left. After a missed jumper by Maurice Cheeks, Bob McAdoo of the Lakers grabbed the rebound and fed Jamaal Wilkes, who connected on a layup to put the game out of reach.

Six Lakers scored in double figures. Wilkes had 27 points, and Abdul-Jabbar had 18 points, 11 rebounds, 4 assists, and 5 blocked shots. Norm Nixon, Michael Cooper, and McAdoo each added 16 points.

The 76ers were led by Erving, of course, who had a game-high 30 points, but in this, his sixth, NBA season, he failed for a third time to earn a championship ring. After the game, Erving was asked if the loss was his most disappointing. "I think so," he said. "We got more disappointed this time than any other year. As to why, I don't know. It hurts more than any other year. It's very painful."

Moses and the Promised Land

In the off-season, the team put a huge championship piece of its puzzle in place by signing Moses Malone, an offensive rebounding machine and the game's most dominating center, to a six-year, $13.2-million contract. Although skeptics believed that ninety-four feet of hardwood was not big enough for both Malone and Erving, the two stars quickly silenced their critics, leading the 76ers to a 50–7 record by March.

"Fo, Fo, Fo," Malone, the first player to leap from high school to the NBA, famously spit out before the play-offs began, predicting four-game sweeps by the 76ers in all three rounds of the 1982–1983 postseason. That season, Erving won the NBA All-Star Game's Most Valuable Player award for the second time, and his popularity had reached such heights that he was a guest on *Sesame Street*, chatting with Oscar the Grouch by Oscar's garbage can and helping a cute little girl throw down a slam dunk.

"Mo has exceeded our expectations in a lot of areas," Erving said at the time. "He's a great clutch player. It seems he's always there at the end of a close game to do something to help us win. If it's not a basket or rebound, it's a steal or a real good pick. Every night you know what you're going to get from him. He's consistently good, night after night. And he's not concerned with being catered to. If he doesn't get the ball for a quarter, he doesn't complain like a lot of guys might. He figures we're doing what has to be done to win."

With Malone rubbing elbows inside and the Doctor skillfully carving up opponents everywhere else on the court during that 1982–1983 season, the 76ers stormed into and through the playoffs, wiping out the Knicks in four games straight to win the Eastern Conference semifinals, then winning four out of five games against the Milwaukee Bucks to capture the Conference Finals and earn another shot at the Lakers.

On playing with Erving, Malone said simply, "I come here not declaring myself a superstar player. I'm a hardworking player. That's all. Doc's a great player, and he wants to win like I do. That makes it easy for us to play together. I didn't come here to cause trouble and lose games."

Nor did Malone go to Philadelphia to be pushed around by opponents or his teammates. "I remember when we began training camp and had our first scrimmage," Erving recalled in the *New York Times*. "Guys were hacking him and he wasn't getting the ball. I said to him, 'You all right?' He said, 'I'm fine.' Then he grabbed an offensive rebound, tossed in a shot, and dropped a couple guys to the floor at the same time. He knows how to get guys off his back without making a fuss about it."

"Dr. Dr. J"

After the 76ers took the first two games of the championship series from the defending NBA champion Lakers, just as they had done years earlier in Portland, Erving made a pit stop at Temple University, where he would become "Dr. Dr. J." That is, he received an honorary doctor of arts degree, his first degree, for what school officials described as adding an entirely new dimension to his profession, transcending the human condition through a new dimension of fine art.

Standing before fifty-eight hundred graduates at the Civic Center Convention Hall in Philadelphia, many of them chanting "Beat LA, Beat LA," Erving began by telling the captive audience how his career had reached such legendary heights. "Because I dared to be great," he said.

"Take a look at the stars and label them your limit," the double Doctor told the graduating class that day. "God instilled in me a desire to explore the boundaries of His wonderful gift to me, and I seek the light of creative exploration, as all artists do.

"Winning has to be a goal," Erving added. "As the result, it can't be denied. But the thing that must be most enjoyable is the work itself. The result cannot be your only enjoyment. If it was, and you played on a losing team, you wouldn't be getting anything out of it. The game is the thing.

"There is too much emphasis," he continued, "on the result: degrees, grades. And as a result, too many take as many shortcuts as they can, such as cheating. Amid all the games being played, the meat of the matter is often overlooked, that without disappointments, hard work, and sacrifice, there can be no gain."

He went on to speak of his time spent with the 76ers to that point, the ups and downs, the championships that seemed near but yet so far. "Those experiences with the 76ers helped me grow," he said. "In looking back, [I see that] maybe some of them were necessary for me. If they hadn't happened, I'd be a different person. I wouldn't be as prepared to handle some of the other things I wanted to do. I've accomplished a lot I can be proud of. So instead of feeling sorry for myself, it's a matter of setting an example. There can be pleasure and satisfaction in that.

"My life, and the enjoyment of it, is not based on the ups and downs of my profession. That's a very unstable way to live. Getting to the brink and not making it was very hard to accept in my first three seasons. But when I looked at it last year, it was clear that rebounding was a real weakness for us. Harold Katz, our owner, committed himself to changing that. Now we are a new creation, and we must carry on."

Erving talked about the addition of Malone, the game's most dominating and intimidating center. "It was proof enough for me that we were one helluva team," he said. "All the questions that I had were answered. I was convinced. We have a new feeling about ourselves. When we're at the top of our game, certain things happen that we can't bottle, uncork, and put out on the floor at any time. But the potential for it is always there. I hope everything goes right, but I realize that it could all go wrong. For us, though, the downside isn't that far down, and the upside is way, way up there."

Erving took his diploma and his bows and went about the business of earning his first NBA degree. He got back on the court and helped the 76ers sweep the Lakers in four games. By now, Erving was the last player left from the team he had first joined in 1976. Billy Cunningham was now the coach, and the new roster featured Maurice Cheeks and Andrew Toney in the backcourt and Erving and Malone in the frontcourt, joined by Bobby Jones and Marc Iavoroni.

In Game 4 of that championship series, Erving pulled off one of the most legendary dunks in basketball history, a powerful "rock the cradle" jam at the expense of the Lakers' Michael Cooper.

After making a steal late in the game with his team trailing by 2 points, Erving came down the court on a fast break, cupping and swinging the ball back and forth in his right arm. He stormed to the net along the left baseline, slung the ball around behind his head, and dunked over Cooper, who ducked out of the way as if a brick wall were collapsing on him.

"Nobody dunked like Doc," Cooper told me. "And that 'rock the cradle' dunk he pulled off on me was one of his best ever. I remember Doc steaming to the basket on that play. I was in the vicinity and caught a glimpse of him, and he had such a look of determination on his face—that was the Doctor, for you. I always thought that if I had been in a better position, I would have tried to get up there and attempt to block it, but

I couldn't get the proper angle on it. When he actually dunked it, I had my head down. All I heard was the roar of the crowd.

"That dunk really excited the crowd. It got them going and believing in their team, and from there, there was no turning back," continued Cooper, who is now the head coach of the Los Angeles Sparks of the Women's National Basketball Association (WBNA). "Players dream of cuffing the ball like that and dunking it on an opponent, and Doc just dunked it, as he dunked most basketballs, with such flair and such force. People still ask me about that, and my kids hate seeing it until this day, but I always say, hey, if you're going to get dunked on somebody, it might as well be the greatest dunker of all time. I'm not too crazy about it, but hey, I'll take it.

"At the end of the series, Doc came over to me and said, 'Hey, Coop, I'm sorry about that, but I had to take care of business. No hard feelings.'" Erving's dunk on Cooper tied the score, and Erving went on to score the next 5 points, driving a long-awaited stake through the heart of the hated Lakers.

"That dunk over Michael Cooper really put an exclamation point at the end of that series," said Dominique Wilkins. "I would say that's the greatest dunk of all time because Julius executed it in a high-pressure environment, in the flow of a game against a great team, and on a great player. I was home watching that game, and when Doc threw it down, I nearly fell out of my chair."

The final moments of that series clincher, a 115–108 defeat of the defending NBA champions, featured more of Erving's heroics. With two minutes left in the game, Erving stole a cross-court pass from Abdul-Jabbar and drove for a dunk that tied the game, 106–106. After Magic Johnson made one of two free throws for the Lakers, Erving took a fast-break pass from Maurice Cheeks, off a Malone rebound, and scored a 3-point play that put the 76ers up by 109–107, with fifty-nine seconds remaining. With twenty-four seconds remaining, Erving put the final nail in the Lakers' coffin by making a jump shot from the top of the key that put Philadelphia ahead by 3 points (111–108).

"That was the big shot," said Coach Pat Riley of the Lakers. "I knew then that it [a victory for the Lakers] just wasn't meant to be. They [the 76ers] really deserve the championship. Philadelphia ranks up there with the top three or four teams of the last decade."

In the critical last two minutes, Erving scored 7 points, finishing with 21 points and 6 assists. "We did it the long way, and we did it the hard way," he said, after earning his third championship ring and his first in the NBA. "But we did it the best way."

Cooper recalled one game during that championship series when he was approached by Erving. "Doc pulled me over to the side and just said softly, 'Hey, Coop, always be a pro out here.' Now, Doc never talked much, but when he did, everybody listened. We always were conscious of him when we were putting together a game plan in the locker room, and we were always aware of him out on the court, but when he was doing his thing out there, there wasn't much you could do in terms of stopping him—maybe slow him down a bit, but you could never stop him."

Erving, then thirty, smiled amid the champagne celebration in the locker room. "I hope now people will remember the numbers," he said. "Twelve times I've started something. Six times, I've been to the finals. And three times I've come out a winner. You either take it all or you don't take anything."

Moses Malone, who racked up a 24-point, 23-rebound effort in the clincher and had averaged a series-high 25.8 points and 18.5 rebounds in the Finals, was unanimously named Most Valuable Player of the play-offs. He was the 76ers' leading rebounder in each of their thirteen games in the postseason, and he led them in scoring nine times.

"I can't believe this is over," a smiling Malone said after the game. "It's great. I'm gonna celebrate all night. I'm not saying we're the best team ever. We're the best team now."

After having been defeated in the Finals by the Portland Trail Blazers six years earlier and left red-faced by the slogan "We owe you one," the 76ers finally got around to paying that debt. In the process, Philadelphia set a record by finishing the 1983 playoffs with a 12–1 record in postseason play, the best mark ever to that point. It was the first title for Philadelphia since 1967, and their last to date.

In fact, no other Philadelphia sports team had won a professional championship until the Philadelphia Phillies defeated the Tampa Bay Rays in five games to capture the 2008 World Series. Earlier in 2008, the Philadelphia Soul of the Arena Football League defeated the San Jose SaberCats, 59–56, to win the 2008 Arena Bowl.

"Julius finally got around to justifying that *yup*," said Dave Anderson, recalling Erving's answer when asked whether he would succeed in the NBA. "He further proved that he had the talent to lead an NBA team to the championship, just as he had once led an ABA team to a title. That championship with Philadelphia really solidified Julius's place in basketball history. You could easily make the case that he is one of the top ten or fifteen greatest players ever, and if you want to say top five, I can appreciate that argument as well."

Erving's teammates, fans, and even the media, right down to the last guy from radio station XYZ, celebrated along with him.

"Everybody was happy for Doc that season," the sportswriter Mark Heisler said. "Over the years, Philly had some good teams with Mo Cheeks, Andrew Toney, Bobby Jones, and Caldwell Jones, but the bottom line was that they finally won with Doc and Moses Malone. Julius was a great player in the NBA, even a star player in Philly, but he wasn't the Julius Erving of myth that he was in the ABA, and he certainly would not have won that championship without Malone's help. You would see flashes now and then of the kind of superstar Erving once was, but he would have to have been Michael Jordan in the NBA to live up to the reputation he had in the ABA."

Signature Slam

After winning his first NBA championship, Erving played four more seasons. The 76ers were eliminated by the now New Jersey Nets (the team's name had been changed from the New York Nets several years earlier) in five games in the first round of the 1983–1984 playoffs. That season, however, the Doctor left his calling card for future generations of players and fans at the Slam Dunk Contest that was a part of the NBA All-Star Break in Denver.

On January 28, 1984, Erving provided one of the most thrilling moments in the history of sports. That season, David Stern replaced Larry O'Brien as NBA commissioner, and the league adapted the Slam Dunk Contest from the old ABA. Erving, the ABA's last slam-dunk champ in 1976, was the sentimental favorite of the crowd of 17,251 that had gathered at McNichols Arena in Denver.

The other dunksters included Darrell "Dr. Dunkenstein" Griffith of the Utah Jazz, Edgar "the Wild Helicopter" Jones of the San Antonio Spurs, Clyde "the Glide" Drexler of the Portland Trail Blazers, Dominique "the Human Highlight Film" Wilkins of the Atlanta Hawks, Michael "Coop-a-Loops" Cooper of the Los Angeles Lakers, Larry "Fancy" Nance of the Phoenix Suns, Orlando "Oh! Oh!" Woolridge of the Chicago Bulls, and Ralph Sampson of the Houston Rockets.

In the final round of the contest, Larry Nance watched Erving miss a dunk. It was Erving's second of three slam attempts, a whirling windmill that bounced off the back of the rim—Erving's only miss in nine attempts.

On his third and last effort of the final round, however, the Doctor delivered a slam for the ages that now lives in cyberspace perpetuity. Standing at the far end of the free-throw line, eighty feet from the basket, Erving revved his engine and began racing down the floor. As he reached the near end of the free-throw line, he elevated and soared toward the rim, like one of those jets leaving Kennedy airport. As he glided on the rarefied air, his right arm outstretched like Superman, Erving dropped a thunderous one-hander through the basket, earning a 50 score for a perfect dunk and a place in history that is reserved for those mortals who rolled off the assembly line in God's basketball factory.

"Don't forget, this was later in his career; he was a much older guy, not the Superman that everyone saw in the ABA," Dominique Wilkins told me when discussing Erving's signature slam. "Now, he was still a great player, but I didn't think he had that kind of lift left in his legs. And yet here he was. He jumped so far and so high that he actually hit his head on the bottom of the backboard.

"Do you have any idea what kind of athleticism that takes?" asked Wilkins. "There are probably only a handful of athletes around the world who could duplicate that dunk today. I'd have to put it somewhere in the top ten dunks of all time."

By the time the ball bounced back on the hardwood, every kid in America wanted to be the next Dr. J.

"He was a king in his era, and that dunk helped put him a little higher on his throne," said Wilkins, who was born in France, grew up in Baltimore with his brother, Gerald (a former Knick), and lives in Lilburn, Georgia. "Julius was a highflyer with no equal who played the game with smarts, poise, finesse, and an intimidating explosiveness that set the benchmark super-high for guys who followed, like myself, Michael Jordan, and Vince Carter.

"In terms of skill and professionalism, Julius is still the standard-bearer. He's what you would like to see in today's play-ers, a combination of skill and grace on the floor and a gentle-man off the floor—the complete package.

"He played the game on a level that only a few guys in the history of the league ever played it. Some people may have looked at him as this high-flying circus act, but he was a com-plete ballplayer, the kind of competitor who elevated the games of all the other players around him, whether they were team-mates or the opposition.

"Growing up, I saw a lot of great ballplayers, but I have never in my life seen a player with Doc's combination of flair, finesse, and power, and he was able to put those skills on display on a nightly basis, no matter who the opponent. There aren't too many small forwards who came before or after who could do the things that Julius could do with a basketball, who could take the ball from one end of the floor to the other with the ability to go by a defender anytime he wanted. You could not guard Julius Erving one-on-one, it was impossible. The best you could do was try and contain him with a lot of weak-side help, but one-on-one, he was murder.

"Professional basketball is a very hard game to play, but Julius made it look so easy. In my lifetime, Julius Erving is the most graceful athlete I have ever seen, not just in basketball, but in any sport."

Asked later to describe his historic dunk, Erving merely said, "The score spoke for itself."

Nance would win the contest and the ten-thousand-dollar prize, with a whirling and high-flying reverse right-handed jam. "Larry Nance was great in that dunk contest; you really can't take anything away from him," Wilkins said. "But all eyes were on Julius. Despite the fact that he lost that day, it was like an entire country was in awe of him."

Indeed, it was Erving, in the twilight of his illustrious career, who had given sports fans one last show, one last breathtaking walk on air.

"Dr. J is the single reason that the NBA Slam Dunk Contest is as popular as it is today, why it's the highlight of All-Star Weekend," said Charles Barkley, who teamed with Erving for three seasons in Philadelphia. "Before Doc made it popular back in the ABA, no one even considered it a happening event, but Doc made it count because all his dunks were beautiful and incredibly hard to duplicate. All the players show up on Saturday night at All-Star Weekend because they do not want to miss that event.

"Michael Jordan came along later and was great at it, but nobody dunked like Doc—not Michael or Dominique Wilkins, especially not in the flow of real games, which is so hard to do. There are two kinds of dunkers: guys who can dunk in the flow of a game and guys who dunk in practices and in competitions. Doc could do both, and not many others could. Even today, after watching a guy dunk, other guys turn to each other and say, 'Man, that was pretty good, but he can't dunk like Dr. J.'"

The Rookie Couldn't Sleep

Days before joining the Philadelphia 76ers for the 1984–1985 season, Charles Barkley, a portly powerhouse drafted from

Auburn University, was nervous about meeting one of his boyhood idols, Julius Erving. "The first thing I'll tell you is that I couldn't sleep in the days before my first training camp," Barkley said to me. "I thought I could handle myself as far as basketball was concerned, but I was nervous about meeting Dr. J, because everyone held him in such high regard. I had seen Moses Malone that summer, and all he said was 'Hey fathead, how you doing?'

"Personalitywise, Moses was so unlike Doc, but he was helpful in his own way. Early in my career, I went over to Moses to ask him what he thought was the reason I wasn't playing as much as I thought I should be. He just looked at me and said, 'Because you're fat and lazy and way out of shape.'

"I had always played in college at 300 pounds, and I got by just fine, but after that talk with Moses, I got down to my playing weight of 255, and my career just kind of took off from there. Now, if I had asked that same question of Doc, he probably would have given me the same advice but in a nicer way, saying something like 'Young fella, it's probably best if you drop a few pounds.' But Moses, he just blurted out what was on his mind, that's just the kind of guy he is.

"Julius wasn't one of those guys. He was a whole different kind of personality. I mean, this is NBA royalty you're talking about. When you're growing up, there are maybe five to ten guys that you and every other kid in the playground want to be like. Magic Johnson, Larry Bird, and John Havlicek were among those guys, and, of course, there was Julius.

"When I walked into the locker room for the first time, after having been up the whole night before, I kept thinking, Should I call him Doc, Dr. J, Julius, Mr. Erving, or Mr. J? I wasn't sure, and I can't tell you how intimidated I was. But then he made it so easy for me. He actually went out of his way and came over to me and extended his hand and said, 'Hey, young fella, I'm Doc.' He was everything I thought he would be: cool, polite, and he had a lot of class. It was a pretty amazing experience."

Barkley, a member of the NBA Hall of Fame and, like Erving, voted one of the NBA's 50 Greatest Players, said that the problem with the league today is that there aren't enough Julius Ervings, savvy veterans with the ability to lead and guide young players both on and off the court. It's not always about setting picks. Sometimes it's about setting examples, about imparting wisdom and being a mentor, like Erving was to Barkley.

"The one thing I hate about the NBA today is that there are very few veterans around that the younger players can actually learn anything from," said Barkley, the man once known as "the Round Mound of Rebound."

"When you first go pro and make some nice money, you sometimes do a lot of stupid things," Barkley admitted. "When I first joined the 76ers, I bought five or six cars, and every day I'd drive a new one into the parking lot when I showed up for practice. I owned two Mercedes Benzes, two Porsches, a BMW, and a sports truck. Then one day Doc pulls me over and asks if he could talk to me. I said of course, and he started telling me how I had to be more careful with my money because I wasn't going to be playing in the NBA forever. When you're young, you do think you can go on and on forever, but Doc was trying to tell me that I was spending my money foolishly and that I should not blow everything because I would need that money later in my life. I still remember the conversation:

Doc: You don't need to drive six cars to be a somebody.

Barkley: How many cars do you drive?

Doc: Just one.

Barkley: You're comfortable with that?

Doc: Yes, because even with one car, everyone knows it's me behind the wheel. It's not about the car, it's about the man driving the car.

"Doc told me that the same applied for me, so I didn't need to drive a new car every day," Barkley said. "I'll never forget that conversation, because it set the financial tone for the rest of my career, and being careful with money is something I preach to young players to this day. But I think young guys today do not benefit from players who possess the wisdom of a Julius Erving. The league is suffering from a lack of maturity because so many players are turning pro after just one year in college, so the veterans are now much younger than they used to be.

"Outside of the San Antonio Spurs, a very unique team, no team has a thirty-five-year-old player who is really willing to share his experiences for the benefit of a younger player's growth. Believe me, something like that goes a long way in the emotional and even physical development of a young player. Trust me, some of these old guys can be real pricks, I mean flat-out pricks, to the younger players, because they resent the fact that the young guys are making more money today than they did in their younger days, and they resent the notoriety that young players get today. Doc wasn't like that, he was always there for me. Thank God I had him in my corner, because things might have turned out differently for me if he wasn't."

Barkley, whose first three seasons coincided with Erving's last three seasons, remembered how gracefully Erving passed the torch to him, that he was so unlike the nasty players who resented the new rich kids on the block. "When I got to Philly," Barkley said, "there were still a lot of veterans there, but it was still very much Doc's team. My rookie year really didn't count so much because I was just finding my way, and in my second year I was just starting to make my mark, but in my third year

I became an All-Star for the first time. That's when I really became a good player, when I really took over the team.

"That third season for me was Doc's last season. He made it such a smooth transition for me, and that's something else I'll never forget. When my playing days came to an end, I tried to pass the torch gracefully to players who would succeed me, just as Doc had done years before for me. Every great player goes through that at the late stages of his career, and some guys are better at giving way than others. Doc was great at it with me. I played with Doc at the tail end of his career, but even though he was on the downside, you could see that there were clearly some traces of greatness left in his game.

"There were certain moves, certain dunks, where he would turn back the clock and remind everyone what kind of awesome player he once was. When I was on the downside of my career, I often thought about Doc in Philly and how he handled himself, and I tried to emulate that. It was very unique for me to have Doc as a teammate; every young guy who came along was in awe of him like I was. But we had so many great veteran guys on those teams, like Moses [Malone] and Maurice Cheeks and Bobby Jones; it was a real good bunch."

Barkley also recalled how nice Erving was to another high-flying rookie who once sought his approval. "I know that Doc was really great to Michael Jordan when he was first starting out. Anytime Mike was around Doc, he appreciated Doc's wisdom and advice."

In fact, here is what Michael Jordan said about Julius Erving very early in his career, long before the accolades, awards, and championships: "There are a lot of similarities between the way I play and the way he played. When he left the game, he left with a lot of class and a lot of dignity and respect from his peers, and that's something that if I don't ever win a world championship or MVP award, that is something I would love to walk away from the game to have. He's been a very good friend to me thus far because his advice has always been very comforting for me to accept, and I just think that he and I are getting close, and it's a great feeling to be around him and learn a lot from him."

Discussing Erving's place in history, Barkley said, "Julius is a playground legend, a slam-dunk legend, an ABA and NBA legend who won championships in both leagues. So when you're talking about the greatest players of all time, I'd say Julius pretty much has it all covered. You know, people think that the NBA started with Magic Johnson and Larry Bird and then took off with Michael Jordan. But to me, the NBA really began with Julius Erving, who was the first to take the sport to another level during an age of basketball purity, before humongous contracts began changing the dynamics of the game.

"In Julius Erving's day, guys played for money, yeah, but it was more about pride and wanting to be great and to play against great players and win championships. By the time I came along, multimillion-dollar contracts began taking the sport downhill. Guys were not so much interested in playing to win a championship as they were in playing to win a big contract. There's something really wrong with that."

Brawling with "Larry Legend"

That season (1984–1985), the 76ers defeated the Washington Wizards and the Milwaukee Bucks in the play-offs before they were stopped by the Boston Celtics, 4–1 in the Eastern Conference Finals. Erving had a dismal performance in the play-offs, and many people believed that Father Time was finally on the heels of the wondrous Dr. J.

Among the hundreds of articles I read in preparing to write this book, no column stood out more on the subject of the aging Julius Erving than one written by Dave Anderson in May 1985, just after Erving and the 76ers were eliminated by Larry Bird and the Boston Celtics. "He'll always be Julius Erving, but at age 35 he's not Doctor J anymore," Anderson wrote. "He got his nickname in the Harlem playgrounds because of the way he 'operated.' But he doesn't make the incision for the Philadelphia 76ers now."

In that particular series against the Celtics, Erving averaged only 14 points. Over the five games, he shot just 32 percent from the field and had a total of only 26 rebounds.

"All those numbers seemed to be symbolized by a frozen moment in the final seconds of Wednesday night's final game," Anderson continued. "Trailing, 102–100, the 76ers had a chance in the final seconds for a fast break that might have forced the fifth game into overtime, but Julius Erving collided with Andrew Toney. Doctor J never would have collided with a teammate in that situation, but Julius Erving did. Doctor J would have swooped downcourt and stuffed the ball or flipped a dazzling pass for the tying basket, but Julius Erving collided with a teammate, disrupting the fast break.

"Moments later, as Julius Erving frantically signaled for a time-out before Larry Bird stole the ball from Andrew Toney, neither official saw him. Once upon a time everybody saw everything Doctor J did on a basketball court, but Julius Erving doesn't require that undivided attention. Those two officials, like everybody else, watch Larry Bird now.

"Julius Erving understands better than anyone that over the grind of the 82-game schedule and through the crucible of the playoffs, he's no longer Doctor J, just as he always understood the difference within himself. In his travels, he accepted being identified as 'Doc' by his coaches, his teammates, and his opponents, but he never called himself that. And wherever he appeared, he never introduced himself as Doctor J.

"'I'm Julius Erving, and I always will be,' he was saying now. 'My nickname and what it stands for will cross over into my professional life, but I keep it out of my personal life. It's dreaming on my part to think I can do all the things I used to do,' he said. 'My game is not as explosive as in past years; it's based on consistency now.'"

For Larry Bird and the Celtics, the 4–1 series victory was sweet revenge in a tense year between the bitter rivals that had reached a boiling point on November 9, 1984, when Erving and Bird, two of the league's most high-profile and highly respected players, became involved in an ugly brawl that emptied both benches in the third quarter of a game that Boston won, 130–119.

Several minutes before the fight began, the referee, Jack Madden, was forced out of the game by a knee injury, leaving Dick Bavetta to officiate by himself. After Bird was called for an offensive foul for charging into Erving, he and Erving, friends off the court who had made several television commercials together, exchanged words near the Celtics bench. At the time of the incident, Bird had scored 42 points to Erving's 6.

The two players shoved each other, then Bird began swinging at Erving, who went right back at Bird. Both players soon wrapped their hands around each other's throats—now a famous photo in memorabilia shops around the country—and a melee ensued. Moses Malone, Philadelphia's hulking center, joined the fight, scuffling briefly with Boston's M. L. Carr. Within seconds, eighteen players and coaches were on the battlefield.

"I'm sure Julius was frustrated because Larry had all those points against him," said Celtics player Cedric Maxwell.

Celtics coach K. C. Jones said that the entire incident was blown out of proportion, "mainly because two of the greatest stars in the game were involved."

Bird and Erving, who at a later date would shake hands before a game, were each fined seventy-five hundred dollars by the NBA for their part in the fight. To that point, the only larger penalty the league had dished out was the ten-thousand-dollar fine and sixty-day suspension given to Kermit Washington for punching Rudy Tomjanovich of the Houston Rockets in 1977.

In a letter notifying Bird of the fine, Scotty Stirling, the league's vice president, described the man Bostonians knew as "Larry Legend" as "clearly the aggressor and the instigator of the melee."

To Erving, Stirling wrote, "While [we] recogniz[e] that Bird was the aggressor and instigator, your continuation of the incident by punching Bird escalated an already serious situation."

Perhaps the most stunned spectators of all during the Bird-Erving clash were all the people who had crossed paths with Erving before that wild day in Boston. After all those years of getting banged around on the playgrounds of Queens and Long Island, in Rucker Park, and in college gymnasiums during his time at UMass and during his heyday in the ABA, the seemingly unflappable Julius Erving had finally had his buttons pushed by someone and apparently was human after all.

"I surprised myself," Erving would say later. "I'm usually a peacemaker. I think, though, that too much has been made of it."

According to Mark Heisler, Erving's reaction had little to do with the fact that Bird had outscored him that day. To Dr. J, still an All-Star in the fading moments of his career, the writing was right there on the Boston Garden wall. Not only was Erving no longer the best player in the game, he was also no longer the best small forward in the game. Larry Bird was.

"When Bird came into the league in 1979, Julius was no longer considered the best small forward in the NBA," said Heisler, "if he ever was to begin with."

The next season (1985–1986), Matt Guokas replaced Billy Cunningham as head coach and led the 76ers to the second round of the playoffs, where they were defeated by the Milwaukee Bucks in seven games. Though Erving had another splendid season by averaging 19.5 points per game, Father Time was indeed beginning to tug at his jersey. This was the first season of his career in which he failed to average a minimum of 20 points per game.

Erving's last season, 1986–1987, brought a financial bonanza for the NBA owners, who staged retirement good-byes. In April of that season, a capacity crowd of 20,149 attended the Nets' tribute to Erving, probably doubling the normal attendance for what would have been a meaningless game.

"People who knew basketball knew what Erving's overall value was in terms of his significance to the sport," Bob Costas said. "They knew what he had meant to both the ABA and the NBA, not to mention the fact that he is on almost everyone's list as an all-time great."

The night the Nets honored their former captain was an emotional one. During the thirty-minute pregame ceremonies, Erving broke down and cried as the arena darkened and the spotlights focused on a banner with jersey number 32, the first number ever retired by the Nets and the same number Erving wore at the University of Massachusetts.

Erving hugged his mother, Callie Lindsey, and Fritz Massmann, the Nets' longtime trainer. Besides Massmann and Erving's mother, also on hand were Jack Leaman, Erving's college coach, and several of his former Net teammates. "The fact that they brought these special people to me in order to express our love for one another was a tremendous factor," Erving said.

Speaking of his banner that flapped high in the rafters, Erving, his eyes filling with tears, said, "I can't bear to look up there. It's been eleven years. I haven't seen it in eleven years, and it's been a long eleven years. It links the present Nets organization with the old. A tree without roots cannot stand. The fans here need to know about me and the Nets of Long Island."

The presentation to the Hall of Fame of the uniform that Erving wore when the Nets defeated the Denver Nuggets, 112–106, in May 1976, to win the last ABA Championship, and the memories of Erving's three seasons as a Net were part of the halftime ceremonies at the game between Erving's old team, the Nets, and his new one, the Philadelphia 76ers, in the Brendan Byrne Arena.

On that historic evening in 1976, the Nets had celebrated wildly in the center of their crowded dressing room in Nassau Coliseum. Erving had hugged Jim Eakins, a teammate who had played a crucial role in the victory, while his red, white, and blue uniform, soaked with champagne, lay at the foot of his locker. Erving would never again wear that Net uniform, and now it would be put on display at the Hall of Fame alongside the jerseys of Wilt Chamberlain, George Mikan, Bob Pettit, and other basketball greats.

Jim Bukata, then an assistant to Dave DeBusschere, the last ABA commissioner, was the man who thought quickly on his feet and preserved a treasured piece of basketball history. "I got the uniform from Doc that night [in 1976] with the idea of presenting it to the Hall of Fame," Bukata explained. "There were feelings at the time that the ABA was headed for extinction, and I wanted Doc to be remembered for his days in the ABA. For many years he was the league's showcase, and in the final years, when teams were folding all around us, Doc was the ABA's spokesman and rallying force. I remember him continuously telling the players, 'We've got to stick together and keep this league going.'"

At a press conference earlier on that day in April 1987, Erving talked about the painful days when he first parted ways with the Nets. "When I found out about the trade, he said, "I had a wide range of emotions. After the three years with the Nets, I really believed I would finish my career there. Then I learned about this business. It was something I had to do. When I left for Philly, I felt a very special something in my heart for the Nets, and that made it difficult for me to play there the next two or three years. It really affected my game. It's been eleven years, and although some of my feelings have passed and I've played some good games against the Nets, I still have emotional ties."

After the game in April 1987, Erving said, "It was a strange night." He was thrilled with his retirement party, but not too happy about the fact that he had made only two of twelve shots and had 6 points in twenty-eight minutes, as the Nets defeated the 76ers, 113–109. "It was very difficult to remain unaffected." He also said that he hadn't been shooting well in practice, adding, "I have a [slightly] sprained wrist. Of course, the emotion today affected me. I was crying, I admit it. I think the way the salute was staged was what did it to me."

At the time of Erving's retirement, Frank DeFord of *Sports Illustrated* wrote, "More than any single player, Erving transformed what had been a horizontal game (with occasional parabolas) into a vertical exercise. Basketball is now a much more artistic game than it was before—than any game was before—because of Julius Erving. The slam, before the Doctor, was essentially an act of power—a *stuff* is what it was usually called—as great giants jammed the ball through the hoop. Erving transformed the stuff into the dunk, and he made what had been brutal and the product of size into something beautiful and a measure of creativity."

Three days after the Nets' tribute, 17,146 fans came to Madison Square Garden for a tribute to Erving by the Knicks.

After a crowd of 19,411 attended the final regular-season game against the Baltimore Bullets at the Capital Centre in Landover, Maryland (a suburb of Washington, D.C.), more than 350,000 people had attended the twenty-two road games in which the teams had bid a bon voyage to the Doctor.

"The one thing I can remember about Julius was that every retirement speech he made at every press conference in every city was a little different. There was always a new twist in whatever city he was playing in for the last time," said Phil Jasner, a 76ers beat writer for the *Philadelphia Daily News* at that time. "I always made sure I was at as many of those press conferences as I could be at, because Julius always had something sincere and interesting to say. If he was in a former ABA city, he would tell some great old ABA stories."

Charles Barkley, a rising star himself in Erving's final season, said of those farewell tours: "They were great for Doc, and we didn't mind them because we knew he deserved every one of them.

"The fans in Philly can be tough on just about anyone," Barkley added. "But with Dr. J, they knew better than to boo him, even late in his career. They knew that Doc was loyal, that he won them a championship, and that he would retire with grace and dignity. Very few players in the history of any sport deserve not to be booed, even in the worst of times out on the field or on the court, but Doc was one of those players and Philly fans knew it. They held him in high regard and apart from most other athletes who went through that town. Very few guys got that kind of send-off at the end of their careers, because very few guys meant as much to their sport as Julius Erving meant to the game of basketball."

In December 1986, Tom Callahan of *Time* magazine wrote a farewell tribute to Erving under the headline "Dr. J Is Flying Away." The article began:

Julius ("Dr. J") Erving, the most watchable basketball player of the past 16 years, has begun to say goodbye to cities: Portland, Seattle, Oakland, Phoenix. At final stops along the Philadelphia 76ers' way, home teams have been introducing their own players first in order to build a crescendo for Dr. J, the National Basketball Association star who plays for everyone.

"Each arena holds its own memories," says Erving, who was not thinking of wine or golf clubs when he announced on opening day that this will be his final season. Dr. J's best going-away present has been the sight of the Phoenix fans bedecked in surgical caps and masks for his last house call. "I'm savoring a lot of old moves and a lot of old players," he says, "because they should be savored. These buildings house so many ghosts."

With a quarter of the season gone, the revamped Sixers are neck and neck with the Boston Celtics, as usual. Since Center Moses Malone transferred to Washington, bulky Forward Charles Barkley has become the dominant figure. After Maurice Cheeks, a whirlwind guard, Erving, at 36, continues to perform probably the third most important role, shifting almost exclusively to the backcourt. By his standards, Dr. J's game has become subtle and subdued. "Man makes plans," he says. "God laughs." But he can still play.

Before Erving's great career was over, he had achieved a milestone realized by only two others in basketball history: Kareem Abdul-Jabbar and Wilt Chamberlain.

On April 17, 1987, Erving reached the 30,000-point plateau in Philadelphia on a night when these words appeared on a fourteen-by-eighteen-foot billboard outside the Spectrum: "We'll never fill your shoes. Thanks for everything, Doc."

The words were surrounded by fifty thousand signatures of Julius Erving's fans. It was Erving's last regular-season home game after eleven years with the 76ers, and a sellout crowd of 17,967 was present to see what final bits of magic he would make against the Indiana Pacers.

Erving made 36 of his 38 points in the first thirty-one minutes of the game, which the 76ers lost, 115–111, to the Pacers. With his 36th point, an eight-foot turnaround jump shot with four minutes and fifty-nine seconds left in the third period, Erving joined Kareem Abdul-Jabbar and Wilt Chamberlain as the only players with 30,000 points. Karl Malone (of the Utah Jazz and the Los Angeles Lakers) and Michael Jordan would later join that group.

Erving, who scored 11,662 points during his five years in the ABA, finished his career with a total of 30,026 points.

"Julius is one of the players who changed the direction of the game," said Mike Fratello. "He changed that direction not just by the way he played but through a personality that was, and is, one of a kind. He will always be earmarked as a guy who carried the greatness torch from one generation to the next. He was an impact player the way Wilt Chamberlain and Bill Russell [of the Boston Celtics] were. Without question, he helped set the stage for other great players who followed, like Magic Johnson, Larry Bird, and, of course, Michael Jordan."

Taking Five

Michele Sharp, the head basketball coach at Kean University in New Jersey, remembered a Philadelphia day in 1987 when she was the head coach of the AAU's Shooting Stars and was walking through Fairmount Park.

"People were filming a commercial that day, and I immediately noticed that Julius Erving was there," Sharp recalled.

"He was doing a public service commercial on behalf of children, and I went over to see if he could give me a hand with one of my clinics."

Sharp, who had never met Erving before that day, waited a while for a break in the filming and then walked up to Erving.

"Hi, I'm Michele Sharp," she said as she extended her hand, which Erving shook. She told Erving that she and her team needed money for a trip to Texas to compete in the AAU National Championships and that they were raising the money by holding a basketball clinic for children in the area. She asked Erving, who was still playing for the 76ers, if he would lend his time by coming over to the clinic and working with some of the youngsters.

"Okay," he said. "Here's my phone number. Call me and we'll set it up."

Sharp was amazed at how courteous and helpful Erving was to her, and she wondered if he was just talking a good game.

"I called the number about a week later," she said, "and I think it was his home number, because he picked it up right away. I asked him again about the clinic and he said, 'Yeah, it looks like I can do it. No problem.'"

Two weeks later, Erving was at Cabrini College in Philadelphia, showing the young players the finer points of the game and even playing one-to-one with some of Sharp's Shooting Stars.

"He was incredible, just so nice, and he stayed there for about two or three hours and didn't ask for a penny," Sharp said. "Some of the kids couldn't believe that they were playing basketball with Julius Erving. It was like they were living a dream."

When Erving was a Net, he spoke with *Black Sports The Magazine* about the day his own basketball dream would end, when basketball would no longer be an option. "There comes a time in everyone's career when they have to be realistic," he said. "There's going to be ten men picked for every team, and you must realize that someday you might not be in that top ten. For some, that realization comes in high school; for others in college, and for others in the pros. I think a great deal of realism has to be considered when you talk about athletes, because you know everybody can't make it.

"I think it's necessary to say that to make youngsters aware of that so they won't put all their eggs in one basket. A lot of black youngsters have a false perception of athletics. They see it as a means to an end and often as the end itself. Athletics can't be that. Athletics should only be part of your total existence, part of your total development as a man or a woman."

11

Swan Song

By season's end, Erving knew that his day had finally arrived. His last official game was in Milwaukee in May 1987, when the Bucks defeated the 76ers in the seventh and deciding game of the Eastern Conference semifinals.

When the thirty-seven-year-old left the floor for the final time, with forty seconds remaining and the Bucks well in control, Erving was replaced by Andrew Toney, who hugged him warmly near midcourt. "I felt like crying," Toney said later in the quiet Philadelphia locker room. "I could only embrace him."

As Erving walked by his teammates, there were more hugs and an increasing din from the crowd of 11,052 as he donned his blue warm-up suit. John Lucas, the guard for the Bucks, left the floor to embrace Erving and whisper some parting words.

"No more tears," Erving said after that last game, a 102–89 loss to the Bucks. "This is a special day, a happy day."

Erving then embraced his wife, Turquoise, and walked away from a storied career that spanned sixteen seasons, two leagues, three teams, and three championships. More important, Erving had left the game of basketball in much better shape than he had found it.

"What makes Doc so special is that he was the only player in history to have saved both the ABA and the NBA," the former Nets coach Kevin Loughery said. "He saved the ABA from sure extinction, because if it were not for him, the league would have folded before the merger. And when he got to the NBA, he did a lot to save the league's image as a boring sport. The magic he brought revitalized the NBA, in terms of energy and entertainment, and made it popular. The league used his image in almost all its promotions, which was a smart thing to do. In that sense, Doc was worth every penny he was ever paid, and more. I was really happy for him when he signed for the big money, because he deserved to be making as much as he could."

Indeed, Doctor J's skywalking tenure in a tank top and shorts, his thrilling theatrics, had breathed life into a stale game. His otherworldly swoops to the hoop and viciously graceful dunks changed the way his contemporaries and future generations of players approached the game, as well as the way future generations of fans viewed modern-day, above-the-rim basketball, from the windswept courts at Rucker Park to NBA arenas to other professional arenas around the world.

"I still look at Julius Erving as the granddaddy of basketball excitement," Dominique Wilkins said. "In terms of greatness, the one thing that separated Julius from the rest of the pack was that he was able to put on a show, with all his great dunks and incredibly twisting layups, in game situations. Some guys can do spectacular things in practice or in exhibitions when no one is playing defense, but to be able to execute those great moves in the flow of a real game, to be able to pull off all those dunks in traffic, is extraordinary, and Julius did that, game after game, throughout his entire career.

"Coming from high school to college and into the pros [as I did], my signature moves were my dunks in traffic," Wilkins continued. "I often tried to back my opponent in and dunk on him. I used the dunk as a mental tool. It was a weapon meant to intimidate opponents, and I'm sure Julius used it as a weapon to intimidate as well. Psychologically, it always worked to his advantage, because it also served to motivate his teammates and get the fans out of their seats and screaming. But Julius's game wasn't all about dunks. It's hard to get 30,000 points on dunks alone.

"Doc was the ultimate showman, but he never did anything to rub it in anyone's face. He did anything he could to win, and you can't penalize a guy for doing that. If he dunked in your face, you didn't take it personally, because that was one of the signature moves in his arsenal, so you just shook your head and rolled with it.

"The bottom line," Wilkins concluded, "is that Julius would be a superstar in any era because he had the most unique set of offensive tools that any player ever brought onto the court."

Michael Cooper, who said that "the Lakers and the 76ers had a lot of very professional battles on the basketball court," said of Erving, "At the peak of his game, Doc was the most exciting player to ever put on a uniform. Elgin Baylor and Wilt Chamberlain came before him and Michael Jordan came after him, but none of them had Doc's flair for the game above the rim; none of them had the kind of hang time and offensive arsenal that Doc had with all his dunk shots, bank shots, and finger rolls. When I watch footage of him from those days, I still get chills."

In his final performance, Erving scored a game-high 24 points. However, he missed his final attempt, a driving scoop shot from the right side of the floor that struck the bottom of the rim. His last basket was a 3-pointer, a fitting conclusion for a player who began his career in the ABA (which instituted the 3-point play).

"Doc was the first guy to fly," Loughery said during Erving's retirement tour in 1987. "He did things with a basketball that no one else had ever done. I honestly believe that Doc did more for pro basketball than anybody on and off the court."

After the final buzzer in the last game, Erving was presented with the game ball, and as he left the floor he held it high in response to the ovation.

"I had a great career, a very productive career," Erving said. "I just feel blessed in a special way, so there's nothing to be sad about. For me this will be a very, very long off-season, the longest one I've ever had."

As Erving so eloquently put it, the time was right to say good-bye. "I pulled the plug on it at a time that I thought was right for me to exit," he said.

After retiring from basketball, Erving became a successful businessman, buying a Coca-Cola bottling business. In 1992, a year before he was hired by NBC as a studio analyst for the network's basketball coverage, he told the Academy of Achievement just how much he believed that basketball was his true destiny.

"I think I was chosen by basketball, although I never really physically got drafted to any team that I played for," he said. "The only team that drafted me, I never played for, which was the Milwaukee Bucks. I think that my God-given physical attributes—big hands, big feet, and the way that I'm built, proportionwise—just made basketball the most inviting sport for me to play. From the first time I picked up a basketball at age eight—I had a lot of difficulty when I first picked up a basketball, because I was a scrub—there were things that I liked about it.

"Although I wasn't good, there were things that I liked about it. I could always handle a ball pretty well, even though I couldn't shoot it straight and wasn't a good defender. I had to spend countless hours, above and beyond the basic time, to try and perfect the fundamentals. So there was a relationship there. It was a two-way street. I liked the game, I enjoyed the game, and the game fed me enough and gave me enough rewards to reinforce that this is something that I should spend time doing and that I could possibly make a priority in my life, versus other sports.

"If someone gave me a choice of playing football, basketball, baseball, golf, tennis, or hockey, I think that basketball would be my favorite, because it was best for me, and it had chosen me. As time passed, that became more and more true."

Erving also told why he chose to retire when he did. "I knew what my standards were, and I didn't feel as though I could continue to play at that standard. Every team I had ever played on, I was either a captain or a cocaptain. I didn't want to become a reserve player or a bench player, and it was time to move on and take on another challenge. That process had already started during the later years of my career. So I was letting go of one thing to be committed to other things, and I thought that was the right move.

"I felt there was a curve that I had to adhere to. I had gone past my prime, and I was at a segment in the curve where there could be a real serious drop-off. I was no longer in control of playing time or my role on the team. I wasn't the one who would have the final say-so, and I had not experienced that before. If you've experienced having control, you don't want to be moved to a subordinate position, if you have your druthers. And I think I had my druthers, so I decided to do something else."

Erving once told *USA Today* that his all-time set of starting five players "was, is, and always will be Oscar Robertson, Jerry West, Elgin Baylor, Wilt Chamberlain, and Bill Russell, with Connie Hawkins coming off the bench as my sixth man to play guard, forward, and center." He fondly recalled the two most memorable games of his career: his first professional game and his first college game.

"The first professional game that I ever played remains, to me, the most exciting moment of my professional career. I had signed a contract with the American Basketball Association, and we had gone through an exhibition season. A lot of speculation had been created about me, and my teammates, and my team, and what our talents were, and that we were an exciting team to watch. We represented something new and exciting in the game of professional basketball because we played at a fast pace. We always pushed the ball, and there was a lot of room for creativity and excitement. Our game was a lot different from what was being played in the NBA. We featured a lot of slam dunking.

"The first professional game was clearly different from the exhibitions and what had happened in the summer. Even though I had been on the basketball court with a lot of professionals, this is when it really counted. This was the beginning of the career.

"I grabbed 19 rebounds in my first professional game, and somehow found a way to score 20 points. I felt real good about it. I felt that this was the beginning of something good. It was something that I had dreamed about as a kid, something that I didn't think was promised me, and I was never sure that it would happen. Yet it was happening, I was here, and it was reality, and now it was time to see what I was made of and what I was about. It became a real good experience. All the things that followed, in 16 years of playing: the playoffs, the excitement of championship play, the frustration of getting knocked out, the frustration of injuries and pain, and becoming close to teammates and then they get traded. The transition from playing with three different teams during 16 years, all those things. I don't think any of those things excited me as much as the first game. Because, once again, I kind of programmed myself: 'This is a business.'"

Of his first college game as a varsity player, Erving said, "I had a 27-point, 28-rebound game. I wasn't a big guy, but I was able to chase rebounds down, and that set a school record in the first game. I wanted to make a good impression. I knew that rebounding was the strongest part of my game and I said, every shot I take tonight I might miss, because sometimes that happens. I didn't think that was going to happen, but I knew that that was a possibility. And that was something that if it did happen, I would have to live with it. So I started trying to think of things that I definitely had control over. And I said, when that ball goes up on the board, nobody is going to pursue it harder than I. With my jumping ability and quickness, I know I can out-rebound everybody on the floor.

"I think [when I was] a youngster the work ethic was there, practicing hard and being dedicated and not, by nature, being a complainer. My teammates have always related to me in that way. I think probably the best compliment I've ever received from a teammate was what Henry Bibby told me after we had played together for two seasons in Philadelphia. He said, 'Of all the guys that I've ever played with, I don't know if you're the best that I've ever played with, but I know you come to play every night. And because of that, I feel like we always have a chance of winning.' I thought it was a great compliment."

On winning both the ABA and NBA Finals, Erving added, "I think the two Finals that I would recall as being the most significant to me were the second one in the ABA and the first one in the NBA. In the first two games against the [Denver]

Nuggets, I opened up with 48 and 45 points on back-to-back nights, but we split the games. And both of the teams (New Jersey and Denver) went into the NBA.

"Of course, ours was intact and proved to be worthy competition for a long time. Then in 1983, sweeping LA, sweeping with Andrew Toney and Mo Cheeks and Moses Malone on the team, was interesting because our team was very dominant, but because we had gone to the Finals three times previously and [had] not [won], there was nothing that could be taken for granted or left open to chance. And I really didn't, until there was no time on the clock. That was big because there's a very thin line between success and failure. So for me, I think the '83 championship, going 12–1, collectively reaching our goal, was the most memorable."

A Good Doctor to Thank

I was covering the New York City Basketball Hall of Fame induction ceremonies for the *New York Times* in September 2008. Among the inductees were two former NBA point guards, Rod Strickland and Kenny Anderson.

Strickland, the former Knicks point guard who led Truman High School in the Bronx to the Public School Athletic League and New York state titles in 1984 before heading to DePaul University and later embarking on a seventeen-year NBA career, was speaking into a crush of notepads and microphones and talking about all the people who helped his career along the way.

"I just think back to all those playground battles," Strickland, who is now an assistant coach to John Calipari at the University of Memphis, said that night.

Just after the pens and the tape recorders retreated, I quietly asked Strickland if there were any players who inspired him on his journey from the hardscrabble streets of the South Bronx to the most prestigious hardwood floors in America.

"There was one player who really turned me on, who really got my imagination going, as far as being a creative player," said Strickland, a soft smile growing on his boyish face. "Julius Erving. When I was growing up, Doc was the guy I wanted to be like. I dreamed of being able to do the things he used to do out there on the court."

Kenny Anderson was walking past when he heard Erving's name being bandied about. Anderson, the former Nets point guard from LeFrak City, Queens, held the New York state schoolboy record for points (2,621) when he left Archbishop Molloy High School for the Georgia Institute of Technology, before the record was broken by Sebastian Telfair of Lincoln High School in Brooklyn.

"I'll be honest with you," Anderson said to us. "I was more a guy who was always out playing the game than watching it on television, so I can't lie and tell you I knew all these players growing up. But the one guy I always made time to watch was Dr J. He was an incredible talent."

I reminded Strickland and Anderson that Julius Erving was not a "New York City kid" like they were; he did not grow up in one of the five boroughs. He was a Long Island kid, and Long Island kids cannot compete against City kids in basketball, right?

"Wrong, dead wrong," Strickland shot back. "Doc is one of the greatest basketball players, if not the greatest, to come out of New York. I don't care that he didn't come out of one of the five boroughs. He was a New Yorker, period. It doesn't matter if you're from Brooklyn, Queens, or Long Island. The only real estate that matters is the ninety-four feet from baseline to baseline, and Doc was phenomenal in that area.

"I grew up rooting for the Nets because I idolized Doc. I wanted to do the things on the court that I saw him do on television.

He made everything look so artistic and so easy out there, and
I always tried to be just as creative as he was on the court, but,
of course, that was impossible for most humans. When he went
to the Philadelphia 76ers, I became a 76ers fan. My loyalty
was to Dr. J—wherever he went, I went. When I got to the NBA,
Doc had already retired. I met him for the first time one day in
Orlando, when he was an executive with the [Orlando] Magic
[basketball team]. I felt like a little kid meeting him that day. He
was very kind to me and very humble, everything I thought
he was when I was growing up rooting for him. It was one of
my greatest thrills in basketball."

A Not-So-Memorable Comeback

In February 1992, Julius Erving and a handful of former NBA
stars made a rather unforgettable comeback. For Erving, it was
one of the few low points of an otherwise illustrious career. It
was announced that the great Dr. J, five years removed from the
game, would be pitted against Kareem Abdul-Jabbar, who was
in the second year of his retirement, in a one-to-one affair; it
would be part of a Friday night, boxinglike, pay-per-view event
at the Trump Taj Mahal in Atlantic City, New Jersey, for $19.95
admission. The undercard would feature Rick Barry against
Connie Hawkins and Nate "Tiny" Archibald against George
Gervin. All were over forty years old, except the thirty-nine-
year-old Gervin.

Richard Sandomir, the sports television critic of the *New
York Times*, harshly criticized the contests. "The first pay-per-
view event devoted entirely to retired, over-the-hill athletes (as
opposed to boxing cards featuring recently unretired, over-the-
hill pugilists) takes to an ersatz basketball court tonight when
Kareem Abdul-Jabbar goes one-on-one in a halfcourt game
against Julius Erving at an Atlantic City hotel owned by the
over-the-hill real-estate developer Donald Trump."

Abdul-Jabbar, readying himself to play four five-minute quarters against Erving, said before his showdown with Dr. J, "One-on-one is part of the game that hasn't been put before the public in the right way. Now we can relate that to the people with great players."

Sandomir noted that "even farther from active duty are the stars of the undercards. Rick Barry, retired for 12 years, faces Connie Hawkins, retired for 16 years. George Gervin, in year six of his retirement, plays Nate Archibald, in year eight of his retirement.

"Maybe these guys are in good shape for men between 39 years, 10 months (Gervin) and 47 years, 11 months (Barry). But $19.95 to watch them approximate their former selves in halfcourt?"

At a press conference before the event, Erving, who always seemed to say the right thing at precisely the right time through-out his legendary career, said oddly, "I'm not a basketball player anymore."

Said Abdul-Jabbar, "I'm trying to get the rust off the hook shot."

Said Barry, "I can't do the things I did in my prime. But if I shoot the way I did last week, I'll beat Connie."

Erving and Abdul-Jabbar, the article noted, were guaran-teed six-figure fees; the other four were receiving five-figure payments. All were to get shares of the pay-per-view gross.

"This is the kind of thing basketball fans dream about," Abdul-Jabbar said. "Let's hope it's not a nightmare to make us ache for *Wrestlemania*."

On February 28, Abdul-Jabbar defeated Erving, 41–23. Barry sank seven 3-pointers and beat Hawkins, 29–17, and Gervin defeated Archibald, 35–14. Gervin then defeated Barry, 29–26. The games, slow and plodding and minus the superskills the players displayed in their heydays, were widely lampooned in the media.

That night, the crowd at the Trump Taj Mahal gave a standing ovation to Magic Johnson, who had left the Los Angeles Lakers three months earlier after finding out that he had HIV, the virus that causes AIDS. Johnson sat courtside for the exhibition, which was dubbed "Clash of Legends."

Other than the ovation for Johnson, none of the rest was very pretty.

"Mark down Feb. 28, 1992," Sandomir wrote. "It was the day pay-per-view TV sank into the bog of virtual fraud, when viewers we were asked to pay $19.95 for the dubious privilege of watching Julius Erving, Kareem Abdul-Jabbar, and four other National Basketball Association retirees perpetrate a one-on-one 'show.'

"The promoters' dream to make this an annual event (coming soon: Bird vs. Magic!) should be tossed aside immediately. David Stern, the National Basketball Association commissioner, has no power over former players, but he should still pronounce such ignominy a taint on the game.

"Viewer response to this brand of counterfeit sport should take care of its future: Based on responses from sample cable systems, a mere .3 percent of the nation's 18.3 million pay-per-view homes bought the event, said Dantia Quirk, whose QV Publishing tracks the pay-per-view market. That translates to about 54,900 homes.

"This so-called 'Clash of the Legends' was nothing more than 'Cash for the Legends.' Only three of the players—Rick Barry, George Gervin, and [Kareem] Abdul-Jabbar—trod on Donald Trump's Taj Mahal Hotel half-court possessing skills that were reasonable facsimiles of their past abilities. But Erving had nothing. Tiny Archibald had nada. Connie Hawkins had even less.

"The one-on-ones proved at least that basketball is a team sport and that even the best head-to-head matchups are part of the fabric of the full-court game. If promoters insist on putting retirees on pay-per-view, maybe three-on-three would be more suitable," Sandomir concluded.

The Hall Calls

On May 10, 1993, Julius Erving, then forty-three years old, sailed into the Hall of Fame in Springfield, Massachusetts. The good Doctor—no, the great Doctor—went into the Hall along with Bill Walton, Walt Bellamy, Dan Issel, Dick McGuire, Ann Meyers, Calvin Murphy, and Ulyona Semyonova. After the induction ceremonies, the eight were further honored at a dinner at the Springfield Civic Center, which was attended by three thousand people.

Erving is also a member of the University of Massachusetts Hall of Fame, which he entered in 1980, as well as the World Sports Humanitarian Hall of Fame, which he entered in 1995.

In comparing the two leagues he starred in—what Dean Meminger called the "slow, white man's NBA" and the up-tempo ABA—Erving defended his style of play.

"The purists cringed at the alley-oop play, but the purists had to give in," he said. "This was not a hot-dog play, it was a good play."

In speaking of his fancy behind-the-back passes and his tomahawk dunks from every angle on the court, Erving said simply, "We're all different in the way we use our gifts."

Upon his enshrinement, Erving ranked in the top ten in the following ABA-NBA combined categories: third in scoring (30,026, or 24.2 points per game); eighth in games played (1,243); seventh in minutes played (45,227); third in field goals made (11,818); fifth in field goals attempted (23,370); third in most free throws made (6,256); and first in steals (2,272).

In eleven NBA seasons, Erving averaged 22 points and 6.7 rebounds per game. He still holds the career record for highest scoring average (28.7 points per game) in a minimum of 250 games, and he is one of only five players in pro basketball history to score more than 30,000 career points, joining Kareem Abdul-Jabbar (38,387), Karl Malone (36,928), Michael Jordan (32,292), and Wilt Chamberlain (31,419).

While Jordan was soaring and scoring en route to his 30,000-point milestone, Nets president Rod Thorn compared him to Erving. "Erving did things that hadn't been done, like Jordan does now," he said. "He was bigger and stronger than Jordan. He wasn't a great shooter, which is what makes Jordan the best ever. But of all the great players, Julius understood the team thing best. Michael will pass you the ball once or twice, and if you don't get it done, forget it. Julius was sensitive to every guy on the team. We had a lot of young, unstable guys on that Nets team, but as long as Julius was there, they stayed in line. He looked out for them. They respected him. When he left, they were lost."

Erving is one of the few players in modern basketball to have his number retired by two franchises: the Nets retired his number 32 jersey, and the Philadelphia 76ers retired his number 6 jersey.

"No offense," Charles Barkley said, 'but I think it's best that Doc finished his career in a major sports city like Philadelphia. A guy that great should not be playing in New Jersey with a team like the Nets; that wouldn't make too much sense. I thought that in the end, he was just a nice guy, and it was an honor to play on his team. I still see him at a lot of functions, and he's still the same old Doc, still the same nice guy he always was."

Asked once for the secret to his great success, Erving talked about resiliency and about dreaming, if not daring, to be great. "The more successful people in life—and I've found this to be true—have this resiliency about them, where no matter what comes down the pike, they're not going to quit," he said. "They're not going to be blown out of the water, and they're not going to exit from the game, unless it's their choice. And if it's their choice to exit from the game, they're exiting because they've got something else to do. It's like the old expression, it's better to not succeed than it is to not try.

"If you don't try, you're guilty of a crime that in business or in sports, or whatever, would be considered the cardinal sin. Always give your best effort, always try. You might come up a little bit short, but have this intestinal fortitude within you. Have this attitude programmed. Understand who you are, what you can bring to the table, and then bring that to the table. Where the pieces fall, they fall. I think that the resiliency to deal with good times as well as bad times, and to still remain focused and purposeful and true in your quest for worthy things in life, is part of the character that one has to have to be successful. There are a lot of technical things that you have to understand, a lot of fundamental things that you need to be a part of your makeup. But you're way ahead of the game if you have the knack for being resilient and resourceful."

Erving was once asked about another secret. How was he able to soar so high above the court on his way to the basket? "I never had any trouble jumping," he said. "The key to jumping is knowing how to land."

There is no question about the time in Erving's life that he most cherishes. "The ABA days were the best," he said, looking back at the five seasons in which his teams won two championships and he was named the Most Valuable Player three times, averaging 29 points and 12 rebounds a game. "For me it was a chance to expose all my gifts, night in and night out, in absolute freedom. It was a time to take chances."

In an interview with NBA officials, Erving once said, "A defining moment in my basketball career was the transition from the ABA to NBA. The five years I spent in the ABA—it's odd how it sometimes gets treated. There are some people who choose to act like it never existed, while others choose to make it seem like it was amateur basketball, and still others look at it for what it is. The challenge for competition, ABA versus NBA, was hot and heavy. Some guys were ABA and some guys were NBA, but they were guys coming out of colleges across the country after competing with each other and just making a decision about which way to go.

"It was very individualized and no special caveats for me, but I was being recruited by the Virginia Squires. I signed a contract with them and that's where I went to play. That's where I ceased being an amateur and commenced becoming a pro. That was a big decision. There were two decisions actually: one was leaving school early, and the other was starting my professional life. It fortunately allowed me to be there for sixteen straight years."

Erving did not recall the NBA through the same romantic eyes. "I was taken aback by the NBA, by the ego-tripping by some of the players, who were not all that good, anyway. I saw jealousies of older players toward rookies. I saw people criticizing the leaders."

Although many players had squandered their NBA fortunes through reckless lifestyles or bad business deals, Erving had parlayed the grace and genius he brought to the court and an unparalleled star quality into successful business ventures. He now sat on the boards of four public companies, including Converse and Coca-Cola. Years earlier, he had formed the Erving Group, a holding company based in Philadelphia.

In 1996, three years after Erving was enshrined into the Hall of Fame, he received professional basketball's highest honor, being chosen as one of the 50 Greatest Players in NBA History. (By 1980, he was one of four forwards named to the NBA's 35th Anniversary Team, along with Elgin Baylor, Bob Pettit, and John Havlicek).

"Julius was Michael Jordan before there was a Michael Jodan," Dave Anderson said. "Nobody knew it when he was in the ABA, because the league lacked the exposure, tradition, and prestige of the NBA. It was just less respected, plain and simple. It was the same for Joe Namath in the AFL—people really didn't appreciate him or the league he played in until the Jets beat the Colts in the Super Bowl. Julius had to go to the NBA and become an All-Star and then a champion before he got all the respect he always deserved."

The 50 Greatest Players, selected by a panel of journalists, former players, former coaches, and former team officials, were the following: Kareem Abdul-Jabbar, Nate Archibald, Paul Arizin, Charles Barkley, Rick Barry, Elgin Baylor, Dave Bing, Larry Bird, Wilt Chamberlain, Bob Cousy, Dave Cowens, Billy Cunningham, Dave DeBusschere, Clyde Drexler, Julius Erving, Patrick Ewing, Walt Frazier, George Gervin, Hal Greer, John Havlicek, Elvin Hayes, Magic Johnson, Sam Jones, Michael Jordan, Jerry Lucas, Karl Malone, Moses Malone, Pete Maravich, Kevin McHale, George Mikan, Earl Monroe, Hakeem Olajuwon, Shaquille O'Neal, Robert Parish, Bob Pettit, Scottie Pippen, Willis Reed, Oscar Robertson, David Robinson, Bill Russell, Dolph Schayes, Bill Sharman, John Stockton, Isiah Thomas, Nate Thurmond, Wes Unseld, Bill Walton, Jerry West, Lenny Wilkins, and James Worthy.

The following year, 1997, Erving was selected by *Sports Illustrated* as part of its fortieth anniversary celebration. The magazine named Erving one of its forty most important athletes.

Commenting on the Doctor

I joined the *New York Times* in July 1986 and began covering basketball games, college and pro, shortly thereafter. That was Julius Erving's last season in basketball, and I never had the thrill of getting to watch him from a courtside press table and interview him after a game. I often wondered what covering Erving from that perspective must have been like, so I reached out to three giants in the business who have been there: Bob Costas and Marv Albert, two men who watched Erving fly while working before national audiences from the best seats in the house, and Mike Fratello, a longtime NBA coach and onetime broadcast colleague of Erving's who would later be known to millions of television viewers, thanks to Albert, as "the Czar of the Telestrator."

"Back in the ABA days, there were teams in certain cities that always drew well—Denver and San Antonio were among those with consistently good attendance," said Costas, a play-by-play man for the Spirits of St. Louis from 1974 to 1976. He was twenty-two years old when he started.

"In my ABA city, St. Louis, the people would be motivated to come out when Dr. J came to town. They would come to see *him*, and not necessarily the team he was playing for. The ABA had no real television contract back then, and because players are so overexposed today, the casual fan can now name over one hundred guys in the NBA. Back in Julius's day, the average fan in a city like St. Louis might have heard of Dr. J and asked, 'Who is this guy?'

"I would categorize the ABA and some of its big stars—none bigger than Dr. J—as the last major sports enterprise in America that had an element of mystique and mythology attached to it. Since that time, everything in sports has been completely overexposed, with ESPN and all the sports shows on radio and television and all the highlights that keep coming into our living rooms. When people say to me that Michael Jordan is a legend, I say, 'What's so legendary about him?' Every single move he ever made was on record. There's no legend attached to his career; we watched every minute of it.

"Now, a guy like Satchel Paige, he was a legend because a lot of the spectacular things he did on a baseball field were handed down from generation to generation by word of mouth. Julius Erving, when he was in the ABA, was in that same boat. You heard about this guy, about these incredible moves that he pulled off in all these cities, but you couldn't verify it, so you had to go on someone's word, and when you finally did see Julius perform so spectacularly in person, you felt pretty good that you had received some solid information about the guy.

"As a broadcaster doing a game that Julius was part of, you knew that there was a very good chance that he was going to pull something off that you had never seen before," continued Costas, who broadcast on KMOX in St. Louis, the same station that carried Cardinals baseball games. "You couldn't always guarantee a highlight-reel type of play from Julius, but you knew the chances were very good that you were going to get one. I can remember all the times he pulled off a spectacular dunk or one of those pretty finger rolls, how the oohs and the aahs and the gasps would start in the audience—and not just the home audience, but on the road. Before Julius came along, there weren't that many players doing the kinds of things with a basketball that he was doing out there."

Marv Albert, a longtime voice of the NBA, caught enough of Erving's aerial act from behind a microphone to categorize Dr. J as "one of those great players who never took a night off."

"I can't think of too many stars I'd put in that category," Albert told me. "Michael Jordan, of course, never took a night off, and that's a rare quality that both guys possessed. A dunk in the NBA back in the early 1970s could be considered an insult, based on who was dunking and what was going on in a particular game."

In fact, some of the best players of the 1960s and the 1970s—Oscar Robertson, Jerry West, and Elgin Baylor—rarely slammed. Rather than dunk, Baylor enjoyed finishing visits above the rim with smooth finger rolls. Robertson, who is six feet five inches, has stated that he was never a fan of the slam.

"A dunk is just 2 points," Robertson said. "I wouldn't spend three cents to go see a Slam Dunk Contest. I watched them reluctantly because my family wanted to see some of them, but a dunk doesn't mean anything to me. It's just another basket."

Darryl Dawkins, who once dunked alongside Erving, disagreed. "Everybody says a dunk is only 2 points, but it gets your team hyped, gets the crowd all excited, and takes the starch out of other teams, especially when you dunk on somebody. And I always dunked on somebody."

Wayne Embry, the NBA's first African American general manager, once told the *New York Times* that dunking may actually hurt the development of players who would rather soar into the headlines than be grounded by fundamentals.

"I wouldn't say that dunking has hurt the game, but the way it's presented has hurt the game," said Embry, the general manager of the Milwaukee Bucks from 1971 to 1979, and later of the Cleveland Cavaliers and Toronto Raptors. "That's all everybody focuses on now. Because it's been made such a glamorous part of the game, I think players have not worked on their midrange game and their jump shot as much. I tell anybody to dunk the ball in competition if you can. But that's just one part of the game. Let's not glamorize it and make it the only way you can score."

The dunk was Erving's hallmark, however. It never got in the way of his overall production, and it never gave him a swollen ego. Like Swen Nater said of Erving, "Don't let all that flash fool you, because Doc was a very fundamentally sound player."

The dunk, in fact, is what Albert called "the very essence of what made Julius Erving a great performer."

"Just think back to the Slam Dunk Contest in Denver," Albert said. "Julius was putting on a show that day, the kind of show that very few others were capable of putting on. Julius enjoyed his celebrity; he embraced it by always being accessible to his teammates, the media, and the fans. I never saw him refuse an autograph. When people ask me where I'd rank Julius all-time, I have to put in context what he meant to the sport—not just his greatness, but how he helped shape the game of basketball for future generations of fans. When you add it all up, I'd say he is among the top ten players of all time.

"Our families would get together from time to time. We were very friendly," continued Albert, whose family lived in Sands Point, Long Island, not far from the Ervings of upper Brookville back when Dr. J was a Net. "I started working many of his games when he came into the NBA, and I really got an up-close and personal look at his entire repertoire. He was a player with so many weapons who could hurt you in a variety of ways. There are a few guys who have come along recently— Vince Carter comes to mind—who could do some of the things in the air that Julius could do, but as far as playing the game with excellence above the rim, I'd have to put Julius at the head of the class. Billy Cunningham and Michael Jordan in their primes could really get up there, but I don't think anyone put on a consistent show above the rim the way Julius did, and that's what made him so much fun to watch.

"[If you were] a commentator sitting courtside, Julius would always get your adrenaline going, because you just sat there knowing that any second, he was about to explode and give the crowd something to cheer wildly about. You knew something was going to happen, you just didn't know when and at whose expense. He had such an incredible connection with the fans, and [at] every game [I saw him play] in Philly, you could feel that connection buzz right through you, you could feel the love that all those people had for Julius. I am so fortunate to have been a broadcaster during Julius's playing days. It was both an honor and a treat," Albert concluded.

When Mike Fratello was starting out as a broadcaster at NBC, Erving was working as a guest commentator and an analyst for the network. "We got to know each other pretty well," Fratello said. "A lot of people don't know that when I got the head coaching jobs at Atlanta and Cleveland, the first guy I called on both occasions was Julius; I called him right away.

"I remember saying to him, 'Hey Doc, please take this the right way. Would you mind being my assistant coach?' I thought, who better to work with my younger players than a guy like Julius whose whole career has been about greatness. He is also a guy who really knows the game, and he is so articulate and genuine, he would have really been a perfect fit, especially when it came to getting our big men rolling. Unfortunately, he turned me down both times. You don't come across a down-to-earth superstar like Julius Erving very often.

"It's ironic, but Dominique Wilkins is also down to earth, and guess who his idol was? Julius Erving. Just like Doc, Dominique would always take the time out to talk to people and sign every autograph. What does that tell you about the kind of effect that a great basketball man like Julius Erving can have on younger players? That's exactly the kind of thing I was looking for when I was thinking about bringing him on board," Fratello noted.

"As far as his game was concerned, I don't think there's any question that Julius set the exciting tone of the NBA during his great career. When he retired, basketball fans everywhere wondered who was going to take his place as the next great superstar. Julius had set the table; he set that bar really high. As it always happens in sports, someone else always comes along, but it certainly does not diminish the great things that Julius accomplished during his career and the fact that he is easily one of the game's all-time greats. If you're asking me if Julius Erving played the game above the rim better than anyone who came before or after him, I'd have to think about that for a little while, and I must say that no one comes immediately to mind.

"I saw Connie Hawkins play at the tail end of his career, so it wouldn't be a fair comparison for me to make. I don't think anyone else, though, could match up with Doc's physique, his overall size and length, and those giant hands. He played the game with a certain kind of easy flair. Dominique Wilkins played with a dramatic, dominating kind of flair; he was an amazing power dunker. But Julius played with a kind of finesse flair; he made everything seem so easy. He was graceful and smooth and covered so much territory with his long strides. He was just a brilliant performer."

Fratello compared two of the greatest dunkers in history. "Julius was bigger than Michael; he had a different physique. Julius was six-seven, but he stretched out and it was like he was six-ten or six-eleven. When he jumped to the basket and went up to block shots, it was like watching a snake uncoil. Michael was explosive to the rim, but he was also a finesse player; he could kind of dish it out any way he wanted.

"As an announcer, you get pumped up when you know you're going to call a game that has a superstar like Julius Erving in it.

It makes it a lot more fun for the commentators, the crowd, and the television audience at home, because you're wondering things like who he's going to dunk on, how many points is he going to score, and will he win the game with some more last-second heroics. I don't really think it's fair to rank Julius in a certain spot all-time, because there have been so many great players from so many different eras. But I'll tell you what: if I were putting together an all-time team, I'm pretty sure I'd find a uniform for him."

So would Albert. "Julius was a guy who could have played in any era," he said. "In the ABA, he was the face of the league. When he came into the NBA, there was a great amount of respect for him from players and fans alike. Not only was Julius a significant factor in the merging of the two leagues, he also became a significant factor in helping the NBA get to where it is today in terms of popularity. He was a rock star in Philly who electrified one crowd after another.

"I have seen a lot of great players throughout the years, and even some of the great ones, when the national television spotlight was not on them, took a day off here and there by kind of mailing in their performances. But Julius never did that. In both the ABA and the NBA, he was a major star, a first-team all-league player. He was younger in the ABA, so obviously he was able to do more things from a physical standpoint, and the offenses used by the teams in the ABA was like the Phoenix Suns times two, so a player as skilled as Julius would often wind up with big numbers in a lot of high-scoring games.

"So really, just the nature of the game afforded him the chance to display every one of his basketball gifts. Julius did bring a lot of those great moves and dunks with him to the NBA, and he was still very much a showman. A lot of guys growing up, like Vince Carter and Dominique Wilkins, patterned their games after Julius's game, which wasn't such a bad idea."

Life after the Final Buzzer

After retiring, Erving became firmly entrenched in the real world, with his businesses and charitable causes as well as stints as a television analyst. He and the former National Football League running back Joe Washington fielded a NASCAR Busch Grand National Series team in the late 1990s, becoming the first ever NASCAR racing team at any level owned completely by minorities. The team had secure sponsorship from Dr Pepper (for whom Erving has been a pitchman) for most of its existence. Erving, a racing fan himself, stated that his foray into NASCAR was an attempt to raise interest in NASCAR among African Americans.

At one point he became a business partner of Bill Cosby and Bill Russell, two older and high-profile black celebrities whom Erving grew up reading about and wanting to emulate.

"For me, the transition from sports person to businessperson was a natural one," Erving told NBA Career Opportunities. "When I went to college, I enrolled in the business school at UMass, took a lot of courses before leaving school after my junior year, and then went back and finished and got my degree in a program called University Without Walls. I studied management and marketing and always had a feeling and a desire to be in the business world.

"As it turned out, my area of expertise or good fortune came more in the mergers and acquisitions area. Being able to get an equity play in the Coca-Cola bottling company—along with Bill Russell and Bill Cosby—Queens City Broadcasting, Garden State Cable, and companies in New York, Pennsylvania, and New Jersey allowed me to get a foothold in the Northeast, which is where I was born and raised and chose to spend many of the years of my life after my basketball career. The teams that I played for, the New York Nets when they were in Long Island

and the Philadelphia 76ers, also made that a natural avenue for me because of the platform that I got from my sports career."

Although Erving sold out of Coca-Cola, he said that his time with the company taught him a valuable business lesson in patience and perseverance. "We sold out of that company, and I would say that during our tenure there for over 20 years, there is a degree of luck involved, but it's not all luck. I think one of the things I could share is that once it was identified that my partners and I wanted to get into the beverage business, we actually pooled money and literally we waited seven years, from 1978 to 1985, before the opportunity came about. We were patient during that time, and we said when it comes, we want everyone to be ready to make it happen.

"It was a seven-year wait—from age 28 to age 35—before that happened. Fortunately for me, I was playing basketball during that time and was able to get in two years before retiring—I retired from basketball at age 37. [In terms of the] Defining moment businesswise, I think the Coca-Cola opportunity outweighs everything. Being a partner with Philadelphia Coke bottling and waiting for it to happen with Bill Russell and Bill Cosby was significant to me. I was the youngest of the three, and here we were, making moves and doing something very groundbreaking for African Americans."

Erving likened the heated rivalry between the Philadelphia 76ers and the Boston Celtics to Coke and its well-known rival, Pepsi. "Boston-Philly is kind of like Coke and Pepsi or Saks and Neiman. I don't deal with Pepsi products because I'm a Coke guy, and I don't go to Neiman Marcus because I'm a Saks guy. And I don't cheer for Boston because of Philly. That is the simple scenario.

"Going a little deeper than that, I think there is a physical, mental, emotional, and spiritual component to the makeup of a person. In sports, you are burdened sometimes by what you can do physically, because many times people don't look at you, your mind, your emotions, and your spirituality. They tend to judge you by what you are able to accomplish physically. But when you transition away from that physically centered arena, it is a totally different game. Your mind now is front and center. How you think, how you process information, and the decisions you make that affect you and the company and others is how you get judged. It is always healthy if all along, during the process while you are in the world of sport, you don't allow yourself to just be viewed physically and you continue to develop yourself in a parallel way mentally, emotionally, and spiritually as well as using your physical gifts. You're going to be better because you're going to be more of a complete package as a person.

"That has to occur simultaneously to your playing, so I think the guys who have made the better transition and who are having more successful business lives have been doing it part-time. They had offices set up. They had corporations set up. They had foundations set up, holding companies set up, and they were learning the game while they were still performing. Great examples are Dave Bing, Clyde Drexler, and Dominique Wilkins. So that transition is less than a major transition, less of a challenge, and something that flows naturally."

Erving has made it known that when his playing days ended, he did not just flick a switch to turn on his brain. In fact, he had been a thinking man's player, on and off the court, all along. "Many people think sports are totally physical, that you don't have to think, everything is done for you, and you're catered to. I found that to be so far removed from the truth that it's almost a joke. The ones who become stars are the ones who have a head on their shoulders and know how to use it. So much of becoming a good athlete involves bringing things to the table other than physical skills. It involves intelligence, it involves many of the things that you learn during the process of being educated, like how to analyze, how to assess, how to equate, how to reason."

Sorry, Fellas

On a January day in 1998, Erving attended a class reunion of sorts. Twenty-two years after he turned the basketball world upside down by being sold to Philadelphia, Erving floated into the Nets' inaugural alumni night to apologize to his teammates from the 1975–1976 New York Nets, the final ABA championship team, which was forced to soldier on without him into the brave new world that was the NBA.

"I'd like to offer my apologies, something I've never been able to do, for not being there with the team when they went into the NBA for the 1976–1977 season," Erving said to the former Nets sitting behind him: Al Skinner, Brian Taylor, Bill Melchionni, Jim Eakins, Tim Bassett, and George Bucci. (Bertha Williamson, John Williamson's widow, was also on the podium, and Erving's ex-teammate Kim Hughes came later.)

"Thanks a lot," chirped Kevin Loughery, the coach of those Nets, which went 22–60 when the Doctor was no longer in their house.

One-on-One with the Doc

I had been trying to arrange a one-on-one meeting with my boyhood basketball idol, the great Dr. J, for the better part of a decade. Finally, through colleagues at *The Source Sports Magazine*, to which I was a contributor, the whole thing came together in an Orlando, Florida, hotel room in 1999.

Suddenly, here I was, face-to-face with the man I was first introduced to by my brother in 1973 as I held that red, white, and blue basketball in front of the Christmas tree in our East

Harlem apartment. All these years later, I had arrived in the presence of the great Dr. J, who three years earlier had been named to the NBA's 50th Anniversary Team. If only the kids from the old neighborhood could see me now.

Despite the flecks of gray dancing in his hair, the Doctor still looked fit enough to get out on a fast break and assault a rim. Appearing to have the body fat of lettuce, his biceps bulging through a white business shirt, the forty-eight-year-old Erving had defied Father Time the way he once defied gravity.

"Just in case you're wondering," he assured me, "I can still dunk it."

Before long, we were schmoozing about the old days on Long Island, playing at Roosevelt High School, UMass, and Rucker Park, and later in the ABA and the NBA—"about some of the things I haven't talked about in years," as Erving put it.

At the time, I was writing a book called *Asphalt Gods: An Oral History of the Rucker Tournament.* Erving is pictured on the cover of that book dribbling up a sideline at Rucker Park in the early 1970s.

At our sit-down, Erving was kind enough to tell me about some of his experiences in the tiny Rucker Park and how they helped him soar to places he could never have dreamed of when he was just a small boy hoisting up all those line-drive shots at the Prospect School.

"It's a time in my life that is near and dear to me," he said. "It was a great journey for me of discovery, of learning more than I had previously known about the game. I didn't know how long I was going to play or how good I was going to be. I didn't know a lot of things, but being able to play in the summers up there was a great journey of confidence building and understanding more than I had known in the previous twenty-one years."

In the book *The NBA's Greatest*, Magic Johnson said, "Erving did more to popularize basketball than anybody else who's ever played the game. I remember going to the schoolyard as a kid, the day after one of his games would be on TV. Everybody there would be saying, 'Did you see the Doctor?' And we'd all start trying to do those moves. There were other big players, talented players, and great players before him. But it was Dr. J who put the 'Wow!' into the game."

Many other athletes, and scores of others from the entertainment industry and other walks of life, were wowed by Erving. Glenn "Doc" Rivers got his nickname when he was at Marquette University because of the Dr. J T-shirt he often wore to basketball practice. The Carolina Panthers defensive end Julius Peppers was named after Erving. The rapper Dr. Dre once performed using the alias "Dr. J." The jazz musician Grover Washington Jr., a Philadelphia 76ers fan, created the song "Let It Flow" in a tribute to Erving, and the actor Will Smith grew up a Julius Erving fan.

Named an All-Star in each of his sixteen pro seasons, Erving attributed many of his great dunks to those valuable minutes he spent fine-tuning them at Rucker Park, the laboratory he credits for much of his success at the big-league level.

"The league and the tournament and the challenges there had a lot to do with it; they let me have the freedom," said Erving, his eyes opening wide. "For me, it was an empowering experience. I loved coming back to the park summer after summer.

"In high school or college, I never went out and scored 40, 50, or 60 points," he said, "but in the parks, you start rockin' and rollin' during a forty-eight-minute game, and the next thing you know, when the smoke clears, somebody is bringing out the stat sheets and saying 'Oh, man, you got 60 today!'

"Sixty? I never got 60 before," Erving said. "But a lot of it had to do with the environment and the freedom and the fact that it was showtime and the shackles were being taken off. You're letting it all hang out, and you're playing the game at another level, and the guys you're playing against are bringing stuff out in you that maybe guys you played with before, in the organized set, didn't bring out in you.

"I probably could have scored 60 in college," Erving said, "but nobody brought it out in me."

The good Doctor recalled one particular game at UMass, against the national power Syracuse University, when he was feeling the freedom. "I had 37 [points] in college once, and the coach pulled me out and said, 'I want you to break the school record when you're a senior,' but I never had a senior year. He was playing God. But it wasn't like that in the parks. If you had 60 [points], people were yelling, 'Get 70! Get 80!'"

"All that competition, all that love those people gave us, it was a good, growing experience for a boy from the suburbs," said Erving, who at that point was the executive vice president of the Orlando Magic team. "Each summer, playing in the park was my urban experience, and culturally, I still feel very connected to that."

We finally got around to Joe Hammond and the disputed 50 points (see chapter 4).

"Not true," said the Doctor.

"Not true?" I shot back.

"Absolutely no truth to it," Doc snapped.

The Doctor told me that he remembered playing against Hammond but that there was no dramatic halftime entrance by the Destroyer, that Harlem's shooting god did not score 50 points, and that the two players did not guard each other for the entire game.

"In all of the six years I played at Rucker, I saw Joe once," Erving said, "and he and Charlie Scott had a little thing. When I first heard the story, I was trying to recall that game. I was thinking, 'Did that really happen?'" He smiled a smile that filled the room. "I called Peter Vecsey, and I asked him, 'Did that guy get 50 on me, or was that on Charlie?'"

Vecsey said he is not surprised by Doc's defensive stance. "I think that with the stuff being written about Joe, that he could get 40 on Julius, that people are putting Joe in the same breath [as Julius]," Vecsey said. "Julius was voted one of the NBA's 50 Greatest Players. His legend is solid. It's real.

"But," Vecsey added, "this was the summertime, and the fact of the matter is that Joe could get 40 [points] on him. Julius was never known to play great defense. But he doesn't like it when you say that Michael Jordan is better, so don't tell him that Joe Hammond is better. You have to understand where he's coming from."

There was, Erving said, one truth to the Westsiders' storied matchup with Milbank. "We beat them," he said. "I don't know exactly what Joe's stats were, I just know we took care of business, that was the main thing. We put on a show, and they put on a show. In fact, they were the masters of putting on a show."

The Doctor did admit, however, that Hammond was a pretty good operator himself back in Harlem's hallowed days. "I thought he was pretty good," Erving said. "He was slick with the ball, had a good shot, and was very cagey. He was the best player on that team, I'll concede that. He was a true playground legend. Thirty-nine in the parks? That's not such a big night, but 50 in a half?

"Look," Erving continued, "I'm sensitive to the fact that Joe and some other playground legends might need [to believe] something like that, and if it's a little bit at my expense, so what? I can roll with it. But if I get an audience, I need to say what really happened, I need to tell the true story."

The Doctor explained to me that in the winter of 1990, when he read my account in the *New York Times* about his legendary battle with the Destroyer, he was careful to not react too harshly.

"I didn't go out of my way to seek an audience," he said, "because sometimes, when you're trying to tell the true story versus something that's put out there, it sounds a little like sour grapes, and all you do is give the story more life."

Erving added that no matter how history writes about his meeting with the Destroyer or any other spine-tingling tale told before or after, it can never fully describe what playing on Holcombe Rucker's stage meant to a man who would become the greatest basketball attraction in the world. He only hopes that he was able to give as much as he took.

"I felt as though I was taking a lot in terms of the competition and all the confidence that was being built, but I was giving as well," he said. "I was a professional player, I didn't get paid for being there, so the exchange really had to be sweat equity, strain, and exhibition of talent in exchange to feed off of what I was receiving. I don't know whether I gave more or took more," Doc concluded, "but I felt as though it became a good deal."

A Man for All Seasons

"Julius brought a whole new level of excitement to basketball, especially to the ABA," said Dominique Wilkins. "He made it a true spectator sport. Before he got to the NBA, the league had never seen his kind of flash, his kind of up-tempo style. The NBA was kind of flat in terms of excitement, but Julius, and guys like George Gervin and other NBA stars, changed all that. Guys like me and Michael Jordan came along in later years to carry the torch, but Julius had already put the NBA on the map. He was the one guy people really tuned in to see. I'm not really much into comparisons, but in terms of creativity in the air, Julius and Michael were very similar, but they played different positions. Jordan is the greatest two-guard that ever played, and Julius is one of the greatest small forwards of all time."

Wilkins remembers Erving terrorizing one of the league's most dominant players: himself. "I remember the first game I played against Julius," he said. "I was in total awe. It was more like I was a fan out there playing against this legendary guy that my brother Gerald and I had idolized growing up in the playgrounds of Baltimore. Now, I was a player who always tried to dunk as hard as I could, especially on those seven-footers. I would take the ball and go right at their chests and attack the rim. But Julius turned the tables on me that first game; he dunked on me that very first time we met. Everyone on my team just sort of looked at me. I was like 'What are you guys looking at? He dunked on the entire front line.' Besides, that was Julius Erving who just dunked on us, the greatest dunker of all time, so if anyone is going to dunk on us, it's him, I'm all right with it. Doc and I had some great battles over the years, but that first one I'll never forget."

Wilkins said that he and Erving still keep in touch and that every now and then Dr. J still has the ability to wow him. "I was with him about two years ago [2006] and we went out on a court just to shoot around. I'm watching Julius, and all of a sudden he just palms the ball, looks up, and just skies toward the rim and throws down a nasty dunk. This is a guy in his mid-fifties, still able to dunk a ball like that. I just turned to people there that day and said, 'Did ya'll see that?' That tells you a lot about the incredible gift he possessed as a young man. All these years later, the gift was still there."

When the Hall of Fame called Dominique Wilkins, his old friend Julius Erving was there by his side. At one point, Erving described Wilkins to a reporter and sounded as if he were talking about himself.

"I'm happy to be here for Dominique," Erving said. "Dominique was a phenomenal basketball player. Even as a young player he was a take-charge player. He had the type of approach, attitude, and style that I really liked to watch. He had a dare-to-be-great style: Let's challenge the standards that were established before me, let me experiment a little out there, let me not be afraid. Let me move aggressively, whether players are bigger or stronger or had reputations. That didn't matter once you stepped over the black line; it was time to go out there and do work. Dominique was all about just getting out there and doing work night in and night out. He always came ready to play."

Wilkins added, "It was a dream come true to have Julius be the guy who brought me to the Hall of Fame. When the Hall called me, Julius was the first guy I thought about. After all those years, I was still nervous about calling him. I felt like a rookie all over again. I asked him if he would introduce me and he said, 'Dominique, it would be my honor.' That was typical Julius, always gracious, always classy, always accommodating.

"Julius is like a big brother to me, and what I admire most about Julius is that he always made the time for people—not just his friends, but the media and fans. He was, and is, as kind to perfect strangers as he is to his closest friends. He's just Julius Erving, and he carries himself as a regular guy, not some out-of-touch superstar. Julius gave me a great piece of advice my rookie season. He knew I idolized him and wanted to pattern my game after his, but he took me aside one day and said, 'Look, young fella, there's only one Julius Erving and there's only one Dominique Wilkins. You do what you can do best out there on the court. Don't try to emulate what I do. Work on your game one step at a time, and trust me, you'll achieve your own level of great success.'"

On April 5, 2004, Clyde Drexler, another NBA superstar who grew up idolizing Julius Erving, asked Dr. J if he (Dr. J) would present him (Drexler) for induction into the Basketball Hall of Fame. Drexler, a six-foot seven-inch guard who was also chosen as one of the NBA's 50 Greatest Players, was nicknamed

"Clyde the Glide" for his swooping moves to the basket. In college, he played in two Final Fours for the University of Houston. In his fifteen-year NBA career, Drexler led the Portland Trail Blazers to the finals in 1990 and 1992, and he won a championship with the Houston Rockets in 1995. He is one of three players in league history with 20,000 points, 6,000 rebounds, and 6,000 assists, and he also won an Olympic gold medal with the Dream Team in 1992.

"I'm dreaming tonight," Drexler declared, after Erving had said yes. "My childhood idol is presenting *me* for induction into the Hall of Fame. It doesn't get any better than this. I am dreaming. I don't want to be awakened. He seemed to fly. I wanted to be like him," Drexler said of Erving.

What set Drexler apart, Erving said, was his ability and imagination to take the game above the rim "and make things happen."

Darryl Dawkins said the following about Erving, his old teammate: "I would certainly say that Doc is one of the all-time greats, but it's hard to rank any of the great players, because different players meant different things to their teams in different eras. People forget how great Elgin Baylor, Connie Hawkins, and Wilt Chamberlain were in their eras, and they forget how great Doc was in his era. But I'll tell you this: anyone who ever saw Doc play can never forget what kind of gift God gave to him and just how dominant a force he was out there on the court. I saw him play. I lived through the Dr. J era, so I know how great he really was.

"Doc is considered one of the greatest small forwards," Dawkins continued, "but don't forget all those times his teams needed him to play power forward or a big guard; these are the skills that Doc possessed. He could play all those positions and be equally effective at all of them. If you look at Michael Jordan, you know that he probably patterned a lot of his game

after Doc's game. Mike could run and he could fly, and sometimes he even reminded me of Doc with some of those leaps to
the basket. But the big difference was that Mike had a better
outside shot than Doc ever did.

"When I was playing, I always ran into guys who never gave
guys like Dr. J any credit for their moves. Guys would throw down
a fancy dunk and say they had been working on it for quite some
time. And I'd say, 'Yeah, since you were a little kid in your backyard and you were practicing all those Dr. J dunks you saw on television—that's where you got that dunk,'" Dawkins concluded.

12

The Ghost of Samantha Stevenson

Several months after my long-awaited one-on-one meeting with Julius Erving, I was flipping through the pages of the *New York Times* sports section when a startling headline brought my fingers to a screeching halt: "Tennis Cinderella's Father Has a Name: Julius Erving."

On July 3, 1999, a story written by James C. McKinley revealed that Alexandra Stevenson, an eighteen-year-old rising tennis star at Wimbledon, was Erving's daughter. The mother of the child, who was single and white, also had a name: Samantha Stevenson.

This was the same Samantha Stevenson who had cozied up to Erving and his wife, Turquoise, years earlier; the journalist who, according to Mark Heisler, had ghostwritten the letter from Turquoise in *the New York Times*. It seems that the woman who helped Turquoise publicly vent her frustrations about Erving not getting enough love in Philadelphia was also helping Erving to get a little of the love he was so desperately lacking.

"Julius was always very discreet about everything he did," Heisler said. "I wasn't shocked when I found out about Samantha and Julius. Samantha was a very pretty woman and very smart, so what was not to like? I never saw her pregnant, though. I had no idea anything had happened between the two of them until everything came out about Alexandra during the U.S. Open. I was only on the beat for two years. I left in 1979 and moved to Los Angeles. I think she went to San Diego, but I'm not sure."

When it came to his personal life, Erving was just as private with reporters like Heisler as he was with his teammates.

"As far as Samantha goes, that was something that Doc never delved into with me," said Darryl Dawkins. "So when the word got out, I wasn't going to intrude on his personal life. Doc is all grown up now, and he's big enough to deal with any situation, and he has dealt with all of it just fine."

After years of stony silence concerning his "love child," Erving finally admitted he was Alexandra's father—doing so, he said, only to help relieve the stress on his daughter as she prepared for a pressure-packed semifinals match, which she would eventually lose to Lindsay Davenport.

"Julius Erving, the Hall of Fame basketball player who had been one of his sport's greatest performers and sturdiest models of personal rectitude, issued a statement acknowledging that he is Stevenson's father and that he had, in secret, provided for her well-being from the day of her birth," James McKinley wrote. "Erving, who was married when Stevenson was born, said that he had kept his wife informed and that their four children were also aware that he had another child."

"I understand they are being besieged because she won her match today," Erving, told the Associated Press. "Getting this statement out will help."

The article noted that Alexandra Stevenson had known her father's true identity but had met him only once. She said she did not feel cheated because she had grown up without her father present. She pointed out that many of her friends had parents who had divorced.

"It has always been normal to me," said Alexandra, who graduated from a high school in California just two months before exploding onto the Wimbledon scene, where she had been a virtual unknown before winning three matches at a qualifying tournament. She then won five straight matches in the main draw against mostly higher-ranked players to become the first qualifier in history to reach the women's semifinals.

When the news broke, courtesy of the *Fort Lauderdale Sun-Sentinel*, which published a copy of Alexandra's birth certificate identifying her father as "Julius Winfield Erving 2nd," Alexandra declined to talk about her father, saying that her mother had served as her only role model.

"I had both parents wrapped into one," she said.

Samantha Stevenson was still a freelance sports journalist, and her work had continued to appear in the *New York Times*. McKinley wrote that she "has written extensively about her experiences as a single mother raising a gifted tennis player, and over the years she has not discouraged speculation that her child's father was a prominent athlete. She has been working on a book project about her daughter's life as a promising tennis player. But yesterday, she said very little about her daughter's father. 'I can't comment at all,' she said. 'The mother maintains her silence.'"

In his statement to the press, Erving acknowledged that he had had a relationship with Samantha Stevenson in 1980, four years after he joined the Philadelphia 76ers. "All matters concerning Alexandra since her birth have been handled privately through counsel," he said.

Erving, who said of Samantha that he applauds her "efforts and courage," told the Associated Press that he had met Alexandra only once, when she was three years old, and had supported her financially since her birth. "She was brought to me at a basketball clinic at a public school," he said.

McKinley's article laid out Alexandra's meteoric rise. Samantha Stevenson recognized early that her daughter had inherited her father's athletic prowess, so she enrolled her in tennis lessons at the age of four at the La Jolla Beach and Tennis Club. By the time Alexandra was nine, she was taken on as a student by Dr. Peter Fischer, the Los Angeles pediatrician and tennis teacher who tutored a young Pete Sampras (who went on to become a tennis champion). Three times a week, Samantha Stevenson drove her daughter three hours to Los Angeles for tennis lessons.

Under Fischer's tutelage, Stevenson developed a classic style, using a wicked one-handed backhand, a giant serve, and lightning volleys in an era favoring two-handed backhands and dogged baseline play. She was, much like her famous father, a throwback to another time. In 1996, at age fifteen, she was ranked the number five junior girls tennis player in the United States.

As she grew up, Alexandra's skills were honed by other prominent coaches in California, including Pancho Segura and Robert Lansdorp. Fischer dropped out of her life in 1997, the article noted, when he was arrested on charges of molesting children at his medical practice.

Lansdorp, who helped Stevenson stabilize her ground strokes, said that rumors that her father was a professional

athlete began circulating years ago in West Coast tennis clubs. Erving's name was sometimes mentioned, he said, but neither mother nor daughter would talk about it. Lansdorp said the absence of her father never seemed to bother Alexandra. "She seems a real well-adjusted kind of girl," he said.

Alexandra described herself as "the epitome of the American dream" because she was brought up by a "single parent, multicultural."

The article ended with these words: "Erving's admission that he had fathered a child out of wedlock is not in keeping with his public image. Many prominent players in the National Basketball Association have been hit with paternity suits from single mothers in recent years, and several have acknowledged supporting children born to women they had not married. But Erving, universally known as Dr. J, has been held apart by fans, not just for his breathtaking play, but as a model family man with deep religious beliefs. He and his wife, Turquoise, have been married since 1972."

And Then Came Barbara

Later that year, during an interview with Barbara Walters on ABC-TV's *20/20*, Alexandra Stevenson, speaking out for the first time about her famous father, expressed no feeling for him whatsoever.

"I don't like people saying 'the Doctor's daughter,'" Stevenson, then eighteen, told Walters, "because I'm really not the Doctor's daughter. I'm my mother's daughter. When you think about a father—a definition of a father is someone who takes care of you and is paternal. And he wasn't really that. So I just don't think of him as my father."

In that interview, Alexandra recalled the first time her mother told her that she was Julius Erving's daughter. "When I was four, she told me," Alexandra said. "I remember her showing me a basketball picture in a newspaper, and she said, 'This is your father.' And I said, 'Okay.'"

Although Erving had said they met when Alexandra was three years old, she remembered it differently. "Actually, I was eight," she said. "So he's five years off. I don't know where he got this three from. At my other school, there were flyers going out about Julius Erving's basketball camp. I brought it home and told my mom that I wanted to go see him. It was my decision. My mom made sure I had a big name tag on. I stood in line for an autographed ball, and I didn't really want to. When I got there, I just stood in line to see what he looked like. When I got up there, he asked me if I wanted a ball, and I said no and I walked away. I think he knew who I was. I was a little upset afterward because he didn't say anything, but that's about it. Then I just forgot about it."

Alexandra told Walters that she thought it was "kind of stupid" for Erving to initially deny that he was her father. "It did appear to make him look stupid after he said, 'Yes, I am her father.' I mean, first he said no, then he said yes. People probably thought, 'Wow, that's not very nice.' Finally he admitted it. Then I just knew that I'd get asked questions and that I'd just say, 'Let's talk about my tennis.' I mean, that has nothing to do with Wimbledon."

Walters asked Samantha Stevenson if she was in love with Erving.

"It was a long time ago, Barbara, and you know in our lives how we move on. It was a long time ago," Samantha said. "I think any time that you get involved with anyone in a relationship, if you're a woman who has passion and a heart, and you understand love, and you have innocence and you're a little naive, I think that you would believe in the Cinderella story."

Walters also asked Samantha why she named her child Alexandra Winfield Stevenson, giving Alexandra the same middle name as her father.

"I wanted to give Alexandra a sense of belonging," she explained. "Actually, it was something done with a lot of thought and care, and I never thought anyone would go in and get the birth certificate. I thought it was private information. I didn't really look into the fact that you could go in and buy a birth certificate. You can't take away the blood [by which] she was tied to him. I wanted her to have that choice, and I thought, again, that was part of the dignity of the situation."

13

Cory Disappears

Ten months after the Alexandra Stevenson saga, trouble found Julius Erving again.

On May 28, 2000, Erving's youngest son, nineteen-year-old Cory, who was fighting a drug problem, went out to buy bread for a cookout and never returned to the family's Orlando home. That morning, Julius and Turquoise had gone to church services and had asked Cory to pick up bread for a cookout they were going to in the afternoon at a neighbor's house. Between one and one-thirty that afternoon, Cory called his parents to say that he had picked up the bread and would be back in about twenty minutes. That was the last anyone ever heard from him.

Cory had begun using drugs and alcohol when he was fifteen, and he was just three months out of a substance abuse program. (It was later learned that he had completed five rehabilitation programs.) The family hoped that this time he was in full recovery mode.

Cory was not the first of Erving's children to get mixed up with drugs. In July 1996, Erving's oldest son, Cheo, then 22, was charged with possessing drugs after police said they saw him buy five dollars worth of crack cocaine in north Philadelphia. An undercover narcotics officer staking out a known drug peddler saw Cheo drive up and make a deal. He was sentenced to one year of probation. (In August 1998, both Cheo and Cory were arrested in Florida, charged with possessing a crack pipe and burglarizing a car.)

"Cheo, who was Turquoise's son from another relationship, was a real problem for Julius," an old teammate of Erving's told me. "Julius and Turquoise were always fighting because Cheo was always in trouble, and he was a bad influence on Julius's other children. It put a real strain on their marriage." Cory Erving had disappeared before on drug binges. Erving initially thought that Cory had suffered another relapse, so he notified the security staff in his development as well as the Orlando sheriff's office, hoping they could help him to bring Cory home.

By the following week, Cory was still missing, and there was no sign of the black Volkswagen Passat with the Florida tag A76LFE that he was driving that day. Cory's case was now being considered more than just a search for a missing person. Foul play, it was feared, may have been responsible for his disappearance.

On the evening of June 23, 2000, Erving, growing increasingly desperate, went on *Larry King Live* to ask America to help him find Cory. "It's tough," Erving told King. "Some days are worse than others. As you mentioned, it's a parent's worst nightmare. This is day twenty-six for us. Since that Sunday afternoon, nobody in the family has heard from or seen Cory. You know, it's just a totally unacceptable situation, so we're full-time trying to find him and bring him home.

"I just think he was in a relapse situation, but you know, we were somewhat blindsided by it. A lot of the signs we saw, demanding of him by me—that he get back in school, which he did; that he hold down a job; and that he maintain proper conduct around family, friends, and the neighborhood—we kind of felt that he was doing a pretty good job, in terms of at least putting on a facade, because there were other things going on."

King asked why the Erving family had waited two weeks before going public. "We thought that listening to the security in our area, looking ourselves as a family for him—as we had done a couple times before in the previous five-year span—notifying the sheriff's department, and hiring private investigators were the way to go," Erving said.

"Then after a certain amount of time, maybe out of frustration and just desperation, we decided to enlist the support of friends and associates outside that circle and also the general public, because we didn't want to eliminate any options. We didn't know whether he was in the area or not, even in the country or not. So at that time, because it was a chip that we had and a card that we had, that we were able to play, we decided to do it."

Erving, who offered a fifty-thousand-dollar reward for any information that led to finding Cory, said that his son had attention deficit disorder.

"This was recognized maybe in second or third grade, early," Erving said, "and he was in a special school, as opposed to a mainstream school, until after eighth grade. Many of the more definitive problems began to occur after he went to a mainstream high school in ninth grade."

King asked if anyone had a best guess of where Cory might be.

"I don't think so, Larry," Erving replied. "I think we've kind of hesitated to do that, because it just sort of weakens our position in terms of objectivity, and you know, all the leads are real leads, and unless you know something certain, you can't eliminate anything. I think that the posture for us is that this is an all-or-nothing situation. I mean, if we don't have him, then we have nothing. So I don't think there's a best guess. I think there are maybe two or three scenarios that are more likely and stronger possibilities, but to venture to say there's one best guess, I don't have that, and I don't think any law enforcement agencies who are involved in this with us have it, either."

King introduced Erving shortly after a commercial break as "one of three pro basketball players ever to score 30,000 points, 16 years a pro, 11 in the NBA, five in the ABA; MVP in the NBA once, twice in the ABA; and enshrined in the Basketball Hall of Fame in 1993." He then quoted authorities as saying that they believed Cory was in danger and that he may have been abusing crack cocaine.

"In danger of what?" King asked Erving. "Self-harm?"

"Well, I think in danger," Erving said flatly. "You don't put limitations on 'danger.' If you're missing, you have limited resources. He doesn't have a credit card. You know, we don't know who he's with. Certainly, he has an appetite for drugs. He has a zest for life, but you know, he's somewhat self-destructive, [and that's] a real contradiction; he's young, and there are mean streets out there.

"I got a card—I kind of keep it close to me—[from] a former NBA player who just divulged to me that he had lost his twenty-seven-year-old son to the streets, and if he were in that situation, he would go get him; looking back on it, that's what he wished that he had done. So I'm taking that posture, that I have to do everything in my power to go and get him. I do feel that he's endangered. I feel that each day he's away from his family and people who love him and who he's always communicated with, he's endangered."

There had been reports, King noted, that Cory was involved in some sort of physical confrontation in a neighborhood north of Orlando known for drug dealing. The reports were that in the course of that confrontation, someone had smashed a brick through his car window.

"Yes, those are facts," Erving said. "And that was about a month prior to his disappearance. I think those leads have pretty much turned up nil in terms of being of total significance here, but they're not ruled out. You know, that door is still open, that lead is still open, those people are still suspects in terms of being involved in some way in a misdeed or just in terms of having knowledge that they're not divulging about his activity there in the weeks prior to his disappearance.

Erving continued, "Cory is a human being. You know, 'recovering drug and alcohol abuser' is a term that's used, but Cory is my son. He's a person who's fun to be around, who has a lot of potential as a person; he's very athletic, he's charming, he's clever, he's kind of kooky at times, and you know, that side of it is what the family thinks about and knows and wants the public to know. So when we make our public plea, we're not making a public plea to bring back a person who is in a downward spiral, who's down and out. We want the public to help us to bring back a person we love very much, who can make a contribution to society and who is trying to do some things to turn his life around, and I think that's the most important thing for us."

After taking a couple of phone calls, King asked Erving if being a "superstar celebrity father" ever led to moments in which "you wonder 'What did I do wrong?'"

"All the time," Erving responded. "All the time—you know, just in terms of having to have a life on the road, having the celebrity aspect be a burden for my family, friends, and extended family. We always tried to rationalize by saying you take the good, you take the upside, then you've got to deal with

the downside. But if you live an affluent lifestyle, there are all
types of traps there that you have to be cognizant of, and you've
got to try and communicate freely and gain understanding and
then keep moving on, because sometimes lifestyles are chosen
for us as opposed to us choosing them."

King then got around to asking about Alexandra Stevenson.
"You had a child out of wedlock. That was tough to live with,
[to] come forward [about]," King said. "By the way, did any of
that have an effect on Cory?"

"Well, it's hard to say," Erving answered. "You know, the
counseling. He was in two programs since that revelation last
June, and I'm sure it came up with different counselors, but he
seemed to be pretty cool with it. But you know, I can't say for
sure exactly what's going on inside his head."

Asked specifically about Alexandra, Erving said that he had
not heard from her, and when King suggested that she was
probably concerned, Erving replied, "I would think so, yes."

King took a few more callers, one of whom said to Erving,
"I wanted to ask if the local church community has been sup-
portive also, in [terms of] accessory prayer?"

"Very much so," Erving said. "As a matter of fact, just last
night, my mom gave me a call. She had gotten a call from my
deceased dad's sister, who is a minister in Chicago. They had
created a prayer circle, and they said that they just felt Cory was
still alive. They've had this prayer circle going since the date
that he was acknowledged as missing.

"And in Orlando I've gotten letters. You know, the church
that I attend, they've been great, they've been tremendously sup-
portive, they pray on Wednesday nights and of course Sundays,
and it's there—the prayer is there, and the faith is there."

When their conversation came to an end, Erving thanked
King for the time, then turned to the camera and said: "Cory,
if you're out there, we love you unconditionally. We miss you.

I know you spent half your time trying to con me. But I want you back, and we need you back, and we love you, son."

More Bad News

On July 7, 2000, an Associated Press report hit the newswires with this story: "The 19-year-old son of Julius Erving, the National Basketball Association Hall of Famer, was found dead in his car Thursday in a pond, the Seminole County Sheriff's Office said this morning. Cory Erving had been missing since May 28.

"Seminole County Sheriff Don Eslinger said the clothing and other details of the body fit that of Erving. There will be an autopsy today to establish the identity.

"Cory disappeared on what was supposed to be a 20-minute shopping trip to buy bread for a family picnic on Memorial Day weekend.

"Cory had been working at a sandwich shop and taking courses geared toward getting a high school equivalency diploma.

"Julius Erving, at news conferences pleading for help, said Cory was born with a learning disability that he described as a mild form of dyslexia and attention deficit disorder. He said his son also had past drug and alcohol problems.

"Julius Erving's stellar 16-year professional basketball career ended in 1987. He is the executive vice president of the Orlando Magic."

The following day, a story in the *New York Times*, written by Charlie Nobles from Sanford, Florida, reported that Cory Erving did not commit suicide, but Sheriff Eslinger declined to dismiss the possibility of foul play.

Seminole County investigators found Cory Erving's car in a pond about a half mile from his family's residence in the affluent Alaqua Lakes neighborhood. They had dragged thirty-six bodies of water in three counties before finding the car about twenty yards from shore. The story said that the windows were up, the air bags had not been deployed, and that Cory was not wearing a seat belt.

The news of Corey's death sent shockwaves through Erving's basketball circles. "I was stunned," World B. Free said. "I started thinking back to the old days in Philly, when Doc's kids used to be the ball boys for the team. They were great kids, man, and to know that one of them is gone, that's tough to deal with."

Bob Behler, a former radio play-by-play man at UMass who teamed in the broadcast booth with Jack Leaman, said that Erving's former coach was "extremely upset."

"When Julius's son went missing, Jack was very concerned," Behler said. "He called Julius as soon as it happened, but all he could really do was offer some words of encouragement. At that point in his life, Jack had become a grandfatherly type. When he heard what was going on, he was extremely upset for Julius and his family."

When Mark Heisler heard the news, he too thought back to the old days in Philly. "I used to see Julius with his kids by his locker," he said. "He seemed like such a great father and that he had such a great relationship with his kids. They were just toddlers at the time, and Julius was so sweet with them. I think that if there were problems with his kids later on, it was because of the lifestyle that Julius lived, especially being on the road a lot. That certainly had a lot to do with it."

Darryl Dawkins was tempted to pick up the telephone and call his old teammate, but then he thought better of it. "When Doc's son died, I can't tell you how sad I was, but I didn't call him to say, 'I'm sorry to hear what happened to you,'" Dawkins said. "In a situation like that, I think it's just best to leave the guy alone. You can't call and say I know what you're going through, because you really don't, unless of course you lost a son or a daughter. He's been hearing that kind of stuff for a few years now, and though I'm sure he appreciates it, he'd probably be better off just knowing that good friends like myself are there for him should he ever need us.

"Doc also knew that there was a great outpouring of love and sympathy from the American public, [which was] mourning along with him, and do you know why? It was because Julius had been such a great guy, such a great ambassador to the sport of basketball all those years, and people never forgot that.

"The one thing I learned from Doc is to take the time to talk to people. I'd see him walking through airports, and people would approach him, but he would never brush past them or just blow them off. He always stopped, even if it was just for a minute, to chat or sign something, and I honestly believe that all that good will came back and paid off, because Doc is one of the most beloved athletes of all time. It's a result of not just how he played the game but how he carried himself off the court all these years, always making time for people, whether they were close friends or perfect strangers.

"I consider Doc a brother until this day," Dawkins concluded, "and if he needs me for anything, all he has to do is shout, and I think I speak for a ton of guys who crossed Doc's path throughout the years."

14

Up Close and
Very Personal

Julius Erving was certainly not the player of myth that he
was after leaving the ABA for the NBA, but he was still an
All-Star player by any stretch of anyone's imagination—except
for *Sports Illustrated*'s, which labeled the NBA version of Erving
as overrated in an August 2001 feature. I had heard and read
slight criticism of Erving's early struggles with the Philadelphia
76ers, but this was a blatant accusation of malpractice.

"As often happens with great artists," Taylor wrote, "Julius
Erving had already done his best work by the time he was dis-
covered by the mainstream public. After five ABA seasons spent
mostly in midair, he came to the Philadelphia 76ers of the NBA
and toned down his game. It wasn't long before even his mag-
nificent Afro was trimmed down to something more conserva-
tive and, dare we say, commercial.

"Erving went from serving up a steady diet of acrobatics in the upstart league to doling out the occasional treat in the established one, but his new fans—and most of the media— gushed. They had heard about how spectacular Dr. J was, so they ignored the fact that as his NBA career progressed, he spent increasing amounts of time shooting jump shots, and not particularly well. Erving produced his share of highlights, but no more than, say, Dominique Wilkins. The fans who came late to Dr. J's game didn't know what they'd missed."

The article did go on to praise Erving as an underrated ABA performer.

"In the early 1970s, genius was on display in the mostly second-rate gyms of the ABA, but precious few people knew about it, and even fewer witnessed it. When the young Julius Erving was traded from the Virginia Squires to the New York Nets in 1973, he remained underappreciated and underexposed, a Long Island curiosity toiling in the shadow of the big-city Knicks. Dr. J played to the crowd, waving the ball as if it were a grapefruit while swooping to the basket like some goateed hawk, but he also won, leading the Nets to two championships.

"The Doctor didn't only make electrifying shots; he also made clutch shots. It's been suggested that the ABA-era Erving was merely part of the evolution of the airborne star, a link in the chain that includes Elgin Baylor, Connie Hawkins, Michael Jordan, and now Vince Carter. That, however, doesn't give the young Doc his due. He married form and function in a way that no player before him had. Every highflier who followed him is in his debt."

It was hard for me, and many others in Erving's orbit, to believe that anyone on the planet could categorize him as overrated at any time in his career.

"The height of Erving's career was, of course, in the ABA," Marv Albert said. "But he was still an All-Star player in the NBA who led his teams to numerous appearances in the NBA

Finals before winning one against the Lakers. He was every bit an NBA All-Star who was far from the finish line. The ABA was such a wide-open freewheeling game where defense wasn't exactly a priority, so it just suited Julius perfectly. The NBA was not as freewheeling, but I thought that Julius did a remarkable job at adapting to the new league.

"Vince Carter loves talking about how he studied Julius's moves as a kid, and how Julius weaved dunking into the strategy of the game. Now, that was the Julius Erving in the NBA, so what does that tell you? There will be future generations of kids who come along and say they studied the way Vince Carter once dunked a basketball, so it's a never-ending cycle, but Julius Erving will always be considered an integral part of that cycle. It was something he started in the ABA and finished in the NBA."

Darryl Dawkins also praised the NBA résumé of his old teammate. "When Julius got to Philly, he still had a ton of game left, and believe it or not, I think that when he got to the NBA he became an even better player. He became more fundamentally sound. The biggest knock on him was that he didn't have a jump shot. But even at that point in his career, as great as he was, he stayed for hours after practice, and sometimes after games, and just kept practicing his shooting.

"Doc's style of play intimidated everybody," Dawkins added. "When you're standing chest to chest with the guy one second, and the next second he's soaring at an altitude of fourteen thousand feet, I'd say that's a bit intimidating. I was a power dunker. I dunked in guys' faces and over their heads. But Doc, he dunked in your face and over your head, and he dunked on you after going under you and around you. There was no path he couldn't take to the rim for one of those beautiful jams. I still think that Doc was the first guy to have air brakes. I remember him flying through the air at different speeds, as if he could stop and go during midflight anytime he wanted. There is no one in the history of the game who glided to the basket with the grace and force of Dr. J."

Dawkins, World B. Free, and many others who teamed with Erving throughout the years still love telling tall tales about Erving, some of which seem better suited for the Sci-Fi channel.

"I remember one game against the Knicks where Doc took off toward the rim, straight at their two big men, Bill Cartwright and Marvin Webster, who was nicknamed 'the Human Eraser' for his ability to block shots," Dawkins said. "Doc held the ball out high over his head with his right hand and went sailing hard and right through them, like a missile. Doc was going so fast and was so high up in the air that he needed to use his free hand to stop from crashing into the backboard.

"Once his free hand hit the backboard and stopped his momentum, he just threw down this incredible dunk," Dawkins continued. "It was like a scene from a monster movie, where Doc just threw the ball down over this giant two-headed monster. It all happened in the blink of an eye, and if I hadn't been there to see it with my own two eyes, I probably wouldn't have believed it. Cartwright and Webster just looked at each other like 'You had him, right?' 'No, I thought you had him.' But nobody had him. Nobody ever had him because he was Dr. J."

Then there is this Dr. J. memory from World B. Free, Erving's former teammate and chauffeur. "Doc had a million different kinds of dunks, I swear. But there was this one night during his second season with us, a regular-season game in Washington against the Bullets that will stay with me forever. It was the game in which Doc threw down the greatest dunk of his life, and in my opinion, the greatest dunk anywhere, at any time. There was about a minute left in the game, and Elvin Hayes, who was known as a big-time shot blocker, was playing defense right beneath the basket along with Wes Unseld. Bobby Dandridge was also near the basket. Doc had the ball in his hands about a step inside the free throw lane.

"Now, over the years, me and everyone else were used to seeing Doc gliding on air or taking off with a force and throwing down one of those incredible dunks. But I had never in my life seen Doc dunk so incredibly high, and hard, from a standstill position. Doc had the ball for a split second, but rather than put it on the floor and try to soar to the rim, he just went straight up, like a rocket, toward the rim.

"Well," Free continued, "Elvin Hayes and Unseld went up too, and their long arms were way above the rim, waiting to block the shot. But Doc, as if his legs had springs in them and his arm was made of rubber, just kept elevating and elevating and stretching that arm until he was high enough over Hayes and Unseld to windmill the ball through the basket. I'm telling you, the place went crazy.

"I know that Doc is known for a few really famous dunks, but believe me, they don't compare to the dunk in Washington, because no human being, then or now, Michael Jordan included, could jump that high and dunk a basketball like that. On a scale of 1 to 10, I'd give that dunk a 100. The sellout crowd just got up and started applauding for Doc, almost as if they forgot what building they were in.

"Those people did not sit back down until the game was over, they just kept applauding," Free recalled. "They had a mascot named Dancing Harry, whose job it was just to cheer for the Bullets and put a hex on their opponents. Well, even Dancing Harry was cheering for Doc after that dunk. I think he might have been fired over that, because I never saw him again anytime I was in Washington.

"I got so giddy, I was cackling and telling anyone who would listen, 'Did you see that? Did you see just see what I saw?' If that game had been on national television, Doc's dunk would have gone down as the greatest in history. I saw some great dunk artists in college and in the pros and even in Rucker Park, but nothing compared to that dunk, and unless people with wings start playing basketball, nothing ever will.

"Back in those days, everyone was living in fear that Doc would 'posterize' them. No one wanted to end up on a Dr. J poster, getting dunked on. When you went up there to try and block one of Doc's vicious dunks, you could also get one of your arms torn off, so it really wasn't a great idea," Free concluded.

Dawkins said that whenever he gets together with other retired players and the subject of dunking comes up, so too does Julius Erving. "We dunked on people in actual games, not just at All-Star competitions and in practices, but during actual games, on big-time defenders, and we dunked that way because Doc did it that way before we came along.

"We were just trying to be like Doc. He taught us to go hard to the rim and just slam it down and that the worst thing that could happen is you get two free throws out of it. It wasn't such a bad strategy. In Philly, we practiced real hard, almost as hard as we played in real games. Doc was always one of the most aggressive guys out there, always running at full speed on both ends of the court and stuffing the ball in your face with authority; [he would be] as hard on a teammate in practice as he would on an opponent in the game."

I asked Bob Costas how much game he thought Erving had left in the NBA after his days in the flamboyant rebel league had ended.

"I think that when Julius first got to the NBA, he may have lost a bit of the thunder that he had in the ABA, but that doesn't mean he was no longer a great basketball player," Costas said. "A lot of people who had the thrill of watching Julius fly in the ABA were really affected by it, and a lot of that had to do with the fact that he was closer to being a pioneer among players who performed above the rim than today's players, many of whom can really get up there. But the highflyers today, a lot of their extraordinary dunks don't seem as eye-opening as they once did when Dr. J was doing that stuff, because no one was really doing it back in Doc's day, so it all seemed so unique.

"It was the stuff of legend, and maybe you only heard about a great dunk but you didn't see it, which in a strange way made it even more special, more magical. But nowadays, you might see the same great dunk twenty-five times in a single night just flipping around the dial, or fifty great dunks in a given week from the hundreds of college and pro basketball games that ESPN and other networks are covering, and that kind of takes the luster off it.

"So some guy in the NBA might make a great move tomorrow which, objectively, would be seen as a great play, worthy of the highlights on the nightly news, but no matter the move, it always seems to be a variation of something you've seen before. Now in Julius's day, everything he was doing was fresh. It was new. It was bold and imaginative. It injected life into every building he played in. All the mystique and legend that surrounded Julius in his ABA days really went a long way in enhancing his basketball reputation," Costas concluded.

In the Shadow of a Legend

In October 2003, Robert Huber, a reporter with *Philadelphia* magazine, delved deeper into the private life of Julius Erving than any reporter before him.

Under the snap-to-attention headline "Julius Erving Doesn't Want to Be a Hero Anymore," Huber got close enough to Dr. J to write about his sons' drug addictions, his numerous affairs, and his mistreatment of his wife, Turquoise, whom he eventually divorced after thirty years of marriage.

"I was trying to square the public image with the real guy," Huber told me in June 2008. "I think the public guy and the private guy are somewhat different, and that the Julius Erving that the public knows is not entirely who he really is."

Huber brilliantly drives home that point throughout the piece, which he wrote after spending some quality time with Erving and a girlfriend named Freddie.

During trips to an airport, a clothing store, and a golf course with Julius and Freddie, Huber peppered Erving with questions about Alexandra Stevenson, the tennis pro whom he had secretly fathered by Samantha Stevenson, one of the first female journalists to report from a men's locker room. It turns out that Turquoise had known about the talented "love child" all along.

A few more revelations had emerged during the divorce trial: Erving's net worth was ten million dollars, Turquoise was spending $1,150 a month on grooming, and Turquoise's cable service was shut off because Erving had not paid the bill.

However, all that paled in comparison to another piece of news that Philadelphians received about Julius Erving, whom many had seen as the league's gracefully graying version of Joe DiMaggio. Now they were talking about him as if he were just another Shawn Kemp, a basketball player who became more famous for his out-of-wedlock children than for the monstrous game he once flaunted for the Seattle SuperSonics.

In addition to Alexandra, the court papers revealed, there was yet another out-of-wedlock child, a then five-year-old boy named Jules, whom Julius had fathered with a woman named Dorýs Madden, who was known as Pearl.

There was even more. "The divorce papers allude to yet another woman Turquoise says Julius is supporting," Huber wrote, "one with a son who lives in Hollywood, Fla."

When Huber pressed Erving on coming clean about little Jules, Erving snapped, "I've removed myself from having to

answer to the general public on certain issues, and that would
be one of them. After it's done, it's done. How that relates to
my children, whether it's children within my marriage or out of
my marriage, are things I have to deal with, be accountable for,
[but] not [to] the public. Not [to] you."

Apparently Erving did not feel accountable to Turquoise,
either. They married when both were just twenty-two years old.
She already had a son, Cheo, with Freddie Summers, a quarter-
back at Wake Forest and one of the first blacks to play that position in the Atlantic Coast Conference, a division of the NCAA.
Julius adopted Cheo, and the couple went on to have three more
children: Julius (usually just called "J"), Jazmin, and Cory.

"I would have eaten his s—t," Turquoise told Huber when he
asked why she turned a blind eye toward Erving's philandering.

Turquoise recalled the day in May 1981 when she discov-
ered her husband and Samantha Stevenson, who were trying to
hide baby Alexandra.

Turquoise, who was eight months pregnant with Cory, had
arrived home after running errands and was told by the housekeeper that a woman named Samantha Stevenson kept calling.
The housekeeper said that she was instructed by Stevenson not
to reveal her name to Turquoise, but she told her, anyway.

"Now that was odd," Huber wrote. "Samantha, a
sportswriter, was her friend. In fact, Turk was the only Sixer
wife who would talk to Samantha, the only one who didn't feel
threatened by her taking notes next to their half-naked hus-
bands. Samantha had even ghostwritten an article in the *New
York Times* [in which] Turk complained that the Ervings' recep-
tion in Philadelphia certainly could have been warmer, which
ruffled feathers, naturally, in the team's front office—really the
problem was that Turk's words had been twisted, made harder.
Samantha had assured her that she didn't do that, it was some
editor out of control.

"Anyway, Turquoise hadn't seen Samantha for months, she hadn't been around, but now, when Samantha called back again, Turk got on an extension as Julius answered the phone and silently listened in: Samantha was in California, there was this baby, and Turk didn't waste any time demanding to be brought up to speed as they talked about how to handle it. 'What the f—k is going on here? What the f—k you doin' callin' my husband?'

"Even with that, the truth in her ear, Julius denied it," Huber wrote. "At first. That was the hardest thing—the lying. It was almost a game. He would tell her anything, always working an angle with her. Tell her she had it wrong, she was crazy. It drove her mad. She'd fight him but cave; when Julius stormed out for a few days, she'd be worried sick: Where was he? Was he safe? He'd be holed up in some hotel, playing golf, maybe Vegas.

"Later, the condo he bought in A.C., or the Islands. She was always anxious, so thin, not only battling Julius but having to play both mother and father to their kids—mid-'80s, they'd finally moved from Long Island, buying a mansion in Villanova, but to the boys the suburbs were milk-toast: So you're the Doctor's kids.

"As soon as they were old enough [and] could get out from under Turk, they hit the streets in Philly. [They wanted] reality, not this fame bullshit. Cheo and later Cory got caught up in drinking, weed, coke. Turk was not having it, her babies were not going this way. But what could she do? [They were in] rehab, and then back out on the streets. [They were] craving their father, she's sure now [that] that was the deal. [They were] needing their father.

"Eventually they [Julius and Turquoise] sent Cory to John Lucas, the player and coach who'd been an addict and had a treatment center down in Houston. The boy's drug problems weren't so bad, really—Lucas saw the challenge as helping 15-year-old Cory become Cory, whoever that might be.

"[It's] a tougher nut when your dad is so good and so famous and so busy. The one thing that Julius was totally dedicated to, that Turquoise gives him credit for even [as she is] in the storm of trying to crawl out, now, from under Mrs. Julius Erving[, is this]: He was always ready to perform. She admires that still. The problem, though, is how everything centered right there. It was all about him, that's the way it had to be. All of them [were] at the beck and call of Dr. J.

"She thought it might get better when he retired. But it was worse, he was around less. [He was either] chasing business or fooling around. They lived parallel lives even when he was in Villanova, Julius always hitting the sack at three or four in the morning, Turk up at six with her kids. She liked Philly, had found a network of lunch friends—Doris Taxin, Joanne Keenan, Riki Wagman, women who schooled her in moneyed class. She was friends, too, with singer Teddy Pendergrass—Teddy's seats were right next to hers at Sixers games—and somehow that became a big rumor about Turquoise: a partyer, in the car with Teddy and the transvestite the night of his accident in '85, the wreck that broke his neck and paralyzed him.

"Turquoise, in fact, was not in the car; she was home in bed with Julius. Julius and Turk were among the first at the hospital early that morning to see him. Teddy himself told her what happened: He was at the game that night with a woman, went out to a club afterward, and ditched her for another. They left, heading for Teddy's place, [with] him driving. Weaving [on] Wissahickon Drive, he put his hand up her dress, and at the moment of getting the genital news [that is, discovering that the "woman" was a transvestite]—a man!—[he] lost control of his car. Really, Turquoise has always liked to stay home, with her children. Julius liked to be out, and it was the same once the kids were old enough to start living on their own.

"Then [came the] Orlando [team]. He called her one day six years ago from Chicago announcing a new life—'I'm signing tomorrow with the Magic. They'll send a plane for you to go to the press conference.' So she moved south with him. Turquoise and Cory—[who was] still in and out of rehab, trying to get a grip—hated Orlando. Their lives thickened with public trouble. Cheo and Cory were busted with a crack pipe, charged with breaking into a car. The Alexandra story broke while Cheo was in jail in Orange County on a drug-related conviction; Julius visited him the next day to explain the deal, but too late: Cheo had already been in a fistfight with another inmate who clued him in to his half-sister by running his mouth about how good she looked, and 'what I'd like to do with that,' and 'how long she been playin' tennis, anyway?'

"Turquoise found out about Julius's young son Jules—though she got hit sideways with this one, too. An acquaintance had told her, innocently enough, about seeing Julius with his grandson. Little Cory, J's kid? That wasn't possible—J and Cory were up in Philly, and Julius barely saw them even when he went north. Turk went to Julius's Magic office [and] asked him point-blank: What little boy you spending time with down here? 'We'll talk about it later' [was his response]. That night he admitted it: another woman, another child. But his attitude was, as always, that she could take it or leave it; this was the deal, take it or leave it.

"Julius was banking on Turquoise folding, letting him off the hook. As always. By this point, she'd been trying to come to terms with herself, who the hell she was in this marriage, for years. Her therapists had been telling her that one day she'd wake up, decide that she loved herself more than she loved Julius—as trite, and as monumental, as that. Then he'd have nothing on her. She could tell him to get the hell out of her house and mean it. And all he could do was stop paying her bills [and] play hide-and-seek with his fortune. That was the only thing he had on her."

Perhaps the most startling aspect of Huber's story was how unremorseful Erving appeared, especially where his love affairs were concerned. "I've had two children out of wedlock, but I can walk down the street holding my head up high," Erving said. "I love all my sons, I love all my daughters."

I asked Huber what he thought about Erving after spending time with him, and after his story had hit the newsstands. "I came to realize that Julius was a lot more complicated than the family guy we sort of saw and believed in publicly," Huber replied. He noted that no one in Erving's camp, or Turquoise's, for that matter, challenged anything he had written about them.

"I've always been fascinated by this hero-worship thing with athletes," said Huber, fifty-four, who grew up in Morrisville, Pennsylvania, as a 76ers fan but fell in love with Dr. J's game, as I did, when Erving was a rim-rocking member of the Nets. "Julius is a very likable guy, and he's pretty good company. Although he admittedly has his share of problems, Julius still seems very comfortable with who he was and who he is."

Calling Samantha

After reviewing James McKinley's article about Alexandra Stevenson (see chapter 12) along with Huber's article, I wanted more, so I reached out to Samantha Stevenson by phone in January 2008. By now, a series of injuries had unfortunately turned Alexandra's 1999 Wimbledon run into fifteen, maybe twenty, minutes of fame.

"Hi, Samantha," I said when she answered the phone. "My name is Vinny Mallozzi and I'm a reporter at the *New York Times* who is writing a book about Julius Erving. I'd like to speak with you about your past relationship with him, which is already in the public domain, and about Alexandra."

"Does Julius Erving know you're writing this book?" she asked in a rather terse tone.

"Yes," I said. "I have contacted his representatives through e-mail and by phone, although they have not gotten back to me." (Later, one of Erving's representatives eventually did call me back to say that Erving had gracefully declined my invitation to be part of this biography.)

She wanted a name of someone I had contacted. I gave her one that she recognized, and then she asked awkwardly, "Isn't he [Erving] divorced now?"

I told her that he was, then she asked, in a rather annoyed voice, why I was reaching out to her and Alexandra.

"You are a journalist, like I am," I reminded her. "If you were in my shoes and you were writing a book about Julius Erving, wouldn't you be making this same call? As a journalist and someone who is trying to paint the fullest portrait of Julius Erving, I owe it to myself, and to him and to you and to my publisher, to try to knock on every possible door, to ask every question. I couldn't write this book in good conscience without even attempting to contact you, and others in Julius's world, for an interview."

I seemed to finally connect with her. She changed her tone but was not about to offer an interview. She politely declined. I asked if she might ask Alexandra if she would be interested in talking to me, although everything I had read about their relationship told me that the mother kept a close watch and safeguard over her daughter.

"I'll ask her for you," she said softly. "I have your number. If she wants to call you, she will."

I never heard from either one of them.

Turquoise Sees the Light

Turquoise hung in there during the Samantha Stevenson affair and during countless other shadowy accounts of her husband sneaking around and sleeping with other women. The last straw, however, came when she heard about Erving having another "love child"—to whose mother he reportedly was paying two thousand dollars a month in child support—and maybe even yet another.

So Turquoise Erving, her family falling apart, what little self-esteem she might have had nearly gone, finally summoned the strength to file for divorce in May 2002 in Seminole County, Florida.

By January 2004, those proceedings had taken an X-rated turn, right into the heart of tabloid land. While the case was being heard, a videotape emerged showing Erving having sex with a woman in a hotel room.

According to the Associated Press story, the tape was delivered to the *New York Post* while Erving was divorcing Turquoise, his wife of thirty-one years. It showed Erving, in a sleeveless undershirt, boxers, and metal-framed glasses, having sex in a hotel room with a young and attractive light-skinned brunette, clad in a negligee, while the song "Sea of Love" played in the background. At one point, you can hear an early morning weather report of fog announced on the radio for San Jose, Santa Cruz, and Monterey.

The *Post* revealed that once in the hour-long video, Erving is seen adjusting the camera. After approximately ten minutes, the couple makes the transition from underwear and sips of wine to kissing and making love. The video ends before the lovers do.

"This is a tape that was made fifteen years ago, while Julius and his wife were separated," Erving's then spokesman Dan Klores said. "The decision by his wife's advisors to release it during their divorce negotiations is disappointing, especially since Mrs. Erving has had it in her possession for all these years."

"It didn't come out of our camp," Andrea Black, a lawyer for Turquoise, told the Associated Press.

Shortly after, Erving was answering questions about the second "film" he starred in (after his bigger but less memorable role in *The Fish That Saved Pittsburgh*) at the Philadelphia Sports Writers Association's 100th Annual Banquet in Cherry Hill, New Jersey.

"The media is always going to be part of my life as long as I'm breathing and even after I'm gone," said Erving, looking dapper in a black tuxedo and tie. "I'm not stressed about it."

Sitting on a dais between then 76ers coach Randy Ayers and the Los Angeles Dodgers legend Tommy Lasorda, Erving spoke of his longtime relationship with the Philadelphia media.

"The waters were calm," he said, "but [they are] not so calm today. I had the option of not coming here, but I feel it is important to celebrate milestones, and my relationship with the media has been so good for so long [that] I did not want to miss being a part of the hundredth year of this banquet and this program."

Erving was the twenty-fifth speaker after a dinner of chicken, salad, and cheesecake. "For twenty-one years, Philadelphia has been my adopted home," he said. "Time has marched on, but memories are forever."

Black told the *Post* that Turquoise was asking the court to enforce the terms of her separation agreement and to sanction Erving for his alleged failure to comply with its terms. As Robert Huber noted in his story, the court had ordered Erving to pay Turquoise fifteen hundred dollars a week plus eight thousand dollars a month in credit card expenses. Both Julius and Turquoise were living in Orlando.

"I'm sad that it has reached this point," Black told the *Post* when she was asked about the video. "We've been trying to resolve this amicably. Making something like that public would help no one. He made agreements to do things. He did not do those things," Black said of Erving. "We're about to have a hearing for enforcement and sanctions."

Even though Florida is a no-fault divorce state, which allows spouses to split without the need to assign fault for things like adultery, abandonment, or intolerable cruelty, sources close to Erving suggested that the timing of the video's leak to the press was an attempt to strengthen Turquoise's hand at the negotiating table for a divorce settlement.

Erving's lawyer, Andrea Cain, denied any knowledge of such a tape, but she said that if it existed, it wouldn't be introduced as evidence. "I can't see any relevance. Florida is a no-fault state. The most valuable commodity I know of is information."

Later at the banquet, Erving was signing basketballs and memorabilia for fans when another reporter asked him again about the video. "I think there's nothing left to say," Erving responded. "I think my comment stands by that."

Losing a Coach—and a Friend

On March 6, 2004, Julius Erving lost his old varsity coach, Jack Leaman, who died of a heart attack at age seventy-two. Leaman, the head coach at UMass for thirteen seasons (1966–1979), was returning from a road trip to Richmond, Virginia, with the UMass basketball team. He was at Dulles Airport when he collapsed in a bathroom. At the time, Leaman was serving as the school's associate athletic director.

"It was the last regular-season game," recalled Bob Behler, the radio play-by-play man whom Leaman had worked alongside as a color analyst. "We had gone to Temple for a game, driven back to Amherst, and flown back to Richmond for our last regular-season game. The one thing I remember was that the arena in Richmond was very hot; it had no air conditioning. I looked at Jack during the game, and he looked a little out of it and was really sweating. But I was sweating, too, so I didn't give it much thought.

"After the game, Jack immediately went with the team to fly home. I had to stick around to do the postgame show, so I had planned to drive to Baltimore-Washington International Airport and take a flight home the next day. I was driving when I got the call about Jack. He never made it onto the plane. He had a heart attack in a bathroom at Dulles Airport. I immediately drove to the hospital and met a couple of assistant coaches there who had gotten off the plane to be with Jack, but we were all told by the medical personnel there that Jack was dead on arrival."

Leaman was a basketball star at Boston University, from which he graduated in 1959 and earned a master's degree in 1960. He moved on to UMass Amherst, where he would work for more than forty years. As head basketball coach, he would lead the UMass basketball program to a career record of 217–126 as he became the all-time "winningest" coach in school history. During his tenure, he guided UMass to eight Yankee Conference titles in six seasons (1968–1971 and 1973–1976) and to six National Invitation Tournament appearances (1970, 1971, 1973, 1974, 1975, and 1977). He was twice named New England Coach of the Year. Later, his many roles at UMass included head coach of the women's basketball team (1986–1987) and radio broadcaster, which is what he was doing at the time of his death.

"To me, Jack Leaman was more than a basketball coach," former UMass team member Ray Ellerbrook said. "Certainly he had an exceptional record as a coach; he had many great teams and recruited many outstanding players to come to the university. But it was his genuine concern for his players as individuals that set him apart. His players meant the world to him, on and off the court during their playing days as well as after graduation."

The following month, the school held a memorial service for Leaman at the Curry Hicks Cage, and many of those outstanding players, including Julius Erving, came back to say one last good-bye.

"It was a beautiful service," recalled Leaman's widow, Rita. "There were so many of Jack's former players, as well as current players and coaches and students who really didn't know him but just wanted to come by and pay their respects."

Erving was one of many who took to the podium to praise Leaman; so did Behler, now a radio play-by-play man at Boise State University. "It was just tremendous," Behler said. "Because it took place a month or so after Jack died, it was more of a celebration of Jack's life than a funeral. Julius was another speaker, and he did a great job. There was a slide show that night with pictures and clips of Jack and his players from different eras. There were so many people who came from out of town. There wasn't a nicer, more loyal and decent person to be around, and Julius knew that, just as we all did, and I think that's why he remained so close to Jack throughout the years."

Other speakers included Ellerbrook, former UMass team member Al Skinner, and University of Memphis coach John Calipari, whom Leaman had mentored when Calipari was a young and unknown coach trying to make a name for himself.

"I really miss him and the fact that I had a mentor, someone who I knew cared about me, [who knew] what I was doing, and [who] was keeping track," said Calipari, who would make a name for himself at UMass before moving to the NBA to coach the Nets and then returning to the college game at Memphis.

"There are not many coaches who retire and then want the next coach to do well," Calipari added. "It just shows the character of the man and the heart of this man."

On February 25, 2006, UMass named the stretch of hardwood at the William D. Mullins Memorial Center the Jack

Leaman Court. The ceremony took place at the halftime of UMass's 66–47 win over the University of Dayton.

"All those years," Rita Leaman said to me in the fall of 2008, in a telephone interview from her home in Amherst, "Julius and Jack remained good friends; they went out of [their] way to maintain their relationship. It was really a once-in-a-lifetime situation, when you consider how Julius fell into Jack's lap. Julius, who never really had a father, was like a son to [Roosevelt High School coach] Ray Wilson, who was very close to Jack, and that's how the whole thing really came about.

"In the end, I think that Jack and Julius were good for each other. Jack obviously received a lot more recognition when Julius was playing for him, and I think Julius got the kind of coaching and guidance that he needed under Jack, that he maybe would not have received had he gone to a bigger program filled with many other star players."

Tearing Down Memories

The year 2004 continued to be unkind to Erving. In August, Callie Mae, his mother and his best friend, passed away at the age of eighty at her home in Orlando, Florida, where she had moved in 1997 and was attending church services at the Community Church of God.

Erving, who lost his younger brother, Marvin, years earlier and his older sister, Alex, in 1984, was now the last surviving member of the family that had grown up together, through thick and thin, in the Park Lake Apartment complex in Hempstead, Long Island. By the fall of 2008, bulldozers would be tearing down the buildings, and the memories, there in order to erect high-rises.

"Callie Mae Lindsay was born on May 10, 1924, to Gilbert and Bertha Abney in Batesburg, South Carolina," the obituary, handed out during her funeral masses in both Orlando and Hempstead, noted. "Mother Callie, as she was fondly known at Community Church of God, was a devoted mother, grandmother, great-grand-mother, sister, and friend. She loved the sport of bowling, the craft of sewing, the art of hairstyling, and the adventure of traveling. Her favorite song was 'Christ is All,' and it showed in her humble attitude.

"Mother Callie was a member in good standing at Community Church of God since 1997, having come to us as a deaconess, by way of South Hempstead Baptist Church of Long Island, New York, with impeccable credentials. Sister Callie continued in service as a deaconess, forever faithful. She was a committed member of the Diana Eubanks Missionary Circle Women of the Church of God, holding the office of par-liamentarian from 1998 to 2002. She shined best as a member of the Golden Girls Fellowship and the choir, being one of the lead soloists.

"This wonderful human being accomplished all of her goals in life. Special memories of her will carry us all the days of our lives. She influenced many from near and far during her tenure here on earth, and as she goes home, we know that she will be a special angel in God's kingdom."

Rita Leaman said that Callie Mae Erving had lived a full and rewarding life. "Look how her children turned out, all wonder-ful," she said. "This was a very strong woman who persevered through the hard times and made so many sacrifices for her family. She was a true role model in every sense of the word."

15

Just Like Old Times

In the summer of 2007, Archie Rogers, Julius's boyhood pal, was continuing to battle drug problems; he said that he was "still fighting the demons." He had last seen Erving in 2004 at a restaurant in Plainview, Long Island.

"We just reminisced," Rogers said about that meeting. "He was the same old Julius, and I was the same old me."

At their last get-together, Erving asked Rogers, as he had done numerous times before, if he could help him financially. Rogers, still as proud as he was back in the Hempstead days when he and Al Williams and Julius Erving were the stars of Don Ryan's Salvation Army team, refused the help.

"I'm doing okay, not great, but I'm not really desperate for money," said Rogers, who by now had lost Wanda Watts, his wife. She died that summer from liver failure. "What meant more than anything to me was the fact that Julius took the time out to meet with me and catch up on old times. You can't put a price on a friendship that special. In fact, I wouldn't trade a friend like Julius Erving for all the money in the world.

"No matter where he has been, no matter how much sadness he has had to deal with or how much success he has achieved, he never forgot about me or his other true friends. Believe me, there are a lot of guys out there who claim to be good friends with Julius just because they grew up in the same neighborhood, but they were just acquaintances. That used to bother Julius, but eventually he just outgrew all the nonsense."

Erving once spoke to *Black Sports The Magazine* about those so-called good friends. "I have always been proud of myself for having common sense, knowing right from wrong, and trying to do what was right," he said. "Those who were my friends treat me the same. Like you grow up with a crowd of, say, 15 people who you would hang with from time to time, and two of them are your friends. The other 13 you just grew up with. They're the ones who say, 'Yeah, I knew him' and this and that, 'now look how he's treating me,' when actually you were only acquaintances.

"Some acquaintances put me on the defensive by saying I've changed. It gave me mental anguish, [it] used to bother me for a while until I thought about the true facts and recognized that I had gone through some changes. And if I hadn't, I wouldn't have grown. When someone says I've changed, I say yeah, I've changed. Now I know what the other side of the ocean looks like. I went over there. I've met all kinds of different people. Of course I've changed! It's not really changing, it's adding on to what you already have.

"Obviously, reaching the highest level in your profession gives you a certain amount of personal clout and power," Erving continued. "But understanding that, and then being able to use it properly, exposes you to the limitations that come along with the territory—the exposure that your family gets, and the things they're subject to that you can't be forewarned about. My sister, for example, suddenly having a famous brother created a certain standard in her eyes, looking at her children and [at] male figures in her life. The same [was true] for my mother, the same for my wife [and] my kids.

"Many times people would approach them, as if they should know everything about me, what makes me tick, what I'm thinking about, what my itinerary is. Lots of times they're put in a position of being defensive, and maybe even a little embarrassed by things that they don't know the answers to. Then [they have to put up with] being approached by people who they thought were their friends, who were trying to use them to get through to me, for whatever reason.

"The first few years, you're not sure what to make of it, and you make a lot of wrong choices and a lot of wrong decisions. As time goes on, you learn how to say no, and you learn how to protect those who are close to you and who you love. You start with your children, not permitting teachers, other students, or visitors to school to use them as messengers, to bring home notes relating to that individual's proposed business with you, keeping those around you from being pawns in the process, and teaching them and advising them to stand up and command respect. If people want to deal with you, let them deal with you one-to-one as an individual and not use [others] to get through to [you]. That's part of the curse."

Earl Mosley, the onetime principal of Roosevelt High School and Erving's junior high school coach, once said that Erving "always had self-discipline. Self-discipline means I pick my friends. I know what's right. I made choices."

Erving attributed his homegrown qualities to his mother, Callie Mae. "I think I started learning lessons about being a good person long before I ever knew what basketball was, and that starts in the home, it starts with the parental influence. I came from a broken home, so my mom was a major influence in my life," he said in a 1992 interview with the Academy of Achievement in Washington.

In the eyes of Archie Rogers, Julius Erving never changed. "He's the same kindhearted guy today as he was when we were running around Long Island playing basketball and delivering newspapers," Rogers said. "People know him as the great Dr. J, some even idolize him, and that's a credit to the kind of athlete he was and for all he contributed to professional basketball. It's funny, but I've always looked up to Julius for other reasons besides basketball. He's a man of integrity who comes from a good family. He has always had a great work ethic and he has always, always made time for people, especially his real friends. I don't know anyone else like him. And I know that if I ever truly needed him, he would be there for me, that's just who he is."

An Unexpected House Call

In the summer of 2008, Erving appeared to old audiences and new in a clever commercial for Dr Pepper soda. (He had first appeared in a Dr Pepper commercial in the early 1970s, and he starred in a Chapstick commercial in the early 1980s in which he signed autographs for a bunch of fans as "Dr. Chapstick.")

"You know, scientific tests have proven that when you drink Dr Pepper slowly, 23 flavors, it tastes even better," Erving said in the most recent Dr Pepper spot. His beard was now a lot more salt than pepper, but he still looked fit enough to give an NBA team solid minutes off the bench.

"Hey, I get it, because half my life's been in slow motion," he says, as a slow-motion clip from the old days shows the Doctor, or at least someone resembling the Doctor, losing an opponent in midair with a slick reverse layup.

"Watch this," says Erving, who grabs an ice cube, fades back from about ten feet, and launches the cube in the direction of a drinking glass. As the cube is in midair, Erving says, "Slower is better," and after the shot hits nothing but the bottom of the net—er, glass—Erving looks into America's living rooms and says, "Trust me, I'm a doctor."

Roy Boe, the former Nets owner, who was battling a second round of cancer at age seventy-two in the fall of 2008, said from his home in Connecticut, "I got a huge kick out of that Dr Pepper ad. I thought it was great. After all these years, Julius still looks great, and I'm glad that his image is still getting out there, because there are too many kids out there who did not get a chance to see Julius play the game of basketball. As an owner, no one appreciated his vast talents more than I did."

Also in the summer of 2008, Wicked Cow Entertainment, a New York–based creative brand management and business development firm, signed Erving to a licensing deal. The company released the following statement: "As part of the agreement, Wicked Cow will work with the Erving Group to further develop current and future business opportunities and create licensing programs for Dr. J." Initial plans included consumer products and licensing programs in apparel and memorabilia, as well as speaking engagements and endorsements.

Michael Hermann, the president of the company, who had reached out to Dr. J., told me that Erving was not interested in talking with me about this project. Nevertheless, after all these years, companies were still reaching out to Erving in the hope of profiting from all the magic that surrounded him in his playing days.

More than twenty years after walking away from the game of basketball, Dr. J was still relevant and still marketable.

The memories of his long, graceful strides, his innovative moves to the hoop, and the thundering dunks that once wowed capacity crowds still resonated on Madison Avenue. The Doctor was still reaping the rewards of a smooth operating style that helped to enhance the image of his sport, allowing it to soar to immeasurable artistic heights during his professional heyday, ultimately pushing professional basketball to a level of popularity it had not previously known.

Best of all, Erving was putting together a few of the broken pieces of his storied life. A December 2008 story written by Tom Friend of ESPN.com revealed that Erving had finally reunited with Alexandra. He invited her down to his home in Atlanta, introducing her at a family reunion to six half brothers and half sisters: Jazmin, Julius ("J"), and Cheo, from his marriage to Turquoise; ten-year-old Jules, from his earlier relationship with Dorýs Madden; seven-year-old Justin, from another relationship; and a baby named Julietta, from his current, revived relationship with Dorýs Madden.

"At the tail end of the evening, seven hours later, she [Alexandra] and Julius sat alone in his car, and he brought up her earlier question about why he hadn't called in 27 years," Friend wrote. "He told her it was because she'd been well-cared for by her mom, and that if she hadn't been, he would've come to rescue her. His eyes were red, he seemed close to breaking down. He told her, 'I trust you, and I need you to try to trust me.' He assured her he'd try to help because he knew what it was like to be an athlete, [to have] the desire to go out on your own terms.

"'It's not how you enter your sport,' Julius Erving told his daughter. 'It's how you exit.'"

Epilogue

For me, the sweetest bit of sports irony took place on a day in December 2006. I had made a deal with a professional basketball team called the Brooklyn Wonders: a newspaper article in exchange for playing time. The Wonders, a minor league team filled with ex-college players and journeymen trying to get one last shot at making it to the big show, played in a new league called the American Basketball Association. Like its 1970s ancestor, this ABA came complete with red, white, and blue basketballs. That gave me and my childhood hero, the great Julius Erving, one thing in common. We each played professionally in the ABA, although my professional basketball career was slightly shorter than his. In fact, it lasted all of ninety-one seconds.

Two hours before our game against the Quebec City Kebekwa, I met with Coach Ron Eford, a former Marquette star who played professionally in the Continental Basketball Association and the United States Basketball League and overseas.

"I once covered Chris Mullin," I told Eford.

"You played in the Big East?" he asked.

"No, I wrote for the school paper at St. John's."

After the national anthem, I was heading to the bench when David Greenidge, an assistant coach, stopped me. "Where are you going?" he asked.

"To take a seat," I replied.

"No you're not," he said. "You're starting."

Starting? Even Rudy didn't start.

Suddenly, everything I never worked for but always dreamed of was coming true. I was about to play in the ABA—well, this ABA, anyway, a distant cousin of the league in which Julius Erving, Rick Barry, and George Gervin once played.

Eford shouted, "Vinny, we're in a 2–3 zone—you're on top!"

Quebec City, which was not aware of my deal with the Wonders, went straight at me, putting the ball into the hands of the six-foot four-inch shooting guard whom I was defending. I am six feet in new sneakers and with a three-week-old haircut, and I am slow enough to be timed in the forty-yard dash by a sundial.

The Kebekwa had little trouble spotting this mismatch. "Go to work on him!" they shouted.

My heart started dancing, but so did my feet, and I forced my opponent to the left sideline. A teammate, Chidi Erike, who grew up in Harlem as I did and played at Erie Community College, cheated from his forward position and closed an opening to the hoop, and my man had to pass.

After an exchange of fast-break layups, Ryan Williams tried to pass the ball to me near midcourt. My teammate Carl Lee, from Utah Valley State College, either did not see me or did not trust me; he intercepted the pass.

We scored a basket on that trip, and after a Quebec City foul, the clock stopped, with ten minutes and twenty-nine seconds remaining in the first quarter; we led, 4–2. The substitution horn sounded, and my pro career came to an end, ninety-one glorious seconds after it began. I never even touched the basketball.

"Nice work," Eford said. "Good defense."

I sat and watched the rest of the game, marveling at the strength, speed, and talent of the ABA players. Eventually, I turned to Karl Sanders, a former St. Francis College point guard, and said, "Was I really out there?"

"Yeah, you did all right," he said.

Sanders and the other players use the ABA as a showcase. They hope that it will lead to a professional contract overseas or a shot at an NBA roster. They did not know until after the game, which we lost, 109–98, that three NBA scouts were among the three hundred or so fans in attendance.

During the drive home, as my wife, Cathy, and our young sons, Christopher and Michael, chatted, I thought about Erving and what it must have been like to play with or against him back in the real ABA days, and later in the NBA. It must have been electric, because twenty years after he hung up his Converse sneakers, everyone in his basketball circle that I had spoken to was still in awe of him; they were still feeling the hurricane-like force of Julius Erving soaring down the lane and putting another dent in yet another rim.

"I'd have to place Dr. J up there in the top five players of all time, with Michael Jordan, Wilt Chamberlain, Magic Johnson, and Oscar Robertson, with Larry Bird knocking on that door," World B. Free said to me. "Those guys really changed the way the game of basketball was played. They made the game much more of a spectator sport. I would have loved to have won a championship with Doc and the rest of them guys.

"When they finally did win it with Doc and a different cast, I remember my heart beating inside my chest and my palms getting all sweaty. I still had a tremendous emotional attachment to the team, and when they won it all, I felt as much a part of that championship as they did. What Julius was doing on the court was difficult to do in practice, let alone in games. Watching him float on the air, the basketball looking like an orange in his giant hand, was like watching an eagle soar.

"It was a beautiful and glorious sight; it really took your breath away. The man defied gravity. He just had this ability to hang in the air longer than anyone else who ever played the game. The game was tailor-made for him in those days, because defenses were primarily man-to-man in a half-court set; all those complicated zones starting coming in years later. So basically Doc was left with just taking one or two guys off the dribble, and that was his strong suit.

"I don't run into Doc too often, but when I see him, it's like yesterday all over again, like were back in that big Cadillac driving from New York to the Spectrum in Philly," Free continued. "That's the kind of guy Doc is, a friend for life. I think it's sad that a few generations of kids have never seen Dr. J play basketball. All those who had the privilege know exactly what the younger folks have missed out on. Doc could never understand how much I really loved him and how much he meant to me in terms of my development as a player and as a person.

"He was the best role model a fan or a teammate could have. I couldn't tell him that at the time, because that wouldn't have been the manly thing to do. But deep inside, I think Doc knew how all of us felt about him, and how special and important he was to his teammates in those days."

He was equally important to his opponents, like Michael Cooper.

"I got to know Doc and his family, and he got to know my family," Cooper said. "He was a gentleman both on and off the court. He was the ultimate pro, always classy in everything he did, especially on the court. He was not a cheap-shot artist or a trash talker. I always admired him from afar, and it was a thrill for me when I joined the NBA and became one of his peers. I had been following his career from his Virginia Squire days, when he had that long, flowing Afro hairstyle and was dunking on anyone and everyone in his path.

"I would try to emulate so many of his moves in my backyard; some of them I could pull off, but many of them I couldn't. As you get older and your jumping skills diminish a little bit, you begin to compensate. Doc compensated by being more of a post-up player, and although people always said he didn't have much of a jump shot, I thought that became one of his best weapons in the latter part of his career."

The NBC newscaster Tom Brokaw once said of Erving, "When they come to write the history of the great cultural impact of basketball on our lives, and it does affect everything from the game itself to the way we dress, the kind of heroes that we have, [they will say that] Dr. J was certainly a founding father of the modern school of basketball."

I am a proud graduate of that school, and I'm glad that I chose Julius Erving as my major. I was raised on sports, but Erving made me gung-ho about the game of basketball. That enthusiasm has never left me, and now I have written four books on the subject. It is a shame that Erving did not want to participate in this project (a number of calls went out to Erving's representatives and to his ex-wife, Turquoise, and their children, but most were not returned), because this entire book is basically a giant Valentine from one of his biggest fans.

Erving has certainly had some difficulties in his life, and it is with the utmost honesty that I have reported such difficulties in these pages. He has made what appear to be a few poor choices along the way, but I felt no need to critically comment on them. I simply stated the facts as they had previously been reported in a variety of well-respected publications.

Since joining the *New York Times* in 1986, I had a few chance meetings with Erving in locker rooms and at the occasional party or press conference, but ten years ago, when I sat down with him in that Florida hotel room for an in-depth conversation on basketball and life, I came to see the laid-back and humble side of him that Archie Rogers, Al Williams, and Jack Wilkinson have known since their younger days. I also saw the fire and passion inside him that Pete Broaca and Jack Leaman surely appreciated at UMass, and I saw the elegance and grace that Dr. J's professional teammates and opponents came to respect back in his heyday.

"We all love Dr. J," Bill Walton said to me. "He is better than perfect on all fronts."

My goal here has been to reintroduce Erving to generations of basketball fans who barely know his name and to introduce him to those who have never heard of him at all. By all accounts, including my own, Julius Erving is even better at being a human being than he was at being a basketball player, which makes him quite a unique specimen.

My only hope is that he enjoys reading this book as much as I enjoyed writing it.

Index

NOTE: Page references in *italics* refer to photos.

ABC-TV, 231–233
Abdul-Jabbar, Kareem, 9, 19, 27, 35,
   63, 74, 79, 82, 205
  ABA and, 56
  in "Clash of Legends," 198–201
  Erving's reverse layup and, 158
  30,000-point milestone reached by,
    184–185, 202
Abney, Bertha, 264
Abney, Gilbert, 264
Aladdin Hotel, 121
Albeck, Stan, 106–107
Albert, Marv, 3, 206, 207–210, 212,
   246–247
Alcindor, Lew. *See* Abdul-Jabbar,
   Kareem
Ali, Muhammad, 31
All-ABA teams, 76, 83, 89
Alverson, William H., 87
Amateur Athletic Union (AAU),
   185–186
American Basketball Association
   (ABA), 51–54, 55, 57
  Bukata on, 181
  Erving as ABA Most Valuable
    Player, 89, 111
  Erving as ABA Rookie of the Year, 71

Erving legacy and, 246–247,
   250–251
Erving signed to Nets, 85–87
  (*See also* New York Nets)
gimmicks of, 51
NBA and, 51–58, 77–83, 201,
   204, 205
NBA merger with, 115–118
Slam Dunk Contest of, 108–109, 209
2006 revival of, 273–275
Anderson, Dave, 2, 65, 75, 91
  on ABA, 52
  on "Doctor J" nickname, 177
  on NBA and Erving, 98, 115,
   117–118, 126, 167
Anderson, Kenny, 196–198
Anthony, Carmelo, 47
Araton, Harvey, 4
Archibald, Nate "Tiny," 9, 65, 119,
   124, 198–201, 205
Arizin, Paul, 205
Arnold, Steve, 80
*Asphalt Gods: An Oral History
   of the Rucker Tournament*
   (Mallozzi), 217
Atlanta Hawks, 80–83, 85–87, *128*
Averitt, Bird, 117

Barkley, Charles, 171–176, 183, 184, 202, 205
Barnes, Marvin, 117
Barry, Rick, 55, 57, 94, 118, 205
  Boe and, 86
  in "Clash of Legends," 198–201
  Erving compared to, 123, 126
Basketball Hall of Fame, 173, 181, 196–198, 201, 222–223
Bass, Bob, 108
Bassett, Tim, 123, 216
Bavetta, Dick, 178
Baylor, Elgin, 63, 66, 94, 95, 115, 205, 208
Beaty, Zelmo, 55, 92
Behler, Bob, 53, 144–145, 242, 261–263
Bellamy, Walt, 201
Berman, Len, 149
Betancourt, John, 35, 36, 37, 43, 45
Bianchi, Al, 71, 72, 75, 83, 88
Bibby, Henry, 125, 195
Biddy Basketball, 5
"Big Julie Is Doing Nicely-Nicely" (*Sports Illustrated*), 101–102
Bing, Dave, 205
Binstein, Mark, 55
Bird, Larry "Legend," 113, *135*, 160, 176–179, 205
Black, Andrea, 259–261
Black Sports The Magazine, 12, 76, 109, 186–187, 268–270
Blocker, Joe, 15–17
Boe, Roy, 54–58, 100, *128*
  on Dr Pepper ad, 271
  Erving-Nets contract dispute and, 122–125
  Erving-Nets contract dispute and, 120
  Erving signed by, 85–87
Boone, Ron, 90, 92, 117
Boston Celtics, 160
Boston Garden, *135*
Bowman, Nate, 22
Bradley, Bill, 52, 98
Brethel, Tommy, 6
Broaca, Pete, 34–35, 35, 39, 44, 49
Brokaw, Tom, 277
Brooklyn Wonders, 273–275
Brown, Arthur, 55–56
Brown, Roger, 9

Brownbill, Dave, 21–22, 59–61, 69–70, 88
Bryant, Joe, 141
Bryant, Kobe, 116
Bucci, George, 216
Bukata, Jim, 181
Buse, Ron, 117

Cabrini College, 186
Cain, Andrea, 261
Calipari, John, 196, 263
Callahan, Tom, 183–184
Calvin, Mack, 90
Campbell Park, 1, 13, 15–17
Camp Orin-Sekwa, 23
Carnesecca, Lou, 21, 34, 54–57, 66, 83, 105
Carr, M. L., 178
Carter, Fred, 125
Carter, George, 86
Carter, Vince, 170, 209, 247
Cartwright, Bill, 248
Catlett, Sid, 60, 63
Chamberlain, Wilt, 66, 72, 74, 124, 185, 194, 205
  Erving compared to, 123
  30,000-point milestone reached by, 202
Chapstick, 270
Cheeks, Maurice, 165, 175, 184
Chones, Jim, 58, 88
Cingiser, Mike, 23–24, 39
Clark, Archie, 78
"Clash of Legends," 198–201
Cobb, Eric "the Elevator Man," 64, 68
Coca-Cola, 204, 214
Collins, Doug, 125, 141
Commack Arena, 56
Conroy, Terry, 6
Converse, 104, 204
Cooper, Michael "Coop-a-Loops," 158, 160, 164–166, 168, 191, 276–277
Cosby, Bill, 213, 214
Costas, Bob, 3–4, 48, 107, 180
  on Erving legacy, 206–207, 250–251
  on NBA and Erving, 117
Cousy, Bob, 115, 205
Cowens, Dave, 205
Cunningham, Billy, 115, 118, 123, 141, 164, 180, 205, 209

Cureton, Odell, 18
Curry Hicks Cage (University of
　Massachusetts), 35

Dampier, Louie, 90
Dancing Harry (mascot), 249
Darnell, Rick, 116
Dawkins, Darryl "Chocolate
　Thunder," 228, 242–243
　on dunking, 208
　on Erving's legacy, 224, 247
　with Philadelphia 76ers, 125, 138,
　　141, 149, 151–152, 154
DeBusschere, Dave, 58, 94, 126,
　181, 205
DeFord, Frank, 182
Denver Nuggets, 73, 99, 111–117, 132
Denver Rockets, 52–53
DeWood, Mitch, 121
"Doctor Opens Up His Medicine
　Bag, The" (*Sports Illustrated*),
　111–112
Dove, Sonny, 22, 57
Dr. Dre, 218
"Dr. J Is Flying Away" (*Time*), 183–184
Drexler, Clyde "the Glide,"
　168, 205, 223
Drossos, Angelo, 100
Dr Pepper, 102, 213, 270
dunking, 2–3, 7, 208
　Chamberlain and, 124
　DeFord on Erving's slam dunk, 182
　Erving on, 12–13, 109–110
　Erving's high school career and, 5
　Erving's practice of, 104
　Free on Erving's slam dunk, 248–250
　NCAA on, 35–37, 39, 45
　"rock the cradle" dunk by Erving,
　　164–166
　Slam Dunk Contest (ABA),
　　108–109, 209
　Slam Dunk Contest (NBA), 168–171

Eakins, Jim, 181, 216
Eford, Ron, 273–275
Ellerbrook, Ray, 35–36, 39, 47,
　262, 263
Elmore, Len, *130, 131*
Embry, Wayne, 80, 124, 208

Erving, Alfreda "Alex" (sister), 1, 20,
　30, 43, 264
Erving, Callie Mae (mother), 1–2, 10,
　13–14, 20, 30, 37, 180, 240
　death of, 264–265
　Erving's move to ABA and, 53
　influence of, on Erving,
　　269–270
Erving, Cheo (son), 138, 236, 253,
　254, 256, 272
Erving, Cory (son), 235–243, 253,
　254, 256
Erving, Jazmin (daughter), 138,
　253, 272
Erving, Julius "Dr. J" Winfield, II,
　*127, 128, 129, 130, 131, 132,
　133, 134, 135*
　as ABA Most Valuable Player,
　　89, 111
　as ABA Rookie of the Year, 71
　as advertising spokesman, 102, 104,
　　178, 185–186, 270–271
　with Atlanta Hawks, 80–83,
　　85–87
　childhood of, 1–2, 4–10
　children of, 227–233, 235–243,
　　251–257, 272
　in "Clash of Legends," 198–201
　divorce of, 251–257, 258–261
　on favorite games, 194–196
　in Halls of Fame, 201–205
　Hammond and, 64–70, 219–221
　hands of, 19, 24, 35–36, 37, 48, 60,
　　114, 116
　high school basketball career of,
　　10–18, 19–29, 33–34, *127*
　on his pro *vs.* amateur playing,
　　63–64
　homes of, 102, 254, 272
　HSBI Report (1968), 26, 28
　knee problems of, 94, 123
　marriage to Turquoise Brown,
　　89 (*See also* Erving, Turquoise
　　"Turk" Brown (wife))
　as NBA Most Valuable Player,
　　159–160
　nicknames of, 60–61, 177–178
　on pay, 148
　playing records of, 48, 184–185,
　　191, 201–202

Erving, Julius (*continued*)
  post-basketball career of, 185–186,
    192, 204, 210, 213–216, 241,
    255–256
  religious beliefs of, 103–104
  retirement of and, 179–185,
    186–187, 189–192, 193–194
  reverse layup by, 157–159
  "rock the cradle" dunk by, 164–166
    (*See also* dunking)
  signed to Nets, 85–87 (*See also* New
    York Nets)
  on speed, 114–115
  on success, 202–205, 268–270
  television/film roles of, 159, 161
  Temple University honorary degree
    awarded to, 162–164
  trade to 76ers, 122–126 (*See also*
    Philadelphia 76ers)
  with Virginia Squires, 51–54, 55,
    57, 71–76, 77–83, 204
Erving, Julius "J" (son), 138, 253, 272
Erving, Julius Winfield, Sr. (father), 1
Erving, Marvin (brother), 1, 16, 20,
    30, 37–38
Erving, Turquoise "Turk" Brown
    (wife), 89, *134*, 190
  children of, 235–243
  divorce of, 251–257, 258–261
  husband's affairs and, 227–233
  letter to *New York Times* and,
    153–156, 228, 253
Erving Group, 204, 271
Eslinger, Don, 241
Ewing, Patrick, 27, 205

Felix, Ray, 8
50 Greatest Players in NBA
    History, 205
Fischer, Peter, 230
Fisher, Lee, 121
Fish That Saved Pittsburgh, The, 159
Fitzsimmons, Coach, *128*
Foreman, Earl, 52, 55, 73, 77–78
Fort Lauderdale Sun-Sentinel, 229
Frank, Barry, 122
Fratello, Mike, 206, 210–212
Frazier, Walt "Clyde," 87, 98, 121,
    129, 205
Free, Lloyd (World B.), 242

  on Erving legacy, 275–276
  with 76ers, 125, 139, 141, 143–147,
    149, 151
Friend, Tom, 272

Gale, Mike, 88, 92, 100
Garfinkel, Howard, 23–29
Garnett, Kevin, 44
Garry, Peter, 82, 100–102
Geronimo (game), 5
Gervin, George "Iceman," 81,
    108–111, 117, 118, 198–201, 205
Giannelli, John, 98
Gilmore, Artis, 55, 76, 89, 108–109
Goldaper, Sam, 78, 121
Golden State Warriors, 86, 122
Grant, Travis, 98
Greenidge, David, 274
Greer, Hal, 123, 205
Griffith, Darrell "Dr. Dunkenstein,"
    168
Gross, Bob, 149, 151
Guokas, Matt, 180

Haggerty, Andy, 7
Hall, Willie, 61–63
Hammond, Joe "the Destroyer,"
    64–70, 219–221
Havlicek, John, 94, 205
Hawkins, Connie, 9, 11, 63, 72, 83,
    194, 211
  as "Big Hawk," 60
  in "Clash of Legends," 198–201
Hayes, Elvin, 205, 248–250
Haywood, Spencer, 52, 118
Heisler, Mark, 142–144, 147–148,
    151, 154, 167, 242
  on Erving and Bird, 179
  on Turquoise Erving's letter to
    New York Times, 156, 228
Hempstead (N.Y.) High School, 10,
    15, 16, 33–34
Hermann, Michael, 271
Hillman, Darnell, 88
Hofstra University, 21–22
Hoover, Tom, 62–63, 72
Houston, Allan, 67
HSBI Report (1968), 26, 28
Huber, Robert, 251–257, 260
Hughes, Kim, 100, 216

Iavoroni, Marc, 164
Indiana Pacers, 87, 116–117, *130, 131*
Island Gardens, 56
Issel, Dan, 55, 90, 113, *132*, 201

Jabali, Warren, 98
Jackson, Phil, 98
Jasner, Phil, 183
Johnson, Earvin "Magic," 113, 160,
    165, 205, 217–218
  at "Clash of Legends, 200
  on Erving's reverse layup, 159
Jones, Bobby, 112, *133*, 164, 175
Jones, Edgar "the Wild
    Helicopter," 168
Jones, Jimmy, 89
Jones, K. C., 178
Jones, Lee, 10–11, 61
Jones, Rich, 100, 111
Jones, Sam, 205
Jordan, Michael, 2, 104, 113, 114,
    170, 175–176, 205, 221
  dunking by, 171
  legacy of, 207–208, 209, 211
  shooting by, 224–225
  30,000-point milestone reached by,
    185, 202
Joyce, Kevin "White Tornado," 19–20

Katz, Harold, 163
Kennedy, Eugene, *129*
Kennedy, Walter, 82
Kenon, Larry "Dr. K," 86, 88, 100,
    108–109
Kentucky Colonels, 80, 88, 100, 117
Kerr, Johnny, 71
King, Bernard, 114
King, Larry, 236–241
Kirkland, Richard "Pee Wee," 64, 70
Klores, Dan, 259
Knight, Billy, 117
Kornheiser, Tony, 140

Ladner, Wendell, 88
La Jolla Beach and Tennis
    Club, 230
Lansdorp, Robert, 230–231
Larese, York, 57
Larry King Live, 236–241

Leaman, Jack, 242
  Behler's views on, 144–145
  death of, 261–264
  at Nets' tribute to Erving, 180
  at UMass, 22, 34, 39, 44, 45, 53
Leaman, Rita, 45, 49, 263, 264, 265
Lindsey, Callie Mae. *See* Erving,
    Callie Mae (mother)
Los Angeles Lakers, 160, 164–166
  Abdul-Jabbar and, 19
  Erving's reverse layup and, 157–159
  Hammond and, 66
Loughery, Kevin, 58, 87–88, 91, 95,
    100, 110, 113–114
  on ABA, 115
  Erving-Nets contract dispute and,
    120, 124
  Erving's 1998 apology to Nets
    and, 216
  on Erving's career with 76ers, 153
  on Erving's legacy, 190, 192
  Turquoise Erving's views on, 155, 156
Lucas, Jerry, 205
Lucas, John, 189, 254
Lucas, Maurice, 149, 150
Lynbrook (N.Y.) High School, 18, *127*
Lynner, Paul, 21

Madden, Dorýs "Pearl," 252, 272
Madden, Jack, 178
Madison Square Garden, *129, 134*
Mallozzi, Vincent, 257–258,
    273–278
  *Asphalt Gods: An Oral History of the
    Rucker Tournament*, 217
  meeting with Erving (1999),
    216–221, 278
Malone, Karl, 185, 202, 205
Malone, Moses, *135*, 161–164,
    166–168, 172, 178, 184, 205
Maravich, "Pistol" Pete, 40,
    80–81, 205
Marquette University, 40, 79
Massmann, Fritz, 180
Mathias, Ken, 45
Maxwell, Cedric, 178
McAdoo, Bob, 160
McClain, Ted "Hound Dog," 107
McDaniels, Jim, 80
McDermott, Jim, 75–76

McGinnis, George, 118
  with All-ABA team, 89
  with Indiana Pacers, 88
  with 76ers, 125, 138, 141–142, 143,
    148–149, 150, 151, 153
  Turquoise Erving's views on, 155
McGuire, Al, 40
McGuire, Dick, 201
McHale, Kevin, 205
McKinley, James C., 227, 228, 257
Melchionni, Bill, 156
  on Erving trade to 76ers, 122–123
  as Nets general manager, 120
  as Nets player, 57, 91, 99, 106
  at Nets tribute to Erving, 216
Meminger, Dean, 20, 40–41,
    78–80, 118
  on ABA-NBA comparison, 201
  on AMA, 52
Mendelson, Barry, 121–122
Meyers, Ann, 201
Mikan, George, 205
Milbank, 64–70, 220
Mills, Ollie, 10, 30
Milwaukee Bucks, 80–83, 87, 162,
    180, 189
Mix, Steve, 140, 141
Moe, Doug, 72
Monroe, Earl "The Pearl," 100, 113,
    121, 205
Morris, Ernie, 70
Morris, Plucky, 67–68
Mosley, Earl, 10–11, 269
Mourning, Alonzo, 27
Murphy, Calvin, 20, 201

Nance, Larry "Fancy," 168–169, 171
Nassau Coliseum, 56, 101, 102, 130,
    131, 132, 133, 181
Nater, Swen, 90, 100, 104, 105–106
National Basketball Association
    (NBA)
  ABA and, 51–58, 77–83, 201,
    204, 205
  ABA merger with, 115–118
  draft and four-year-college rule, 80
  Erving as NBA Most Valuable
    Player, 159–160
  Erving legacy and, 98, 115,
    117–118, 126, 167, 176

50 Greatest Players in NBA
    History, 205
  Slam Dunk Contest of, 168–171
National Collegiate Athletic Associa-
    tion (NCAA), 35–37, 39, 45
NBA's Greatest, The, 217–218
Neal, Lloyd, 149
New Jersey Americans. See New York
    Nets
New Orleans Jazz, 121–122
New York Islanders, 123
New York Knicks, 79, 87, 97, 121,
    162, 182–183
New York Nets, 3, 54–58, 128, 129,
    130, 131, 132, 133
  championships of, 92–93, 111–117
  Erving as ABA Most Valuable
    Player and, 89, 111
  Erving's apology to (1998), 216
  Erving's contract dispute with,
    119–126, 120, 182
  Erving's first season with, 85–95
  Erving's second season with,
    97–104
  Erving's third season with, 104–118
  NBA merger and, 116–117
  tribute to Erving by, 180–182
New York Post, 259
New York Times
  on Cory Erving's death, 241
  Mallozzi and, 220, 257, 278
  Nets-Knicks game advertisement
    in, 121
  Turquoise Erving's letter to,
    153–156, 228, 253
Nixon, Norm, 160
Nobles, Charlie, 241

Obama, Barack, 3
O'Brien, Larry, 168
Olajuwon, Hakeem, 205
O'Neal, Shaquille, 4, 205
Orlando Magic, 241, 255–256

Parish, Robert, 15, 205
Park Lake Apartment complex
    (Hempstead, N.Y.), 1, 7, 264
Paultz, Billy "the Whopper," 58, 59,
    67, 88, 100, 101

Pendergrass, Teddy, 255
Peppers, Julius, 218
Pettit, Bob, 205
Philadelphia, 251–257
Philadelphia 76ers, 115, *133, 134, 135*
  Barkley and Erving with, 171–176
  Bird and Erving with, 176–179
  championships of, 157–159,
    167–168
  Erving as NBA Most Valuable
    Player and, 159–160
  Erving's first season with, 137–156
  Erving's retirement and, 179–185,
    186–187
  Erving's reverse layup and, 157–159
  Erving's "rock the cradle" dunk
    and, 164–166
  Erving's trade to, 122–126
  Malone and Erving with, 161–164
  Turquoise Erving's letter to *New
    York Times* on, 153–156
Pippen, Scottie, 205
Pitino, Rick, 48
Portland Trail Blazers, 148–153, 167
Potvin, Dennis, 123
Prospect School (Hempstead, N.Y.),
  4–6
Putnam, Pat, 111–112

Quebec City Kebekwa, 273–275
Quirk, Dantia, 200
QV Publishing, 200

Ramsey, Cal, 11, 65, 67
Ramsey, Jack, 149
Ray Felix Tournament, 8–10, 33
Reed, Willis, 205
Reverend Arthur Mackey Park, 15
reverse layup, by Erving, 157–159
Riley, Pat, 160, 166
Riordan, Mike, 59, 67, 78
Rivers, Glenn "Doc," 218
Robertson, Oscar, 74, 194, 205, 208
Robertson, Pablo, 64
Robinson, David, 205
Roche, John, 58, 88
"rock the cradle" dunk, by Erving,
  164–166
Roe, Lou, 49

Rogers, Archie, 5, 6, 10, 27–34, 42,
  102–104, 267–270
Rooney, Wally, 110
Roosevelt (N.Y.) High School, 10–18,
  20–23, 33, *127*
Roosevelt Park, 15
Rucker Park, 11, 61, 78, *127*, 217
Rucker Tournament, 59–70, 78
Russell, Bill, 185, 194, 205, 213, 214
Ryan, Don, 5, 6, 9, 20, 43

Salvation Army Center (Hempstead,
  N.Y.), 6, 9–10, 34
Sampson, Ralph, 168
San Antonio Spurs, 100, 110, 111,
  116–117, *129*, 138
Sanders, Karl, 275
San Diego Conquistadors, 98–99,
  106, *130*
Sandomir, Richard, 198–200
Saunders, Leon, 60
Schayes, Dolph, 205
Scott, Charlie, 59, 67, 68, 70, 71–74,
  80, 219
Scott, Ray, 72
Seals, Bruce, 91
Segura, Pancho, 230
Semyonova, Ulyona, 201
Sesame Street, 161
Sharman, Bill, 205
Sharp, Michele, 185–186
Shooting Stars, 185–186
Shue, Gene, 140, 155, 156
Silas, James, 106, 117
Simon, Walt, 57
Simpson, Ralph, 53
Skinner, Al, 48, 53, 144, 216
Slam Dunk Contests
  ABA, 108–109, 209
  NBA, 168–171
Smith, Bill, 47
Smith, Will, 218
Sojourner, Willie, 86, 98
Sonny Boy (neighborhood bully), 32
Source Sports Magazine, 216
South Hempstead (N.Y.) Baptist
  Church, 1
Spirits of St. Louis, 3, 100, 117
Sports Illustrated, 91, 100–102,
  111–112

Sports Illustrated (continued)
  on Erving legacy, 245
  fortieth anniversary celebration
    of, 205
  on Virginia Squires, 82
Sprewell, Latrell, 67
St. John's University, 21, 25, 54, 61
Stallworth, Dave, 22
Stern, David, 168, 200
Stevenson, Alexandra, 227–233, 240,
    252, 256, 257–258, 272
Stevenson, Samantha, 154, 227–233,
    252, 253–254, 257–258
Stirling, Scotty, 179
Stockton, John, 205
Strickland, Rod, 196–198
"stuff," 182
Summers, Freddie, 253
Sweet and Sour, 62
Syracuse University, 47–49, 219

Taylor, Brian, 58, 99, 106, 113, 216
Taylor, Ollie, 59, 67
Taylor, Roland "Fatty," 72, 78
television coverage, of basketball,
    122, 125
Telfair, Sebastian, 197
Temple University, 162–164
Terry, Chuck, 100
Thomas, Isiah, 99, 205
Thompson, David, 73, 108–109,
    113, 126
Thorn, Rod, 106
Thurmond, Nate, 205
Time, 183–184
Tomjanovich, Rudy, 179
Toney, Andrew, 160, 164, 177, 189
Trump Taj Mahal, 198–201
Twardzik, Dave, 150
20/20 (ABC-TV), 231–233

University of Massachusetts (UMass)
  Erving and, 35–37, 39–41, 43–49,
    51, 76, 213, 219
  Erving in Hall of Fame of, 201
  Leaman and, 22, 34, 39, 40–41, 44,
    45, 53, 261–264
University Without Walls, 213
Unseld, Wes, 205, 249

Vecsey, Peter, 59–60, 69, 70, 219–220
Veterans Memorial Coliseum, *130*
Virginia Squires, 51–54, 55, 57,
    71–76, 77–83, 204
  demise of, 117
  Erving in Nets game against, 88

Walters, Barbara, 231–233
Walt Frazier Enterprises, 78
Walton, Bill, 148, 149, 151, 201,
    205, 278
Warren, Bob, 100
Washington, Grover, Jr., 218
Washington, Kermit, 86, 179
Washington Wizards, 147
Watkins, Cecil, 8
Watts, Wanda, 33, 267
Webster, Marvin, 248
Weiss, Richard, 93
West, Jerry, 66, 74, 194, 205, 208
Westsiders, 59, 68, *127*
White, Barry, 21
Wicked Cow Entertainment, 271
Wiener, Irwin, 78, 120
Wilkes, Jamaal, 160
Wilkins, Dominique "the Human
    Highlight Film," 2, 114, 165,
    210, 221–223
  on Erving's legacy, 190–191
  in NBA Slam Dunk Contest, 168,
    169–170
Wilkins, Gerald, 169, 222
Wilkins, Lenny, 205
Wilkinson, Jack, 17–18, 93
Williams, Al, 8, 23, 30, 33, 42–43, 75
Williams, Bernie, 78, 107
Williams, Pat, 125
Williamson, Bertha, 216
Williamson, John "Superfly," 86,
    123, 216
Wilmore, Henry, 37
Wilson, Ray, 10, 21, 34, 53, 264
Wingo, Harthorne, 72
Wise, Willie, 90, 92, 95
Woolf, Bob, 55, 77–78
Woolridge, Orlando "Oh! Oh!", 168
World Sports Humanitarian Hall of
    Fame, 201
Worthy, James, 205